A Letter from North Ronaldsay 1990–1999

IAN SCOTT

ORKNEYOLOGY
PRESS

Published by Orkneyology Press
Stromness, Orkney Islands

ISBNs:
978-1-915075-06-2 – hardback
978-1-915075-07-9 – paperback
978-1-915075-08-6 – ebook

www.orkneyology.com
Book Sales:
https://shop.orkneyology.com/collections/orkneyology-press-books

Extracts from 'The Difficult Land' and 'Merlin' taken from *Collected Poems* by Edwin Muir © Edwin Muir and reprinted by permission of Faber and Faber Ltd.

Quotations from Robert Rendall are used by kind permission of the Rendall family.

All rights reserved. The contents of this book may not be reproduced in any form without written permission from the publishers, except for short extracts for quotation or review.

Typeset by Main Point Books, Edinburgh
www.mainpointbooks.co.uk

Poems by George Mackay Brown are reproduced by permission of the Literary Estate of George Mackay Brown

Text © Ian Scott 2024
Cover image © Fionn McArthur: Start Point Media

Table of Contents

Acknowledgements	9
Foreword by Peter Titley	11
The Old Memorial Hall *April 5, 1990*	13
Merry Dancers at the Hall *August 6, 1990*	14
Sheaves and Lanterns for the Harvest Home *December 6, 1990*	16
Christmas Films and New Year Norwegian Links *January, 24, 1991*	20
Spring Time *May 30, 1991*	24
Silage, Haymaking and Dancing *August 8, 1991*	26
Days to Remember *August 16, 1991*	29
Summer Seems Far Away *November 28, 1991*	32
Storm Blows Away Old Year *January 9, 1992*	37
Splendid Evening *January 23, 1992*	40
Remembering the Primroses *April 30, 1992*	41

Remembering the North Boats *July 23, 1992*	44
Captains and Commodores *October 26, 1992*	48
A Harvest Home *November 19, 1992*	52
Will our Heritage Survive the Years? *January 21, 1993*	55
The Navy Take Their Leave of the Shore *March 25, 1993*	60
Midsummer Memories from the Past *July 8, 1993*	64
Fleeting Memories of an Island Summer Past *October 14, 1993*	69
Celebration as the Harvest is Safely Gathered *December 2, 1993*	73
A Summer Sky and a Frozen Loch on Christmas Day *January 13, 1994*	77
Old Farming Practices Survive Centuries *July 21, 1994*	82
Heritage Trust Launch Appeal for Memorial Hall *August 11, 1994*	86
Cavalier Creel Boats *December 1, 1994*	90
'May most of your dreams come true, and let us hold the hand of the past' *January 12, 1995*	95

Island Remembers Those at War 50 Years Ago *May 25, 1995*	100
Farewell and Welcome to Head Teacher *September 2, 1995*	105
The Invasion of Local Fishing Grounds *November 23, 1995*	110
A Serious Case of Burns is Celebrated *February 8, 1996*	147
Epic Boat Trips of Our Schooldays *June 20, 1996*	153
The Harvest is in for Another Year *October 17, 1996*	159
From America … for Harvest Home *December 5, 1996*	165
Will the Angels Play Their Harps for Me? *February 6, 1997*	171
Sailing Away in Realms of Fantasy *June 5, 1997*	178
Changing Times and Changing Seasons *November 6, 1997*	183
Looking Back to Past Harvests and Past Wars *December 4, 1997*	189
Standing Stone Dancers Welcome the New Year *February 19, 1998*	194
The Man with the Friendly Smile *March 26, 1998*	200

Well, Well … *June 25, 1998*	206
Religion, Education, Healthcare *November 19, 1998*	212
Reflections of Past Times *December 24, 1998*	217
Que Sera Sera *February 11, 1999*	225
Burns Supper is a Memorable Occasion *March 25, 1999*	230
Remembrance *June 10, 1999*	236
School Open Day *July 15, 1999*	241
Slideshow *August 5, 1999*	243
Yemen Slideshow *September 16, 1999*	244
Community Functions *October 14, 1999*	246
Thoughts During the 'Heuld' of the Night *November 4, 1999*	248
Millennium Needs a Touch of Magic *December 30, 1999*	254
Appendix Days at Sea	263

Acknowledgements

Away back in 1990 the island decided to carry out repairs, after serious storm damage, to the Memorial Hall. In the following letters I gave an account of the building's history both past and present.

The island's return to celebrating our Harvest Home in the Memorial Hall took place in 1990 and it was then, when I wrote up that occasion, that I began writing my 'Letters from North Ronaldsay'.

Various folk, over the years, have suggested that I should make a compilation of those letters into book form, either as a selection or alternatively, now going into the thirty-fourth year, a record, albeit a personal one, mainly of community life, special events and other noteworthy occasions over a period of time and change. The final choice was to publish in three decades.

VAO (Voluntary Action Orkney) very kindly supplied me with photocopies of all my island letters from 1990–2000. The first decade all had to be typed into a Word system in order that they could be edited and available for publishing. For that somewhat tedious task I must mention my grateful thanks to my cousin, David Scott, his relatives and other friends of theirs in the USA who undertook the typing. David also proofread letters and efficiently compiled all my thirty-four years of letters into available, workable files. I must also gratefully thank both Howie Firth and Peter Titley (Peter, now sadly deceased) for proofreading the first decade of my letters.

Then there were the photographs that I received, or were forwarded to *The Orcadian*, that often accompanied a letter. Those contributors, as well as I can remember, I have named below their photographs. Many others I cannot recall, but to all those suppliers of photographs, or those I have used with the photographer unknown, I also express my grateful thanks. (I may say many were from Dr Beatrice Garvie's collection, early 1930s–1945, inherited by Bessie Muir, who gave them to the Orkney Archive and they have been subsequently digitised.)

Also I must thank the staff at *The Orcadian* office for their help, and *The Orcadian* who, with various editors, have undertaken to publish all my letters over the years. There are many other friends and relatives who have been encouraging me to 'get on with it', and I must make mention of Beatrice Thomson (island archivist), an islander now living in Finstown with a great knowledge of NR who has, many times, answered numerous questions connected with my Letters. My niece, Ingrid Tulloch, who has been another 'encourager' and has patiently helped to solve and manage my inadequate computer skills and other problems, when making the procedures necessary for getting my book underway.

Lastly, but by no means least, I must also especially extend thanks to Rhonda and Tom Muir, publishers, for without their encouragement, and wanting to publish my 'Letters from North Ronaldsay', I do not think any book would have appeared.

In my own editing of years of writing I have carried out a little 'polishing' and one or two very minor changes and correcting, one way or another, the inevitable mistakes pointed out by knowledgeable readers. Looking back over so many years at one's writing I felt my final presentation was more to my satisfaction.

I hope that my writing will bring some enjoyment and bring back memories to those who have lived through those changing times and serve as a chronicle of island life as the generations come and go.

Foreword

For more than thirty years, Ian Scott has been sharing his vision of life as it has unfolded on the remote island of his birth. This is North Ronaldsay.

The island lies at the northernmost tip of the Orkney archipelago at the convergence of two mighty oceans and it sits, low-lying and defiant, in the face of challenges both from the elements and from the outside world. Through the columns of *The Orcadian* newspaper, Ian Scott has charted the everyday events of a small community living at the edge; a fiercely independent people on the fringe of the British Isles with strong historic links to Scandinavia; a community proud of its traditions and striving to value its heritage.

His regular Letters from North Ronaldsay have, across three decades, provided a unique insight into island life; written by one who knows and feels the emotions of a strong communal existence. In the background of his Letters he describes a journey of inevitable change and the pitfalls and barely perceptible threats he sees along the way.

Ian Scott is a farmer, a fisherman and an internationally renowned artist. He is also a keen observer of life, of people and of the wider world. Here he paints pictures with words; pictures which take the reader to his island, into his world where he shares his unique view of events – sometimes with a wistful air of longing for times past and sometimes with a prophetic vision for the future.

Ian Scott has given us an unalloyed first-hand account of a community built on enduring strength and determination.

Peter Titley

The Old Memorial Hall
April 5, 1990

1990 celebrates the 70th anniversary of the Memorial Hall in North Ronaldsay, and the Community Association plans to run some functions throughout the year to mark the occasion and to raise funds for repair work. The first function took place on the evening of Friday, March 30, and lasted well into the early hours of next morning. The Old Hall rang once more to the sound of accordions and dancing feet.

The evening began with an illustrated lecture on 'Wildlife of the Antarctic' by Jim Conroy, at present working for the Institute of Terrestrial Ecology in Banchory. This lecture proved to be most informative and entertaining. Alison Duncan, the resident warden from the Bird Observatory, introduced the speaker and proposed a vote of thanks at the end of the lecture.

A sketch, based loosely on an old folk tale, then followed. It was produced and performed by a few of the island's young folk. The players were John Payne, Evelyn Scott, Jane Donnelly, Peter Donnelly and, not least, Albert Scott. Fiona Muir introduced the scenes and generally helped backstage. The sketch, produced at short notice, proved to be a great success. Bessie Muir, now resident on the Orkney Mainland but still a great supporter of the old hut, proposed a suitable vote of thanks for the players.

During the evening a bottle of whisky donated by John Payne, Principal Keeper of the North Ronaldsay Lighthouse, and a box of chocolates donated by Billy Muir were raffled. The donations and raffle collection amounted to over £100 and will go towards the repair work and general renovations carried out these past three weeks.

The Memorial Hall was erected for the use of the island and commemorates those who served in the First World War. In 1981 a modern New Community Centre was built on to the existing school buildings. Since then the Old Hall has been somewhat neglected, and we have recently been trying to remedy this.

All islanders living in North Ronaldsay and elsewhere will always have happy memories of the Old Hall, and many have expressed a wish that the building should be looked after. It cannot, of course, replace the fine new centre, but it will be fun from time to time to return to the Old Hall and perhaps recapture the spirit and memories of those past years. In some strange way, it holds a part of all islanders' lives who were lucky enough to be part of its history.

Merry Dancers at the Hall
August 6, 1990

In the New Community Centre, towards the end of April, Peter Davis gave an illustrated talk on his Easter visit to Israel. A fairly large selection of quite excellent slides of the Holy Land were shown. Tea and homebakes were available halfway through the show. The second part of the talk then followed, and the evening's entertainment was informative and most enjoyable.

On Sunday, July 1, the new Kirkwall Lifeboat *Mickie Salvesen* made a visit to the island. The crew were served tea and homebakes by the North Ronaldsay Ladies Lifeboat Guild in the New Centre, and trips were organised through the island with a visit to the lighthouse. Despite the day being somewhat windy, the lifeboat made a trip round Nouster Bay with island passengers. The lifeboat's visit was much appreciated, and a collection was taken up for the Institution, amounting to over £80.

To date, a total of £200 has been received for repair and renovation work for the Memorial Hall which is now more or less complete, making the hall look as good as new. The long-term future of the hall is at present under review, and a number of constructive ideas have been put forward for its preservation and community role. After consultation with the islanders we hope to present a multi-purpose community use which will retain its excellent dance floor and the homely atmosphere which is so characteristic of the building.

At the Memorial Hall on the beautiful summer's evening of Saturday, July 28, we continued our celebrations to mark the 70th anniversary of the Old Hall with a slideshow and dance.

Ann Manson, the sound archivist for Orkney, gave an illustrated talk on 'Women at Work in Orkney Early This Century'. The slides were made from a selection of Tom Kent's important photographic record of Orkney life, which he compiled after his return to Orkney from the USA in 1898. Tom Kent died in 1936.

Ann Manson's selection of photographs was very interesting, and she gave us some fascinating information on the life of Orcadian women in those days of long ago.

Interspersed through her talk, Ann told one or two stories learned from her own valuable work with which she has been engaged for some years. This work she manages with tact and understanding.

In the Orkney Archives will be stored the voices of Orcadians which, at the touch of a button, will tell the stories that were part of their lives and which will, in years to come, become part of the continuing history of Orkney.

Following the slideshow tea was served, with a grand selection of sandwiches and cakes. The dance then began. Above the roof of the Memorial Hall, and high in the late evening sky, an unusual and ghostly display of the Merry Dancers shimmered and rippled palely in gossamer trails – almost in strange harmony with the merry dancers who moved within the hall.

A crowd of between seventy and eighty, made up of islanders, ex-islanders and visitors, enjoyed rather a splendid evening. One ex-islander home on holiday, Tammie o' Howatoft, now in his late seventies, intended to have, as he said, one more dance in the Old Hall, and then proceeded to dance all night long. No doubt he remembered old times and will, as he said, remember this evening for the remainder of his life.

Accordions continued to provide music to which the well-sprung floor vibrated in time to dancing feet. A further serving of tea was given during the night, and after the last dance cups of soup were also served.

Hands and arms were then linked in turn to the final and traditional performance accompanied to the singing of 'Auld Lang Syne'.

The light of the summer dawn was already spreading across the morning sky when the company broke up and left. The lighthouse still flashed but with a less intense beam sweeping over white clouds of mildew which stretched coldly here and there through the island.

For everybody – but particularly the young folk who attended our 70th anniversary celebrations – we hope that such evenings will be remembered and valued, as we used to do when we were young.

We hope also that it will awaken an interest in our fast disappearing traditions and way of life. It's worth holding on to, for in the last analysis it is the young folk who will be the guardians of our Orcadian heritage.

Sheaves and Lanterns for the Harvest Home
December 6, 1990

Since last I wrote giving an account of our memorable summer dance held in July, various events have taken place in North Ronaldsay.

The first of two lectures held in the New Community Centre took place on Thursday, September 27, when Dr McCormack from the Museum of Alberta gave an illustrated talk entitled 'Indian Boats of the Hudson Bay and their Orkney Connections'. At the conclusion of a very interesting and speculative discourse, tea and light refreshments were served by members of the Community Association.

The second lecture (Aberdeen University Lectures), with the title of 'Sea Birds in the Bear's Kingdom – A Spitsbergen Summer', was given by Dr K. Taylor. This was held on Wednesday, October 10, and proved to be extremely good with some very fine slides.

On Saturday, November 3, a bonfire and fireworks display was arranged by the Community Association with assistance from the Parent Teacher Association. About thirty to forty children and adults watched the display on the Links. The evening then continued in the New Community Centre when hot soup and baked potatoes, prepared by Mrs Payne, the school cook, were served. Tea and a grand selection of homebakes followed. The PTA arranged this enjoyable part of the evening, also supplying the homebakes.

Over an eight-week period during the summer, a warden, Michael Scott, was appointed by the association to supervise activities at the Centre, with John Payne (junior) as deputy. During that time, a total of 403 people were recorded as having used the building. Of that number 152 were visiting children, with 143 attendances by local children. Excellent facilities are available for badminton, snooker, table tennis, etc., throughout the year, with a total attendance since April of well over 700.

The Centre also provides suitable room for the bank, coastguard, fire brigade, bird net finishers, and many other users.

The third event to be held in the Memorial Hall this year marking its 70th anniversary took place on Friday, November 9, when the Harvest Home was celebrated. About eighty people attended, with well over eighty per cent of islanders turning out. A number of guests, ex-islanders and visitors gave an extra attendance otherwise difficult to achieve at this time of year.

Over a decade has now passed since the Harvest Home was last held in the Old Hall, and it remains the ideal meeting-place for this function. The low ceiling and compact area make it possible to transform the inside into a magical atmosphere of harvest for the children and adults alike.

In order to achieve this transformation, many days and nights of work by the association and other helpers were given. On a grand simmans-making night over 600 feet of straw rope was wound. Another night's work produced many other straw and hay decorations. Other days and nights were spent collecting various other items which, all put together, transformed the hall into a proper celebration of harvest.

On the night of the Harvest Home three long tables decorated with flowers and lit by many candles could be seen when entering the building. From the couples, six old oil-burning steading lanterns hung, providing the only other light for the supper.

Garlands of straw simmans stretched from couple to couple in geometric patterns. From each join, clusters of brightly-coloured buoy-heads representing the fishermen and the three island creelboats were hung, and served as a reminder of the Harvest of the Sea.

On each wall and suspended from the ceiling were large round straw and hay constructions symbolising the sun upon which the harvest depends. Straw crosses, pleated straw, and evergreen displays completed the main decorations. Finally in each corner of the building seven-feet-high arrangements of New Zealand flax brought the hall together in a harmonious finish.

Shortly after eight at night when the gathered company were welcomed and the guests thanked for coming, John Cutt, on being asked to give the grace, did so in the words of Robert Burns. The supper then began with a serving of North Ronaldsay native sheep mutton (cooked by Winnie Scott) and clapshot. The second course was cheesecake with cream, followed by tea and assorted homebakes. Cider was provided for the accompanying drink, with whisky for the toast.

When the supper was over, Bill Carstairs, the North Isles vet and guest speaker, was asked to give the address to the harvest. This he did with his usual characteristic flair, and we were treated to a most informative talk tracing the origins of the harvest celebrations, and other important land festivals whose beginnings go far back into early human history.

The speaker than asked the company to toast the Harvest Home. Bill was thanked for his speech, and the supper came to an end.

Once the tables were cleared away, the old dance floor was dusted with Slipperine and the dance began. On stage were Lottie Tulloch and Ann Tulloch playing accordions as they did for the summer dance. Accompanying them were our guests who also performed together on their own to give a long evening of musical entertainment.

Billy Jolly sang a number of songs throughout the evening, accompanied on the guitar by his wife Ingirid. Three of his songs were 'Jock o' Hazeldean', 'A Pair o' Nicky Tams' and 'The Wild Mountain Thyme'. Ingirid Jolly, as well as playing with the band, sang beautifully the Shetland song 'The Lang Boats o' Delting'. Both performers are of course well known in Orkney and elsewhere, and were greatly appreciated and applauded.

Susan Stout, another guest, also played on stage from time to time, and gave us a fine fiddle selection of Shetland and Irish Reels, with Ingrid providing the guitar backing.

Bill Carstairs accompanied the band on the electric keyboard, adding to the sound of accordions, guitars, fiddles and drums. Our other guests Roy and Susan Russell (guitars, fiddle and accordion), with the rest of the family, Sarah, Andrew and James (on fiddles), are of course well known in North Ronaldsay as former teachers, and remembered for their Christmas concerts which always hosted the main dance of the festive season. All the family played very professionally along with the band, and throughout the night gave a grand selection of bluegrass music, marches, reels and waltzes, with a lively rendition of 'The Midnight Special'.

As the evening progressed, a bottle of whisky donated by John Payne, principal lighthouse keeper, and a box of chocolates donated by John Payne (junior) were raffled and made a total of £48.10. Later John Payne was sponsored in a bid to raise money for the Children in Need appeal by having his beard partly trimmed prior to complete removal. Annie Tulloch, Milldam, skilfully carried out this operation, and a sum of £54.49 was collected. James Lyon, lighthouse keeper, very generously offered to equal the amount collected. This he did, making a grand total of £108.98. Further donations given before, during and after the evening for the Memorial Hall amounted to £80.

Tea, sandwiches and cakes were served late in the night, and finally between four and five in the morning after the singing of 'Auld Lang Syne', cups of soup were offered, bringing this special Harvest Home of 1990 to a close.

Outside in the dark November sky, the Plough could be seen shining only dimly in a hazy sky, its name a reminder of the first work on the land which finally leads to harvest and the yearly celebration. Slightly to the left of that familiar star formation stands the War Memorial, its tall granite cross silhouetted against the winter sky.

On the north-facing side are carved the names of those who died in the 1914–18 war. At this time of remembrance of the Harvest Home and the two great wars, it seems appropriate, in this the 70th year of the Old Hall, to remember that it is a memorial to those who died and to all other islanders who served in that great conflict.

Finally, a special thanks to the many people who in a collective effort ensured such a homely and happy occasion. All the members of the association and others who made and hung the decorations, and removed them. Bertie Thomson and Billy Muir who supplied the native sheep. Winnie already mentioned for her splendid cooking and other chores. Ann Tulloch, Evelyn Scott and Jane Donnelly for their sterling overall work. Bessie Muir, who fulfilled her wish to return for the Harvest Home and very competently took up her old duties. Another ex-islander, Ruth Edwardson, helped as she often used to do for many years in the Old Hall, and all the others, not least Loganair, who helped in any way with this, the highlight of our anniversary year.

Christmas Films and New Year Norwegian Links

January 24, 1991

Four main events have been held in North Ronaldsay's New Community Centre since last year's Harvest Home.

On Friday, December 14, the Community Association held the second of two whist drives to raise funds for the children's Christmas party. An excellent collection of just over £100 was received, and at the end of the whist drive and prize-giving, tea, cakes and biscuits were served.

Four days later the Youth Theatre gave a presentation of the familiar folk tale 'Hansel and Gretel'. This production began rather slowly but livened up considerably with an exciting climax in which the children participated with obvious relish. Without a stage, the props were cleverly adapted for everything to be seen at ground level. A good attendance, helped by the numerous visitors to the island, enjoyed the evening's entertainment, and this standard of production will surely attract the sort of audiences to bring success for the Youth Theatre.

The extra numbers on this occasion ensured a collection of about £90, made up from a combination of donations and a raffle. The raffle was a magnificent version of the witch's gingerbread house artistically created by Christine Muir. This sum of money, along with £30 given by the Community Council, helped to cover the Youth Theatre's expenses. The association as always offered facilities, transport and arranged accommodation (kindly provided by Dr Kevin Woodbridge). Finally, the Parent Teacher Association organised tea and a splendid assortment of homebakes.

On Sunday, December 23 the School concert took place, and although this event has already been covered elsewhere, I should like to add a little to that account. After the production of the play 'Hats for Jizo' which was admirably presented, there were Bible readings by Mary Lyon, Linda Davis and two Kirkwall Grammar School scholars, Ruth and Gillian Swanney. Apart from the school children's excellent singing, Mary Swanney gave a beautiful rendering of a Christmas carol accompanied by Linda and Peter Davis on guitar and flute.

After the singing of 'We Wish You a Merry Christmas and a Happy New

Year', Linda Davis thanked everybody who had helped, and a member of the association, who praised the very fine efforts of all concerned, asked everyone to show their appreciation.

The next event to take place was the children's Christmas party held on Christmas Eve and organised by the association. This eagerly awaited affair began in the afternoon. Various games were played, with sandwiches, cakes, trifle and sweets being served. At about five thirty a loud knocking was heard, and on opening the door Santa advanced slowly into a darkened Community Centre shimmering with long green and gold wall hangings. A Christmas tree sparkling with coloured lights stood to one side, and stretched across the room were garlands of multi-coloured and variably designed decorations.

Adding to the general effect were numerous wall murals made by the school children, and from the high ceiling 200 balloons hung in a number of colourful clusters along the length of the hall.

After walking round the room, accompanied by Winnie Scott, and passing near the circle of seated young folk, Santa took up a stance by the Christmas tree. All the children including the newly born baby, Richenda Brookman, received their Christmas gifts along with an orange and apple. Santa then left waving goodbye, bringing the Christmas party for 1990 to a close.

The last occasion of the year took place on Friday, December 18. This was a film show followed by the Christmas end-of-year dance. Originally planned for the New Centre, the venue was changed as many requests had been made to have the dance and film show in the Memorial Hall. As it happened this decision proved a fortunate one as, on the night of the event, there was a power failure which lasted until the next morning (the Old Hall has its own independent power supply).

This new arrangement meant a very great amount of work transporting the decorations, Christmas tree, dishes and chairs from one hall to another, but it was all accomplished cheerfully, transforming the old Memorial Hall into a sparkling and colourful display for Christmas.

The evening began with a film show. Three films were shown beginning with *The Queen's Visit in 1960* – one among the many which are now part of Orkney's history filmed by Douglas Shearer (a silent film kindly loaned by Kenneth Thomson). The second film was the outstanding documentary *Bank Ahead*, a film about the boat *Otter Bank*, which sailed round the North Isles bringing banking facilities to the islanders. The film was kindly loaned by William Groat who had actually sailed on the *Otter Bank* as the bank cashier. And finally *The Fiddlers of James Bay*, an excellent film which we were pleased to receive from Len Wilson. The film show, reminiscent of the old days of the rural cinema with John Tulloch operating the projector, was very much enjoyed.

Immediately after clearing the floor the dance began. Ronnie Swanney played accordion with his usual irresistible swing. Ann Tulloch also played accordion, with accompaniment by Peter Davis on guitar. Drums provided a supporting beat to the music. The dance was a great success, with Ian Deyell's persuasive MC work keeping the dancers on their toes. About fifty or more people attended the function, and through the evening, tea and a large selection of sandwiches and home-bakes were served. A bottle of whisky donated by John Payne senior and a bottle of vodka donated by Billy Muir were raffled for the Romanian Appeal and amounted to, with donations, £92.

A further raffle plus the rest of the year's contributions reached a sum of £100 for the Memorial Hall. This very generous sum, along with the rest of the year's contributions, will help with the various renovations, survey, and investigations into the building's future. The dance continued until between two and three in the morning when, with everything still swinging with festive spirit, the last community function and dance for 1990 was brought to a close.

On Saturday, January 19, at the New Centre, the Orkney Norway Friendship Association organised a grand evening's entertainment. Very many people turned out on rather a wild night of weather. Before the proceedings began everybody was offered a delicious hot Norwegian drink. Ian MacLeod (who had just completed a School Board training course in the island) began the evening with a wonderful slideshow on Norway. He gave a very interesting and sometimes amusing account of the association's Norway visit.

Bill Crichton, playing guitar, worked with some of the North Ronaldsay School pupils and together they sang, rather well, a song from Norway in Norwegian. This surprising achievement was followed by Lenore Brown, who has many connections with Norway. She talked at length about how Norwegians celebrate Christmas and added information on different types of food. This latter subject was further discussed by Elma MacLeod who in addition read out a number of Norwegian recipes.

The inspiring, atmospheric music of Norway's great composer Edvard Greig provided appropriate background music for an excellent video on Norway – a land of beautiful mountains, fjords and seaways. A further short video, a Norwegian comedy, completed the main part of the evening's programme.

No better ambassadors for Norway could be asked for than those already mentioned, along with Connie Grieve and Jean Crichton who helped to serve a tremendous assortment of Norwegian food. It was nice also to see Mary Ann Thomson (formally from North Ronaldsay), a primary school teacher in Stromness, travelling north with committee members and helping with the various related duties – handling the sale of raffle tickets, badges, and membership forms.

After the supper and raffle Dr Kevin Woodbridge proposed a warm vote of thanks, bringing this special Norwegian evening to a close.

Spring Time
May 30, 1991

It seems unbelievable to think that in a little more than four weeks 1991 will be half spent, and without doubt the next half of the year will pass even more quickly.

These last days of late spring can still have the feel and effects of winter with gale-force winds blowing from the high west. The sea retains its ever-present potential power, breaking as it did recently in heavy, angry runs against the island's rugged west side. Exposed grass, dandelion and nettle leaves have turned black, and the old-fashioned lily, whose distinctive scent is evocative of May and past years, has been reduced to sad remains of this year's short-lived elegance.

Through my bedroom window, which is always open far enough to suit the weather and the time of year, I can easily hear the menacing sound of the sea for, as I write, it still remains in a restless mood. From time to time this never still or silent element gathers itself into a cold green and white fury of island turmoil. Sometimes it lashes the east side, then the north, but mostly the west from where our predominant winds blow.

Unfortunately, but inevitably, at times combinations of spring tides, heavy seas and strong winds can cause extensive damage to the surrounding sheep dyke, and late last year it took almost two weeks to rebuild considerable areas of devastation. A much-reduced work force worked in rain, wind and hail, through cold, cheerless November days – only stopping when the sky turned an even darker steel-blue or grey as the winter night closed in.

Serious sea-dyke damage repair was always without question an island affair, and as long as there are North Ronaldsay men left (and hopefully would-be islanders who share the same responsibilities) I hope that this communal work will be carried out with the same commitment and attitude of mind necessary for island life.

Since last I wrote about our social events, not much has happened. The period after Christmas always tends to be quiet and as the spring advances folk are busy with calving responsibilities, closely followed by the work on the land, and at this time of year attending to animals going out on the grass for the summer, and the many other chores necessary in May.

However, apart from a whist drive, some of our ladies from the Parent Teacher Association have been busy organising events to liven us all up.

On May 10 the Youth Theatre, who were doing some work with school pupils, stayed overnight and gave an evening's public performance. The presentation was entertaining, but for various reasons only a modest number of folk were able to attend the function. Traditional refreshment followed. I missed this event as at that time I was attending a reunion of art graduates which I had organised in Aberdeen where, thirty years before, we had each gone our separate ways. As I travelled south I felt, and maybe even looked, like Rip Van Winkle, who, though he only slept for twenty years, experienced a similar reunion with former friends and colleagues.

The success of this venture has set me thinking of a possible grand get-together of North Ronaldsay folk along with the many friends and people who shared our island way of life. Well anyway, that may be possible someday, but I remember with considerable pleasure those days of thirty or more years ago, and the life I came back to in North Ronaldsay when – even still – the islanders shared a life of relative comfort and independence.

On Saturday, May 25 the Parent Teacher Association organised a video show which began with a recently made video (lent by Helen Swanney) dealing with the establishment of a new flock on the island of Linga Holm set up by the Rare Breeds Survival Trust. After a cheese and wine break two other (silent) videos were available. One was made during the Thirties and shot in black and white by cine camera. The other one covered events during the late Fifties and early Sixties.

There was a fairly good attendance helped by visitors to the island at the time. Unfortunately, this is a busy time of year for islanders, and only a few were able to attend – a pity since much of the fishing and general farming material would have been enjoyed by those who remember the work of past years.

Silage, Haymaking and Dancing
August 8, 1991

One night in June a waning moon rose slowly in the eastern sky. It finally cleared the horizon, appearing more like a hairst moon, its colour a luminous pale rose and its light much less intense than the brilliant cold white of winter seen against darker skies.

The reflected moonbeams still sparkled across the summer sea, making a path like moving silver and gold from shore to skyline, and from those surrounding shores, about a week or more before, the North Ronaldsay creel boats had begun their season's fishing.

Two weeks later, before the new moon began her cycle, the island's silage got under way. Now that work is finished and midsummer has come and gone. Gone also are two islanders, both over eighty, whose funerals were held within a week of each other.

The last two parting days were warm and clear in the sun of high summer. In the blue sky far above the kirkyard skylarks sang clearly in the still air, seemingly unaware of the sombre occasion unfolding below, and from time to time the call of the oystercatcher would sound sadly in the distance.

On May 29 a children's picnic was arranged by the Community Association – a week later than planned, owing to the well-attended Runrig concert held on the Mainland. About forty adults and children enjoyed and participated in a variety of events which included egg and spoon race, sack race, high and long jump, 100 yards, three-legged and wheelbarrow race, and rounders. For a time adults returned in spirit to earlier days.

James Lyon, lighthouse keeper, competently arranged those events, and Jane Donnelly's pony and trap rides proved a great success. Throughout the proceedings, lemonade, sweets and biscuits were served, finishing with a delicious fruit trifle made by Evelyn Scott and Bethia Scott.

One warm and sunny day early in July, a helicopter arrived literally out of the blue. Its flight was sponsored by a local company in Dorset, and on board were some Sixth Form pupils from Corse Hill School, Bournemouth. The aim was to fly as far north as possible and back in one day raising money for various charities. The journey took from eight in the morning till nine-thirty at night. Before leaving North Ronaldsay, souvenir presentations of locally designed mugs and cards were made.

Later in the month the Kirkwall Lifeboat visited the island and an account will be given by the North Ronaldsay Lifeboat Guild of that enjoyable event.

Over the past weeks a team of six men from the Special Projects Unit of Orkney Islands Council have been busy laying cement foundations inside and along a few areas of sea-vulnerable sheep dyke, and a sound job they have made of this work.

A second team of over twenty volunteers from Scottish Conservation Projects arrived later, and were able to rebuild, very well, some dyke on the ready-made foundations. This group were mainly young people, many university graduates, coming from England, Ireland, Wales, Scotland, Germany, Czechoslovakia and New Zealand.

When the work of both teams was more or less complete, and before they left the island, the Community Association arranged a barbecue and dance. This function took place in the New Community Centre on the calm and sunny evening of July 12.

Workers from both units and visitors from the Bird Observatory (outnumbering the islanders) took part in a very cosmopolitan and lightsome get-together. Ann and Lottie Tulloch (with the drum beat) put in a hard night's accordion playing. John Payne, principal lighthouse keeper, agreed to MC, working very hard at his job throughout the night. Although many of the visitors were unfamiliar with the dances, they absolutely swung into action, keeping in time at least to the music, and making the floor a swirling mass of happy revellers. Tea was served twice with sausages and rolls, salad, sandwiches and fancies, and between two and three in the morning a crowd of from seventy to eighty, arms linked, sang the parting song, 'Auld Lang Syne'.

Unsettled weather has meant a difficult haymaking season but, at last, the weekend following the dance gave us two necessary working days. A light wind blew from a northerly direction and the afternoon's steady drouth improved the hay, but as evening advanced two 'jacks' appeared rainbowed and bright before and after the sun. The wind then fell light. Clouds, dark purple and indigo, became tinged red by the rays of the setting sun. Two curlews, piping loudly, flew swiftly east.

On the horizon a tanker sailing westwards seemed far away and entirely removed from the shadows of the newly forked hay. Over the still air came the cries of seabirds sounding sharply in the quietness of the approaching night. Finally the sun disappeared, leaving the long line of the sea showing darkly against the July sky.

In the Memorial Hall on the beautiful evening of Friday, August 2, Martin Gray, who is now well known in Orkney, gave a very professional account of his recent working trip to the Gulf. Although this affair is a sad episode in human and environmental history, Martin was able to paint a fascinating first-hand picture – differing from the political version. A carefully selected series of excellent slides accompanied the talk.

Immediately afterwards, for some four hours, the old Memorial Hall rang to the music of accordions, drum beat and the sound of some seventy folk (made up of islanders, ex-islanders and many visitors) dancing, swinging, talking and all taking part in what was a very splendid summer dance.

A young visitor from Lancashire (staying at the Bird Observatory) afterwards described the evening as one of the best she had ever enjoyed.

Halfway through the night Bessie Muir, who had returned specially to the island for the affair, attended, as of old, to the tea. Sandwiches, homebakes and biscuits were served, with many of the young folk helping.

A bottle of whisky, donated by the new shop owners, Anne and Sidney Ogilvie, was raffled. The winner, Marion Muir, then offered the bottle for auction. The price rose until Kathleen Scott finally bought the whisky for £18.52, making a grand total of £37.62 for the association funds; extra to that was the door collection of £115.

MC and announcements were a combined effort – mainly carried out by John Swanney, with Ian Deyell and Kathleen helping. Two more hours of even more lively dancing followed until the final traditional close of an island function.

Outside, the pearly grey light of approaching dawn lit up a broken sky. The moon's last quarter shone faintly through high cirrus. Quite suddenly, dark menacing clouds passed quickly over the Memorial Hall and were gone.

Days to Remember
August 16, 1991

This is Sunday, August 16, and as I write, just a few minutes before 9pm, the sun will disappear beneath a pale blue sea. Outside my west-facing window there is a glorious fuchsia tree festooned with countless flowers of the deepest and richest red showing up beautifully against the dark green of the leaves, and in the still air above this fuchsia and a graceful honeysuckle, bees are humming away as they work among a treasure trove of red and purple flowers and the fragrant honeysuckle. Myriads of small flies are playing in endless patterns of up-and-down flight, above the low trees, and far away above their little world a few clouds are lazily drifting across the sky, their edges tinged an orangey yellow by the rays of the setting sun.

I am going to tell you about two memorable days which have come and gone on the island, the first of which was two days ago and was a marvelous experience of sun and clear blue August skies. A few clouds drifted past from time to time in the cool wind blowing lightly from the northwest. That day's stream flood tides saw two good and lightsome pundings – one at Snaetin and another at Trindly. Many shears clicked away busily for a few hours.

Then at sea, after the heat of the day, a North Ronaldsay praam worked away, at times gliding over a sea of pale powder-blue – like that wonderful blue of the starling's egg – stretching away north and west as smooth as silk. Passing between Seal Skerry and the land and moving into deeper water, the boat jumped briefly in a minor blue-black tidefall before passing the tall, banded tower of the North Ronaldsay lighthouse, which, as the praam moved swiftly south, looked for an instant to be almost cut in two by the blaze of the setting sun. All the time in the east, the moon was rising and becoming brighter, until an hour or two later her yellowish face reflected a wide path of gold glittering upon the night sea. Once round Dennis Taing, with the golden path following the boat, the darkening line of the island appeared stretching north and south with winking lights showing up here and there from silhouetted houses.

Then, in sudden contrast to the colourful sea and sky, I saw down on the darkened 'tulfers' of the boat, a small, slim, exquisite sand eel, glistening in pale silver.

Later from a happy and busy Community Centre in the process of being redecorated, and where over the summer between 500 and 600 attendances had been recorded by the warden, 300 balloons had been blown up and tied in clusters. They were then carried down the old school brae towards the venue for the following night's venture, the Memorial Hall. Imagine for a moment such a sight. By this time a brilliant moon lit up the island and reflected brightly on the floating, bobbing balloons, their various colours still easily seen. A warm south wind kept them streaming and dancing away as we walked along. Then an oystercatcher called sharply as it winged past. To the west a slight land sea rumbled quietly away, its sound echoing over the night air.

So my second day arrives – Saturday, August 15. In a hall decorated with balloons, flowers and evergreens, a great night began. It was planned and introduced by this year's warden, Ingrid Tulloch. In only three days a concert was conceived, practised and carried out with considerable style and dash. The two teachers, Liz and Trevor Baxter, with others helping, had worked extremely hard to successfully achieve this. Trevor on guitar accompanied ten young folk made up of North Ronaldsay School pupils and some visiting children, who sang and mimed their way through a selection of songs with wonderful confidence and enjoyment. Then twenty performers appeared on stage – with the addition of ten made up by students from Kirkwall Grammar School and one or two others. All sang delightfully together before the older group gave an audience of between seventy and eighty a number of enjoyable songs with Trevor accompanying.

At the end of the concert the warden and a member of the Community Association proposed a vote of thanks before tea, and a magnificent selection of homebakes and sandwiches were served. Then without a moment's delay the dance began. Three accordion players, made up by Ronnie Swanney, leading in fine fettle and style, and accompanied by Lottie and Ann Tulloch (plus drums) began playing for what was to be last dance for the summer. Ian Deyell and Kathleen Scott acted as Masters of Ceremony in an atmosphere that must have borrowed something from the great days of the past. The quality and mood of the evening was enjoyed by young and old alike including a very spry lady, Mrs Dax from France, aged ninety-eight. Through the night an island couple in their seventies and early eighties took part in a Scotch Reel, and so the dance went on with great enjoyment until the early hours of a new day. Donations for the Community Association amounted to over £80.

Outside the dark and silent hall, the moon, just fading slightly on the west edge, lit up the scene and threw shadows of a little parting company across the road. There below the great dome of the sky, eyes turned towards the stars. Cassiopeia, or the Lady of the Chair, could be seen directly above the hall. Further east the Seven Sisters glittered coldly, and in the north the constellation of the Plough dominated the heavens. One or two young folk, for the first time, were helped to pick out a great star of the northern hemisphere. They followed an imaginary line from the two pointers of the Plough upwards, there to connect with another line drawn from the Plough handle, and at the peak of the triangle, one could easily see this star – a star so very far away, but through time and from generation to generation, it will remain fixed for the next few thousand years always pointing to the north. It is of course, Polaris, or the Pole Star.

I am finishing this letter on Sunday while looking through our east-facing window. In the background I can hear Trevor Elliot playing 'The Carnival is Over' which sounds rather sad. A few garden trees are being blown backwards and forwards by the remains of last night's southeast gale. Rain also lashed down in the blackness and fury of the night, and the sea today, in brilliant sunshine, seems to move in a living, sweeping mass to the north. I am ever more aware that summer has been slipping away, as time is, bringing with its passing inevitable changes. Trevor now plays the traditional tune 'A Bunch of Thyme' and I feel there is little more I can say.

Summer Seems Far Away
November 28, 1991

Summer seems far away, as does the memorable dance I wrote about early in August. Since the last account of events, the island's communal punding, clipping, and the work of harvest is now well behind us.

During those hairst operations one magnificent day remains in my mind – I suppose because it somehow evokes memories of some great hairst days. The autumn sun shone with as much warmth as on any summer day. Only a few clouds passed by across a brilliant September blue sky, and the wind blew cool and fresh from the northwest. The sea to the windward sparkled here and there in white splashes blown from the tops of wind-tossed waves, and the wind, moving inland, sent the oats dancing in rippling sweeps up and down the length of our last field.

Imagine on such a day sitting, wind-swept but warm enough, on that marvellous machine, a McCormick binder – now fifty years old – and watching those last sheaves of our crop fall neatly, one by one, in long, easy lines. And imagine for a moment the hand-sown seed flying through the spring air, and falling on to ploughed and harrowed fields, growing, being cut, bound, and finally, before this day ended, being 'stooked' to the tune of the west sea and the northwest wind.

In the New Community Centre two lectures have been given lately. The first was on September 15 when Dr Eric Voice, a lecturer with the Orkney Science Festival, gave a well-attended and informative talk on the serious consequences of the greenhouse effect. The Community Association arranged the evening and provided light refreshment and an opportunity for further discussion.

On October 10 Bill Hewison gave a fascinating account of life in Orkney in the 18th century. Afterwards those who had attended had an opportunity to see some of Bill's research documents and enjoy tea and cakes.

Also in the Centre on November 2, the association arranged a social get-together, which began with a bonfire and fireworks display on the North Links. James Lyon, lighthouse keeper, coordinated these events, which proved to be as successful as last year. Parents generally helped with this enjoyable affair, with Mary Swanney, Kirbist, making the soup and Mary

Payne, school cook, attending to the baked potatoes. Tea and homebakes brought this pleasant evening to a close.

This year's Community Centre warden was Ingrid Tulloch who organised various events over the main summer holiday period. A total of 538 attendances were recorded.

I am writing this letter on November 14, and through a southwest-facing window I can see the half-grown moon set against a dark and faintly clouded sky but special to see, and it reminds me of one other marvellous day when returning from fishing at the Reef Dyke – the sort of day one experiences but seldom, and never quite repeats again.

A set sea had been a pleasure to work upon, and the grandest sunset was fading slowly through wonderful colours of bright orange and red. In the east the moon had already risen, shining with an almost luminous green light on the broken sea surface. Every moment the sea and sky became darker, with the orange-tinged clouds changing to deep red and finally showing up purple against the western sky. The moon rising ever higher became brighter, with its reflected sea path a most beautiful sight to see. Suddenly, in the path of silvered light, a North Ronaldsay praam, *Diana*, our companion fishing boat, appeared silhouetted for an instant against the shimmering sea, and then passed by. The lighthouse flashed steadily, with darkened oilskins and gunwales alike reflecting the cold moonbeams. Far above in the eastern autumn sky, a star appeared small and bright, but light-years away.

Since that unforgettable night, southeasterly gales have pounded the Reef Dyke and the drifts of creels alike, and scattering those that remain unsought after three weeks of gales. The sea will always be an element which demands respect from those who work upon it, and respect shown to those who bring service to others upon it.

On November 8 in the Memorial Hall the Harvest Home took place. After welcoming between sixty and seventy islanders, guests and visitors, John Cutt, Gerbo, was asked to say the grace. The supper then followed with native sheep mutton (again cooked by Winnie Scott, North Manse) and clapshot. After a most pleasant, candle- and barn lantern-lit three-course meal, Councillor Howie Firth, our guest speaker, began his toast to the Harvest. The speech was most interesting and most enjoyable – a mixture of reminiscences, apt quotations, and nostalgia, telling as he did of that great character and well-known Orcadian John D. Mackay, who for some years taught in our island school, and who Howie knew in Sanday where Howie was the itinerant North Isles science teacher. 'John D' also ran a drama group, helped with many concerts, and along with everything else was Scoutmaster in North Ronaldsay. Howie, concluding his speech, asked everyone to toast the Harvest, and the supper came to an end.

Our performing guests this year were Jenny Ellis and Carolyn Drever, who sang quite beautifully a number of songs with Jenny providing guitar accompaniment. On stage were Owen Tierney and Micky Austin, playing guitar and banjo respectively, and accompanying Ronnie Swanney, Trebb, who played with his usual grand swing hour after hour.

Later, Micky and Owen (who were our two other performing guests) gave some fine toe-tapping guitar and banjo music, and Howie, playing recorder, warming up to the proceedings later in the evening, joined the band. At one stage he played two recorders simultaneously whilst dancing a samba. Drumsticks tapped to the inviting rhythm with John Swanney, Westness, acting as MC. Through the evening a bottle of gin donated by John Payne, principal lighthouse keeper, and a large box of chocolates, donated by Sydney and Anne Ogilvie from the shop, were raffled and made a combined total of £35 for the association's funds. Tea, North Ronaldsay mutton, sandwiches and homebakes were served later in the night, and finally, eight hours after the evening began, the proceedings came to an end with the hand- and arm-linking singing of 'Auld Lang Syne'.

Outside, a cold, strong November wind blew from a northerly direction, bringing from time to time sleet showers flying from the dark, freezing sky. Only a memory remains of the Harvest Home – the soft dancing light of candle and lantern, warm straw simmans crisscrossing the hall, sheaf decorations, flax and flackies. The red, blue, yellow, green and white buoy heads, music and song, all combining together over the hours to weave a splendid mosaic of harvest thanksgiving and communal enjoyment.

It only remains to thank everyone who helped. Members of the association and others whose combined efforts ensured such a successful night: Billy Muir and Sinclair Scott for providing the native sheep, Bessie Muir and Edna Cowe (not forgetting James) returning again to the island and helping. Jane and Evelyn for largely organising the catering. Our guests already mentioned, Ronnie for playing magnificently, Ann Tulloch who helped earlier until she caught the 'bug' (as did others on the island). Bob Tullock and his staff from Loganair, those who supplied the grand selection of homebakes and finally those who gave donations for the Memorial Hall.

Storm Blows Away Old Year
January 9, 1992

How often when walking on beach or land does one come across bits of broken pottery or coloured glass? Each piece, if it could reconstitute itself and move back through time, could tell a tale of past generations and days gone by, and the bits of coloured glass – bottle-green or amber, red or deepest blue – when looked through against the seasons' skies, can instantly change summer to winter or winter to summer, or give the effect of twilight, sunset or moonlight.

These colours (and often sounds or simply an airt of wind or a certain type of day) can bring back a past experience or memory – just like one recent calm and mild December night when the moon was full and the sky seemed almost like a summer day viewed through a darkened glass.

Clouds, a faint white, still stood out against the palest blue sky. To the west, white moonlit breakers rolled landward from a restless dark blue/black sea. Quite suddenly a 'teewup' (lapwing) called as it rose and flew, moving to a safer stance. Its call brings to mind spring days and marshy ground. Then a car passed by with rear lights shining red.

Almost whenever I see those receding rear lights they remind me of Christmas and take my memory back to thirty years or more ago, when one night in Kirkwall some of us who had shared digs during earlier schooldays were once again together in the same house waiting for the five or six o'clock morning sailing of the *Sigurd* or *Thorfinn* to Stronsay and North Ronaldsay. It was the only time I remember that any of us shared a night together when passing through on our way home for holidays.

Through the familiar and much looked-through window which covers the length of Broad Street, I could see the many red car lights moving, stopping, and being reflected from a dark wet street, turning left and right and winking brightly in a darker and more old-fashioned and homelier Kirkwall.

In preparation for the children's Christmas party the Community Association arranged a film show on Friday, December 6, followed by a short whist and beetle drive. The following Friday saw the Orkney Youth Theatre's evocative and versatile presentation of *Peter Pan*.

Over the past weeks since the October break, Isobel Muir has been the head teacher – filling in until the arrival of the newly appointed head of the school, Mrs Baxter, along with her husband (also a teacher) and family in time for the new session. Isobel, in addition to her teaching duties, was able to organise a short Christmas programme with the six pupils. This function took place on December 19 in the Community Centre which was specially decorated for the occasion. Anne Ogilvie, Evelyn Scott and Mary Lyon helped to keep things moving in rather a delightful and colourful sketch entitled *Finlo* – the story of a clown.

Despite the fact that they had to compete with the sound of gale-force winds from outside, all the children managed quite nonchalantly to act out their parts gaily dressed in circus costume. Some fine old Christmas carols followed, with Alison Duncan providing piano accompaniment.

Sadly, for various reasons, not least the weather, this had to be a daytime performance, which of course meant that many islanders did not manage to attend. Still, those who were able to come along came away feeling that in the midst of stormy weather and power cuts there was the sparkle and spirit of Christmas.

On December 24, as always, the children's Christmas party was held, and 250 balloons with streamers of various designs, wall murals made by the pupils depicting the twelve days of Christmas, and six-foot-long shining wall drops transformed the hall into a bright and cheery atmosphere for the festive season. After an afternoon of games, everybody enjoyed the usual party refreshments and then, in subdued light and beside the sparkling Christmas tree, Santa, chuckling from time to time, handed over a present to each child and left ones for those not there in the capable hands of his experienced assistant, Winnie Scott.

The last community function for the year was held on December 27. In the New Centre a slideshow and dance was arranged. Between forty and fifty folk attended the occasion when Dr Kevin Woodbridge, assisted by Alison Duncan from the Bird Observatory, presented the 'Birds of the Year Review'. Kevin gave an informative account of bird activity, patterns of development and progress – such as the tern (which has done much better this year), fulmar, black guillemot and others.

It was also interesting to learn that there lives in North Ronaldsay a fulmar aged about twenty-nine. Excellent slides and graphs of bird movements accompanied the talk. Martin Gray then followed with his review of the more exotic birds which have passed through the island during the migration season – birds such as the isabelline shrike, red-backed shrike, pine bunting, and others. He illustrated his interesting account with some excellent slides.

The dance then followed, and although beginning rather slowly developed into quite a grand and successful end-of-the-year occasion. Ronnie Swanney played all night, accompanied by Ann Tulloch, and then for the second half Lottie Tulloch joined in. Three accordions were then playing together, giving more volume and making the dancers swing even more energetically. John Swanney acted as MC, working well in his efforts to get people dancing.

Through the evening tea, sandwiches and even Christmas cake were served. Anne and Sid Ogilvie again donated a large box of chocolates for the raffle, with James Cowe and Luke Woodbridge attending to the selling of the tickets. The chocolates, along with a bottle of whisky handed in by a member of the committee, raised a total of £320.60.

Ian Deyell arranged the presentation of the raffle prizes, calling upon the three eldest ladies present to help. Janet Tulloch picked the winning tickets, with Mary Thomson and Bethia Scott handing over the chocolates and the bottle of whisky. The combined age of the three islanders was 231 years.

Before ending this account of the evening I must mention that two Scotch Reels were danced in an attempt to learn and revive this dance. Three senior members from the old days in their early seventies, and one over eighty, were right there on both occasions. Between two and three in the morning, watching from the stage, above and through the Christmas decorations, one could see, in the subdued and coloured lighting, the widening and closing circle of islanders and visitors, hand in hand, bring the last dance for 1991 to a close.

On Hogmanay a furious storm of wind blew from the southwest, becoming stronger by the minute and whistling away the old year without ceremony. I doubt if it would have been possible for the men of Linklestoon (Linklet Toon) when they were in full Hogmanay swing some thirty years or more ago, to have made the round of the toonship houses, and on the second day of the New Year when visiting the island's oldest man – now ninety-one – I put this point to him.

He couldn't recall such a night on a Hogmanay but went on to talk about other nights of wind and rain (when there were no proper roads), or when the snow lay white on the ground, and once, when a hard frost gripped the island, the company walked across a frozen Ancum Loch to visit the farm of Sangar. On that special night the danger of this venture would not have been topmost in their minds.

We continued to talk about this and that, and stories of great Hogmanay and New Year nights. One concerned a neighbour, well fortified with North Ronaldsay ale, as all the company were as the night progressed, when he asked the local teacher (who was one of the company) if he could tell him what Heaven was really like. The answer he got was that probably that night he was as near Heaven as he would ever be.

As the hours passed, many another tale was told with sparkle and memory of a lifetime's experience. All the while a less violent southwest wind continued to whistle round the chimney and door, blowing 1991 – who knows where or how – even further away into the far northeast.

Splendid Evening

January 23, 1992

Two days after 'Old New Year's Day' almost fifty folk attended what turned out to be a splendid evening in the New Centre. Howie Firth began the night with an excellent lecture on the 'Folklore of Orkney's North Isles'. North Ronaldsay featured prominently in the first half of the evening, and in the second half Howie went on to deal with the Orkneyinga Saga and others (using an overhead projector for relevant passages) to suggest differing interpretations of those great accounts of Orkney's connections with our forefathers of some 700 years or more ago.

After he was thanked for his informative and interesting lecture, the new teacher, Elizabeth Baxter, her husband Trevor, and family Christopher and Emily were welcomed to the island. Isabel Muir, on behalf of the Community Association, presented Elizabeth Baxter with a basket of flowers. This ceremony began an enjoyable and lively welcoming party with drinks being served, followed by tea, an assortment of homebakes, and, even still, some festive cake.

Although the old festival of Yule, which began on December 21 and finished on January 13, was at an end, this evening very appropriately celebrated the end of Yule and the beginning of a New Year.

Remembering the Primroses
April 30, 1992

In another few days (as I write) one-third of the year will have gone. How quickly the days and weeks pass – it must be true as they say, that as one gets older time moves faster. And yet for me it seems hard to believe that in the summer of 1952 I first left North Ronaldsay, to spend a year in Holm where I attended the school in that parish.

Often when the west wind rattles my window it reminds me of those days for, at the schoolhouse where I stayed, my bedroom window also faced the west and the wind played a differing tune according to the season.

When I remember Holm, I think about the smell of the smoke coming from the peat fires which I suppose almost every home burned. Then there were the kindly and entertaining neighbours from whom we received milk, cheese and butter (eggs came from relations in North Ronaldsay).

I also remember the wonderful display of primroses that grew in profusion about this time of year below the little stone bridge that spans the Graemeshall burn, but particularly I remember the singing of the telephone wires – especially on frosty nights, how this wind would play a thousand different tunes through that mass of wires stretching from pole to pole, and yet, marvellously, they would also carry the voices of Orcadians far over the sea and land.

On looking through my North Ronaldsay diary, I see that towards the end of January there was a good attendance at repair work being carried out on the sheep dyke which had been damaged earlier by heavy seas. That work took about a week to complete – but in contrast to the last time such repairs were done, the weather looked more kindly on our activities. Shortly afterwards nine punds were organised to choose sheep suitable for butching, this being a time to remove animals for such a purpose.

Here I might say that those people who attempt to market North Ronaldsay native sheep meat, belonging to animals which are not feeding in North Ronaldsay in winter on the various exposed seaweeds and other sea-driven weed, give the innocent buyer an impression which cannot be the same flavour as our unique North Ronaldsay mutton. The conditions on this island are unmatched elsewhere and remain the main, if not only, proper habitat of these primitive sheep.

Then on the 30th day of January, with as fine a day as that time of year can conjure up, part of a day's fishing near the Reef Dyke brought fish, silver and dark green, spinning into the boat on hand-pulled line – enough to fill a basket and to provide the grandest taste of the cold Atlantic. In March a heavy fall of snow blown by winds from the Pole suddenly fell, and was transformed overnight into high drifts and sculptured forms by the wind – almost covering the island, and reminding one of the weather which can still occur even in early spring. I hope this year when May comes, that the lily – that most graceful of flowers whose scent seems the very essence of spring and summer – will surely survive and stand in all its glory.

The New Community Centre has been transformed into a lively area of activity and enjoyment – not least because of the inspiration and drive of our new headteacher Elizabeth Baxter and Trevor, her husband. Apart from the netters' use of the hall, three planned activity nights are now established, with a mixture of events including badminton, carpet bowls and table tennis, with the ladies having a night on their own. The success of these evenings is evident as in the short time since Christmas well over £100 has been collected for the Community Association.

By way of a celebration for Easter, on April 18 Elizabeth Baxter's idea of a 'bunny hop' took place. The association financed the children's Easter eggs and the drinks which were served after the main event. Despite this very busy time of the year and a night of gale-force winds and rain, a good turnout of over forty, made up of islanders, children and visitors, attended this social get-together.

The evening began with the bunny hop, with various prizes being won by the differing age groups (including an adult hop). A treasure hunt followed for 100 Easter eggs, and although planned for outside, proved to be a great success within the complex of the hall.

Next was the competition for the best decorated Easter egg and Easter bonnet. Liz Forgan (Director of Programmes for Channel 4) judged the various categories and presented the prizes. After this event, Jenny Tulloch, Scottigar, presented each child with an Easter egg given by the association. She also picked the winning raffle ticket and handed over the large Easter egg presentation donated by Elizabeth and Trevor Baxter. This raffle was planned for the Macmillan Cancer Fund and raised a figure of £25. Further fundraising activities will continue for this appeal.

Once all these events were completed everybody enjoyed a feast, beginning with baked potatoes with various fillings and followed by a grand assortment of homebakes. Drinks were afterwards served, thereby giving the adults a chance to relax and enjoy the remainder of the evening.

Finally, special thanks must be given to Elizabeth Baxter who planned and ran all these events so competently, and to the children, Jean Tulloch, Mary Lyon, Ann Tulloch and the association members, parents, and others, who helped in any way to make the evening such a great success. A collection of £50 was taken at the door.

April is drawing to a close as I write these last lines – a month which has sadly seen the passing of one of our senior and knowledgeable islanders, Sarah Deyell. Today, Sunday 26, a morning of rain and wind has suddenly become mild, sunny and quite calm for the moment. Down by Ancum Loch, flies like miniature helicopters hover and dance. Already the segs are turning the marshy ground green again, and here and there, along with the water horsetail and growing marsh plants and moss, marsh marigolds are flowering, their cupped leaves beaded with the remains of the morning rain. Soon their display will carpet the loch area in a blaze of yellow gold. All around, the air is full of the sound of birds. Coots, calling here and there, are feeding in the loch, their white heads plunging from time to time beneath the water.

Oystercatchers, snipe, curlew and 'teewup' (lapwing) add to the chorus of sound, but perhaps most evocative and beautiful of all is the song of the skylark. They seem to be everywhere, always beginning their song as they climb steadily until they reach their chosen height – quite high above the island's fields. Once there they seem to sing away time with glorious ease. But the background sound remains always that of the restless sea. It changes according to the weather and the season, but it goes echoing back through time to a period when even North Ronaldsay did not exist.

Remembering the North Boats
July 23, 1992

The marsh marigold and the lily that I talked about in my last letter have gone, but both this year survived happily, heralding in some glorious early summer weather. One held cups of shining gold to the sky and the other stood tall and graceful, dressed in cool, scented white.

The skylarks that I listened to in April are still singing – one I timed at over four and a half minutes' continuous song. When the lark reaches its height, and in order to conserve energy for what seems a remarkable achievement of combined song and flight, the wingbeats are too fast to count, but after a second and more they miss a few beats, then continue, and so the pattern goes on until the skylark plummets earthwards – free-falling some of the way to regain its chosen territory.

North Ronaldsay has been a busy island since April. In that month, and later, the spring work was completed. Boats were painted and creels made ready. Children's activities continued on Saturdays, supervised by teachers Liz and Trevor Baxter. The school term advanced with Alison Duncan, the Bird Observatory warden, bringing in a long-eared owl and a red-backed shrike for the pupils to see.

Orkney Enterprise and some island councillors visited the island on May 19 and met with the public during a pleasant evening exchange. On the last day of May a solitary corncrake was heard, bringing back memories of past days, but sadly only calling for a night and day before disappearing as mysteriously as it had arrived.

As May ended, the North Ronaldsay creel boats got under way again, setting creels in waters that had already been ruthlessly fished by the bigger lobster boats from other islands throughout the winter and spring. The lobster stocks are as surely being destroyed in just the same way as the world's fish numbers are being depleted. It's necessary, they say, to make a living, but for how long? A few years with oar and sail would soon solve the general problem of overfishing.

One Sunday a special walk was organised to raise money for the Macmillan Fund. After the walk, tea and homebakes were served. £110 was raised for the fund.

As June spent, silage work and hay came round, beginning in time with the most marvellous curing weather – days of blazing sun and fresh northerly and northeast winds, the sort of weather one dreams about for hay. As I write, we are back to more typical Orkney weather.

On June 27 a musical evening arranged by the head teacher Liz Baxter took place for the purpose of raising funds for the school. The Community Association ran the dance which followed, but the evening was a team effort of teachers, guests, Parent Teacher Association and whoever also felt like helping. Tim Geddes, travelling music teacher (synthesiser), the singer Jenny Ellis, Jimmy Leisk (bass guitar) and Keith Wright on drums, from the group Anastasia, arrived in North Ronaldsay for the weekend, their way paid by the North Ronaldsay Community Council.

A full programme began in the evening in a Community Centre decorated with over 250 balloons and wall decorations from the school's term project. The group Anastasia sometimes accompanied an extensive repertoire of songs, recorder and percussion music given by the primary school. Songs and instrumental work had been learned at school under Liz Baxter's direction, with Tim Geddes setting three songs to music. The pupils had made their own costumes, designed to fit in with the theme of the school term's study project and their musical evening: 'Mini Beasts' – grasshopper, spider, centipede and others.

Later the children sang a number of well-known songs – 'This Old Man', 'London Bridge', 'Old Macdonald'. The musical items were splendidly performed with confidence and enjoyment, and the head teacher deserves full credit for this part of the evening. A collection of over £110 was collected for school funds.

The entertainment continued with the group Anastasia taking over. Jenny Ellis (one of last year's Harvest Home guests) sang a variety of songs. The various skills of the accompanists were there to be enjoyed.

Some magnificent food was available, and once the chairs were cleared a rather grand dance continued the evening's entertainment, with the musical guests accompanying the accordionist Ronnie Swanney, assisted by Ann Tulloch. Between 2 and 3 in the morning 'Auld Lang Syne' was sung with three cheers for the evening and for the band.

Outside, the dawn had already broken behind ribbons of purple cloud. The Fair Isle stood clear and coldly blue above the horizon, and in the eastern sky the last sliver of the dying moon disappeared behind the gathering morning cloud.

Wednesday, July 1 saw an open day at the school. Primary Seven from the Holm school and their teacher Mrs R. Whittles were guests for two days, and they also enjoyed tea, coffee and homebakes, which were available as refreshments. Here was an opportunity to see what had been achieved over the summer term. Roald Dahl's book *James and the Giant Peach* formed the basis of the term's work. A field and school study of 'Mini Beasts' such as the centipede and earthworm (overgrown characters in Roald Dahl's story) were looked at, including the complete life cycle of a beetle. The book also provided the inspiration for English and maths, along with the previously mentioned musical interpretations.

Children's work books were laid out for inspection along with wall charts and other items. My trip up the school brae was enjoyable, rewarding and educational.

A little earlier in the term Liz Baxter, assisted by Evelyn Scott, took the pupils away for a week's stay on the Mainland. Both the Community Council and the Community Association helped with costs. Many places of interest were visited including St Magnus Cathedral, and St Magnus Church in Egilsay (where a treasure hunt was held on the island). Stromness and the Pier Arts Centre were also covered, but all of this was not achieved without some drama, since lightning struck the bus on the way to visit the Tomb of the Eagles in South Ronaldsay. Earlier their journey from North Ronaldsay was by sea, travelling in the Kirkwall Lifeboat which visited the island on an RNLI exercise. All in all, it was an interesting combination of experiences.

North Ronaldsay enjoyed rather an unusual occasion on July 3 when Ann Manson, curator of the Pier Arts Centre, came out to the island with the *North Boats* exhibition. It opened, very suitably, in the Memorial Hall with wine being served to upwards of fifty people, and through the week supervised showing by Martin Gray recorded a further thirty-five attendances. There, those of us who had experienced such days or who knew something of the history, were taken back in time – for example to the story of the epic voyage of the Earl Thorfinn in 1953 when, in hurricane winds, the ship survived a fourteen-hour enforced sea journey to Aberdeen. I wonder if our newfangled ferries would have withstood such a storm.

Photographs, original paintings and ship models made the show memorable, and on a wooden table stood, silent, the ship's bell of the *Earl Sigurd*, bringing back memories of nights spent sleeping aboard prior to an early morning's sail: the sound of anchor chains rattling, the heat of the funnel on cold winter and

Easter mornings, and the smell of smoke on the lee side of the steam-driven ship, of grey seas rolling past and fulmars gliding over the wavetops.

Then there was the agony of seasickness, and sometimes having to suffer a return journey when sea conditions prevented a landing. A few trips such as we experienced when travelling home (once in each school term and back again – sometimes crossing the North Ronaldsay Firth in an open boat) would very soon silence any critics of our shipping service to Orkney and the crews of these boats.

Ann Manson and the Pier Arts Centre have to be congratulated on providing the islands with such an exhibition and I know more are planned – an excellent idea which our celebrated artist Stanley Cursiter would have approved, had he been alive. More power to Ann Manson and her supporters, and to further worthwhile and good exhibitions.

Over a period of ten days a team of thirteen volunteers from the Scottish Conservation Projects rebuilt a section of the sheep dyke, leaving a piece of good strong work behind them. They enjoyed fine weather and were invited to the opening of the *North Boats* exhibition, going from there to a barbecue at the Bird Observatory. On their last night a party was organised by the Community Council when a number of islanders enjoyed meeting these young people – mostly university students coming from England, Scotland, Germany and the USA.

As the market time of year draws near there is still some hay to be handled. The nights are noticeably darker and the colour of the sea and sky has changed from that of high summer. One night when enjoying some scything, I was able to watch the sunset. The wind was in the northwest, and in the distance a large cargo ship moved slowly north. With the still bright light of the setting sun, the sheep dyke was silhouetted against the sky and the dark blue of the sea, and in our 'mire ground' below the dyke, a curve of ragged robin made a stunning display of pink among the orchids, forget-me-nots and many other flowers and grasses that grow there untouched.

Quite suddenly, for the first time, at last I saw the phenomenon of the 'green flash'. Just as the sun finally slipped below the horizon, its last light changed to a brilliant luminous green, shimmered for an instant and disappeared, leaving a dark line of sea against the night sky.

Captains and Commodores
October 26, 1992

Well, the glorious display of our fuchsia tree has gone, and so has the song of the skylark. For most of the day (Sunday, October 11) I have been trying to put together a different type of letter.

The time is now about 12 midnight, and outside the night is still and cool with hardly a breath of wind. It is possible to write easily as I make some notes for this introduction, for according to the calendar the moon is full and rides high in a cloudy sky. At times her light floods down brilliantly through parting clouds, leaving her dark-edged against the dark vault of space. Even when partly hidden by high, thin clouds, her form is still visible shining palely, but also beautifully encircled by a luminous collar of rainbowed light.

Looking towards the southwest I can see the dark silhouetted forms of both the Old and New Kirks, with lately-built stacks adding to the familiar landscape. In the northeast the lighthouse flashes every ten seconds, her beam sweeping out to sea and over the island. No ship's lights relieve the dark horizon, but beyond the slowly moving clouds a few stars sparkle from time to time. From time to time 'teewups', plover and wild duck call from far and near, and the wind has died down to the merest whisper. From the west comes a dull, low pounding of a heavy and powerful land swell, while from Linklet's east-facing sandy strand small waves make a sighing, splashing sound which travels musically through the night air.

Summer is, without doubt, part of this year's memories, as is, very sadly, the relater of the Hogmanay story of 'Heaven' I told earlier in the year. John Laverty, Barrenha, aged ninety-one, who died recently, was that storyteller. More than once he told me how he had seen the German Fleet scuttled when he was a young man working on a farm in Orphir. That story led on to talk about North Ronaldsay men, and a woman, who had served in the Great War.

Remembering these stories leads me on to relate more of the achievements of an island which, despite its small size and isolated position, has turned out islanders who have over the decades distinguished themselves in many fields and contributed to society generally. During the Great War there were men who were decorated and Mentioned in Dispatches. There were men and women who served in both wars and those who died in that service.

It is an island where two of its islanders received recognition for their achievements in the form of an OBE and an MBE, where many others became skippers, with six coming from one house. Another became Commodore of the Granton Trawler Fleet. There were two deep-sea captains, ship's engineers and many who have carved out careers stemming from service in the RAF, Police, GPO, Lighthouse Service and many other occupations on land and sea in this country and abroad.

Amongst those occupations was that of a minister and a lawyer, a matron, and many nurses and teachers. There have been doctors of philosophy, a professor, and university and college graduates taking degrees in English, science, agriculture, architecture and the fine arts generally. It is an island where in the past its boatmen have risked their lives to save shipwrecked crews, where it still has experienced and able boatmen, and where the island's reputation for providing fine cattle by its capable and astute farmers is maintained.

In these days of controversial shipping services in Orkney, and in a country facing the worst recession since the 1930s, I suppose finally that economics and common-sense will rule the day. But in the first context it is still worth remembering that once a sailing ship struck bottom in the North Ronaldsay Firth and was lost, with pieces of wreckage coming ashore in Sanday. On more than one occasion Orkney Islands Shipping Company ships have been on their beam ends in that same firth, and there are still seamen who remember those trips, including Kirkwall School scholars who think back about such homecomings, locked for safety in their cabins. On two memorable occasions watchers from the island thought the ships had gone, hidden as they were from time to time down in the deep troughs.

Anyway, almost thirty years ago a writer from the island, who had earlier experienced sail-boat crossings to Sanday, wrote: 'Consideration of our subject [North Ronaldsay] from almost any angle inevitably leads us to the sea; there is scarcely a single aspect of life on the island which does not show its influence; for here, as everywhere, it's both a barrier against, and a link with, the world.'

North Ronaldsay is an island surrounded and isolated by the North Sea and the Atlantic Ocean, and to reach its main pier, ships from Kirkwall must make the approach either from the west or the south before entering the North Ronaldsay Firth – a piece of water particularly dangerous with a westerly-running sea. On approaching from the south a ship has to face the possibility and danger of southeast and north sea, and the effects of the former on the pier.

Those of us who have experienced crossing that formidable piece of water in spring, summer and winter, sailing in an open boat to Sanday or in the steam- or oil-driven ships from Kirkwall – sometimes waiting days in Sanday for suitable post-boat weather or returning to Kirkwall without a landing by the larger ships – have no difficulty in understanding that the sea, and the captains in charge of their ships, will dictate the possibility of making, as the island writer puts it, that 'link with the world'.

Fortunately, though now under threat, Loganair still provides the other link by air, and to an island which Captain Fresson in his book *Air Road to the Isles* says: 'Undoubtedly the outstanding air conscious island was North Ronaldsay.' That service, both for perishables and passengers, must be retained for an island where the surrounding sea holds sway.

On September 15 as part of the successful Orkney Science Festival programme, Professor Archie Roy gave a well-attended lecture on astronomy, showing some magnificent slides of the planets. More recently on October 10 a wonderful exhibition of prizewinning wildlife photographs from the British Gas Wildlife Photographer of the Year international competition was on view for five days. Brian Elliot, from Environment and Resource Technology Ltd in Stromness, very kindly set up the exhibition and also, by way of opening the show, projected excellent runner-up photographs. Both events were held in the New Community Centre and were well attended. Refreshments were served at the end of each function.

Otherwise, the harvest work is more or less completed apart from some tattie picking. The North Ronaldsay School is working away very happily and busily indeed. On Saturdays the children's activities continue, and once a month the pupils, accompanied by Liz and Trevor Baxter, travel to Kirkwall for swimming lessons given by the swimming instructor John Leslie.

More recently in the school the children participated in a Musical Singalong specially arranged for Age Concern Week. Fae Watson, the itinerant music teacher, was there to help with the singing. Then there was an open afternoon at the school for National Book Week, when pupils read from books they had chosen. Sponsorship in this connection was arranged to raise money for the Malcolm Sargent Cancer Fund.

Both functions were well attended and the various entertainments (including looking through old photographs) were enjoyed by old and young alike. Tea, coffee and some grand homebakes were served, pleasantly rounding off the two successful afternoons.

On November 6 the North Ronaldsay Harvest Home will take place in the Memorial Hall, and in connection with the preservation of that building a charitable trust has been set up, about which I will be writing again. An island development investigation, conceived by the Community Council, has also been put in motion with the support and finance of both the Islands Council and Orkney Enterprise.

It's about a week since I stood outside and began this letter. Tonight the contrast is great, as the wind whistles down from the Arctic, bringing every now and again vicious pelts of freezing rain and hail which lash the island mercilessly. The sky is a turmoil of wind-torn cloud, sweeping south, dark and menacing. Through brief rifts in the clouds a few glittering stars appear, as does a fading moon. They seem to fly through a dark and stormy sky, while below unabated heavy seas crash thunderously all along the exposed shores of the island. Those seas are rushing west and south, where through the day they could be seen breaking heavily all along the Reef Dyke, showing the power and majesty of the encircling sea.

A Harvest Home
November 19, 1992

When the fun is at its highest, reads the old Irish proverb, it's time to go, and that is how the North Ronaldsay Harvest Home came to an end sometime between three and four on November 7.

I do not think anything can quite surpass the light of the living flame. It goes back to the earliest civilisations, but still, with lantern and candle, it flickers and lights up our thanksgiving supper, creating, for an hour or two, an atmosphere that conjures up past images and memories, and concentrates the mind, for a short period at least, on the meaning of the Harvest Home. Peter Donnelly's evocative photographs, as they do capture moments in time, should convey some of the atmosphere of what was undoubtedly a great night.

At around 8pm in the Memorial Hall everybody was welcomed to the evening's proceedings. Apart from islanders, there were friends, acquaintances, and a number of former islanders who had arranged specially to be home for the occasion.

Among a company of between seventy and eighty were the association's invited guests. They were the Harvest Home speaker, OIC Convener Jackie Tait and his wife, Alison, our island councillor, Howie Firth and the liaison officer, Ronnie Tulloch, along with their wives Sidsel and Elma, two musicians, Lesley Mcleod and Elsie Linklater, and finally the station manager for Loganair, Bob Tullock and his wife Lena.

Bob Tullock's presence was particularly appropriate as this year was Loganair's 25th anniversary. It was also an opportunity for the island to show their appreciation of Loganair's service to the island, and to Bob Tullock for helping these past years with our Harvest Home arrangements.

After the North Ronaldsay welcome, John Cutt was asked to say grace. Then a supper of native North Ronaldsay sheep mutton, clapshot, cider, sweet, tea etc., began. At the finish of a most agreeable and pleasant meal, Jackie rose to propose the toast to the harvest. He described his very favourable impressions of North Ronaldsay during his summer visit and on this occasion, his admiration of the cattle he saw, and the sheep.

He talked about the island's future and the importance of a development plan, but emphasised the desirability of retaining the island's unique character and way of life. He also said that his colleagues on the council were very much aware of, and sympathetic to North Ronaldsay's problems. At the end of the speech, with glasses in hand, the company rose and repeated the convener's toast to the harvest. The speaker was then thanked and applauded, as were the ladies who had arranged and served the meal.

Once lanterns, candles and tables were cleared and Slipperine dusted on the floor, the dance began with Strip the Willow – a dance which always seems to get everybody up and swinging. On stage were the two guest musicians, Lesley McLeod on fiddle, and Elsie Linklater on keyboard. Also there were our three familiar island accordion players, Ronnie Swanney and Lottie and Ann Tulloch. All played together with fine swing and enthusiasm with Ronnie leading. Drumsticks tapped out the dancing rhythm.

Through the night Lesley and Elsie played some beautiful, slow airs followed by a selection of grand reels, strathspeys and marches. Howie also swung into action playing two recorders for his performance and thereafter played along with the band. Twice, three sets of Eightsome Reels whirled found the floor with many a heuch.

On went the dance and on again after tea, sandwiches and cakes. John Swanney performed in his own unique way as MC. Through the evening a raffle collected by the ever-helpful James Cowe amounted to over £40. Sydney and Ann Ogilvie had kindly donated a bottle of whisky, with Elsie Linklater and Lesley McLeod also very kindly donating a tape. A box of chocolates made up the third item for the raffle.

The three oldest island ladies (whose combined age totalled 233) Bethia Scott, Mary Thomson and Janet Tulloch, under the direction of Ian Deyell, picked the winning tickets. Ian then presented the prizes. And so with the Irish proverb in mind, the time came for Robert Burns' great parting song. This song never fails to bring back memories of past years and old acquaintances, and this night a number of the company remembered the very recent passing of two former islanders and another lady who spent many happy times on the island. But as the last note of music and words died away, three cheers were given for the band and three for the MC and the night, bringing the Harvest Home for 1992 to a close.

Before completing this account I have, on behalf of the association, to especially thank all the many people, islanders, visitors and guests, who together made the Harvest Home such a memorable one: the ladies who attended to the catering, the speaker and two musicians, the band, the many folk who helped with the decorations and those who supplied the native sheep, homebakes, neeps and tatties, gas heaters, lanterns, transport and accommodation.

As I walked home, an almost full moon had quite disappeared behind low-lying dark cloud. A more moderate wind blew cooly from the west. Stars, now gaining command of the winter skies, shone brilliantly, one drawing my attention as it appeared to twinkle and flicker in changing jewelled colours. This vast dome of the sky certainly captures one's imagination, magnificent and mysterious as it is.

I have lately been reading selections from *A Scottish Land Anthology*, and thinking as I walked north, about the Harvest Home and the galaxy of which this world is an infinitesimal part. I remembered a short piece written by Lewis Grassic Gibbon. It seems appropriate to quote part of it at the end of my account of the Harvest Home.

> *'I am a Jingo patriot of planet earth. Humanity right or wrong. Particularly in Autumn. At noon I crossed a field off which the last of the stooks had been lifted and led captive away, the gaping stubble heads pushed through the cricks of clay, the long bouts of the binder wound and wheeled around the park ... And each of those minute stubble stalks grew from the seed men had handled and winnowed and selected and ploughed and harrowed the earth to receive, and sown and tended and watched come up in the rains of Springs and the hot Summer suns – each and all of these – and out beyond their kindred trillions ... This is our power, this the wonder of humankind, our one great victory over nature and time. Three million years hence our descendants out on some tremendous furrowing of the Galaxy, with the Great Bear yoked to the Plough and the wastes of space their fields, will remember this little planet, if at all, for the men that conquered the land and wrung sustenance from it by stealth and shrewdness and a savage and surly endurance. Nothing else may endure in those over-human memories: I do not think there is anything else I want to endure.'*

Will our Heritage Survive the Years?

January 21, 1993

In a thousand years from now what will Orkney be like? Will North Ronaldsay still exist I wonder?

It is said the land and sea endure, but what sort of society – if any – will people these islands in 500 years, let alone a thousand, or even a more easily imagined timespan of 200 years?

If there is a 'Brave New World' will our Orcadian history with its customs, traditions and way of life be respected and understood, with its best values retained?

Anyway, I am thinking back to one or two events missed before my account of the Harvest Home. Ernest Marwick, when referring to ritual bonfires, says that the old bonfires were lit on four occasions in the year: Yule, Beltane, Midsummer and Hallowe'en. On Hallowe'en evil forces were thought to be abroad and fire was considered to be a protection against such forces.

I read also that Hallowe'en falls on the old Gaelic season of Samhain, which represented the end of the half year containing the long days of summer and the cold second half of the year's start. In the North Ronaldsay within minding it seems bonfires were lit on that night, and so on Hallowe'en we revived an old custom by combining a magnificent bonfire with a firework display and thus doubly ensuring that any lurking evil spirits got short shrift.

Later a good turnout enjoyed May Payne's roasted potatoes and warm bowls of soup in the Community Centre. The children present were dressed in suitable costume for the occasion and had, along with adults, produced various homebakes for the tea which followed. To end rather a unique evening, dooking for apples in the old-fashioned way brought considerable amusement.

Before Hallowe'en, Dr T. Stowe gave an illustrated and most informative lecture on the corncrake. Refreshments followed. On November 7 the Harvest Home took place, and through the remainder of the month several successful punds were organised. Also a dancing class began under the professional and elegant direction of Wilma Taylor from Kirkwall. Liz Baxter's idea for an island Christmas dinner proved a great success, with over fifty folk attending. The dinner was provided for a very modest charge with May Payne, the school cook, and Winnie Scott cooking a magnificent three-course meal.

Serving in the brightly-decorated Community Centre was carried out by the combined school staff including Avril Cromarty, PE teacher, and invited school catering manager Heinz Ziegert. After the dinner Trevor Baxter accompanied the school children as they sang quite delightfully a number of Christmas carols, and in addition they played very well on recorders and percussion.

Two days later on December the 19th the children's Christmas concert took place in the New Centre. The evening event meant that the majority of the islanders had the opportunity once again to enjoy the highlights of the festive season, with the Christmas dance to follow. This year the school gave a performance of *The Tinderbox*, an ambitious and fairly complicated piece, bravely tackled and admirably put over by Catriona Lyon, Kirsten Payne, Lorna Tulloch and Christopher and Emily Baxter – five of the six available pupils who rose to the occasion.

Much work has gone into the production, with Evelyn Scott attending to scenery and costumes and the rest of the school staff – Trevor Baxter, Isabel Muir, Anne Ogilvie and not least Liz Baxter, who had provided the inspiration and drive for the concert – helping to keep the play moving. Kenneth Cutt very kindly taped the concert on video.

Immediately after, tea, coffee, sandwiches and homebakes were available. Before the dance began, a suitably inscribed book was presented to the retiring lighthouse keeper, James Lyon. Thanks were expressed for his work for the association and the children of the island over the years. At an earlier date the school staff, children and parents, had presented his wife Mary Lyon, the care assistant, with a clock and their daughter Catriona with a wall hanging.

As the next day had to be an early steamer's morning a short but very successful dance followed, which saw two new dances – the Barley Bree and the Seven Step Polka – being introduced, and the revival of previously known dances such as the Dashing White Sergeant, the Pride o' Erin waltz and the Scotch Reel. An excellent collection amounting to £90 was taken for the school funds.

On Christmas Eve the association's Christmas party for the children took place. An earlier, specially run whist drive had raised £70. With further donations a total of £120 was raised for the party. After the usual games, tea, drinks, cake and trifle the afternoon came to an end with the appearance in the sparkling hall of Santa, who seemed in fine fettle, accompanied by his cheerful attendant, Winnie Scott. The thirteen children present were each presented with gifts from Santa.

And so Christmas came and went, as did Hogmanay and New Year's

Day. But on the 2nd a New Year's dance was held in the Community Centre, thus reviving another occasion of not so many years ago. The evening began with two RSPB films kindly supplied by Eric Meek, the RSPB officer for Orkney. Both films were excellent, but particularly the beautifully-shot film of puffins made on Shetland. What happened in Shetland a few days later made a terrible contrast between the film's wonderful and colourful images and the tragic scene from those islands of our northern neighbours.

The dance – which included another of Wilma Taylor's newly-taught dances, the Cumberland Reel – was again a great affair lasting until about 3am on the third morning of the New Year. A bottle of whisky donated by a member of the association along with Anne and Sidney Ogilvie's Christmas cake was raffled, taking in about £30. Added donations gave a total of £73.66 for the association's funds.

John Swanney acted as MC. James Cowe acted as a raffle collector with Ian Deyell arranging for the winning raffle tickets to be picked by Norman Scott (North Ronaldsay) and his Australian wife Maree, both home on holiday from that far country. Ronnie, Ann and Lottie provided swinging music for the two dances, with Norman doing a little banjo picking.

I have been thinking back to about this time last year when I made my New Year visit to Johnny o' Barrenha. Lately I retraced my steps to the very door of his old home, but only darkness and silence reigned there. I think of visits made in the past around this time of year to Barrenha, when Hogmanay and the New Year nights were almost always remembered and talked about.

Some thirty-three years and more ago, I was privileged to take part for a short time in what was, for 'Linklestoon' (Linklet-tun) in particular, the great nights of Hogmanay and New Year. At about 7pm after an early suppering of the inside farm animals, Milldam was the house where the 'crood' (crowd) collected.

In the late Fifties there would have been about ten houses to visit with a crowd of upwards of twenty men, both young and old. Each succeeding house followed mostly in accustomed order. Light in the homes would mostly have been the old-fashioned Tilley lamp providing both light and extra warmth. Smoke from the older men's pipes would have wreathed the lights and kitchens (the main living room, or 'but'). Home brewed ale, the making of which was a ritual in itself, was to be tried – sometimes mulled for certain older members – latest events discussed, and stories told with good-natured banter thrown in when the opportunity presented itself. Food was also available and after a suitably judged time, for there were some ten houses to visit. Usually one or two of the more senior experienced men would make the move for the next house in line.

And so the night would spend. The short distances between each farm house would be walked by the crowd by the light of the moon or by flashlight, or simply by the light shining down from the stars. Each house would wait its turn, with the remaining folk setting up for the arrival of the Hogmanay visitors.

Through the night songs would be sung, mostly Scottish, with a few by Robbie Burns and Harry Lauder. There would also be World War I songs sung such as: 'It's a Long Way to Tipperary' or 'Pack up Your Troubles in Your Old Kit Bag', all of which were well known, particularly by the veterans of the Great War who had served at sea or in the trenches in France.

Eventually the turn of the last house would come. By this time the crowd would have been in fine shape having sampled various strengths of homebrew. In my minding, Antabreck would have been the last farm to be visited, and it was not unusual for the first cold light of New Year's morning to be in the sky before our last neighbours left.

On New Year's Day there was another round of visits for Linklestoon, but on that night the older men went visiting on their own. It would have been a much smaller company, more intimate and more reflective. 'The Braes o' Balquidder' or 'The Dark-eyed Sailor' and other old songs would be sung. Many stories would have been told, with a favourite subject of the older generation – relationships – being remembered.

On that night also there would be a much younger company of both sexes who might have numbered twenty or more, but they were made up of folk from other districts. The best nights I recall started on 'Bustietoon' (Buistie-tun) and took in houses on 'Nesstoon' (Ness-tun) 'Linklestoon' and Aby or Ancumtoon. An accordion would have provided music for singing or a bit of confined dancing. Sometimes it happened that when the crowd got to Linklestoon both the young and old companies would be together at the same house, filling up the kitchen and spilling out into the passageways for a short time, before leaving the older men to resume a more dignified and wiser exchange.

In other districts similar visits would have taken place, but on Linklestoon Hogmanay was to survive longest and remained to the last a memorable and very special night. Well, those were great days, great nights, wonderful ale, good company and great times, the like of which will not be again.

Old New Year's night is fast approaching as I finish this long letter. An extremely violent wind is blowing and seems to shake the very house from time to time. The sky is constantly changing from dark to light as storm clouds sweep cross the seemingly flying moon – a moon encircled by a great warning halo.

The white of heavy seas is being thrown high into the winter skies, breaking all around the island with damaging power. This combination of low pressure, stream tides and unremitting storm force winds has resulted in tragedy in Shetland, and the devastation of substantial areas of our surrounding sheep dyke.

1993 has certainly established itself with vengeance in a sorry and troubled world.

The Navy Take Their Leave of the Shore
March 25, 1993

I often think that the snowdrop leads a cold and lonely life: no flies or bees to visit their white petals and yellow centres, no summer sun or warm winds to make their short, early existence more enjoyable. But though now gone, they are after all the first heralds of spring and the summer to come.

Today, Thursday, March 18, a few early daffodils are being battered by occasional hail showers and gale-force winds. The west sea is hammering away, rising and churning over in viridian and dark green volumes of water before breaking up into a brilliant white sea, then rushing rock-wards to explode and rise far above the line of the steel-grey horizon. All the time a finer sea-spray sweeps over the island in great, moving drifts. Still, the spring sun is shining in sudden bursts of bright light appearing from time to time through flying cloud, and on the few small tree branches to be seen, green shoots are appearing. The skylarks have been singing again, with occasional songs from a visiting blackbird and a melodious wren. Oystercatchers and teewups have also been calling, their familiar voices sounding sharply through spring days and starry nights. Soon, it seems, King Winter must retire to his northern kingdom – the sooner the better, as we've had enough of his batterings for one season.

Recently the Ronaldsay school spent a weekend on the Mainland. It was a few days packed with diverse activity under the guidance and organisation of the head teacher Liz Baxter and her husband Trevor. The island pupils shared this experience with our Papa Westray neighbours, whose primary school teamed up with North Ronaldsay. A lot of swimming was managed both in Kirkwall and in Stromness, and all the children had a great time participating in an art workshop at the Pier Arts Centre.

Visits were made to the Corrigall Farm Museum, the Brough of Birsay and the Earl's Palace. While staying in the school hostel, a video of *Peter Pan* was watched, and on Sunday evening Tim Geddes and his band led a lightsome sing-along. Over the days in Kirkwall, the Post Office and Radio Orkney gave the pupils a combined school tour of their buildings, and when visiting the library each child was able to choose their own books for the term's reading. Before leaving for their return journey a tour was made of

Kirkwall Airport where the children particularly enjoyed their inspection of the new £250,000 fire engine. Well, for any others – young or old – the above would certainly have been a weekend to remember.

Wilma Taylor's dancing classes came to a close on Tuesday, February 23, bringing to an end a most enjoyable winter interlude. Her professional teaching and graceful demonstrations were a joy to all of us who attended the lessons. On her last night's teaching she went through as many dances as possible.

Over the weeks some of the dances learned and revived were the Circassian Circle, Dashing White Sergeant, Pride of Erin Waltz, Scotch Reel, Axum Reel, Rory O'More, Seven Step Polka, Barn Dance, the Friendly Waltz, Cumberland Reel and Barley Bree, along with the more familiar dances such as the Eightsome Reel, Strip the Willow and Gay Gordons. In total we have a repertoire of over twenty dances.

At the end of our last class Wilma Taylor was presented with a beautiful display of flowers by Bethia Scott, one of the three oldest islanders in attendance. Their combined ages totalled 229 years – an example indeed for the younger Orcadian generations. After this ceremony a very memorable little closing party took place with tea, coffee, cake and biscuits being served, followed by drinks, which very enjoyably brought the evening and the dancing classes to a close. The following morning Wilma changed her dancing shoes for rubber boots and worked for a short time on rebuilding our sheep dyke.

This brings me to tell you about the building of our now famous sheep dyke, articles about which have appeared in various papers and television programmes. The devastation I referred to in my last letter was the worst seen for over fifty years and, although a mile shorter than the three miles flattened in 1937, presented in many ways a more serious problem. For instance, much of the damaged dyke was badly scattered and involved the movement of some very heavy stone, apart from the fact that there were extensive areas where no stone remained at all. The other comparison, of course, is the lack of manpower, since the island can only turn out less than a quarter of the workers who were available in 1937. At that time eighty to ninety builders worked on the three-mile stretch for full days at a time, but yet were able to leave sufficient numbers at home to carry on day-to-day work on the small farms.

The rebuilding of sheep dyke around the exposed shores of North Ronaldsay requires experience, knowledge of vulnerable areas and where to move inland if necessary. It requires the knowledge of exactly how to build – not ornamental dyke but a properly bound structure designed for sea, sand and storm-force winds. It has to be built sufficiently high and straight on the seaward side to prevent the agile native sheep ('loupers') from jumping inland. In short, it is a dyke built by or certainly supervised by, islanders who know their terrain and who consider such work – as long as they are able – a duty, an obligation, necessity and even a pleasure. Its maintenance, along with that of the sheep, remains one of the last examples of the old communal system of agriculture in Orkney.

With such principles in mind, and for more than seven weeks, a work force of mainly islanders, both men and women, turned out day by day and week by week to help, and to deal with a serious problem which affected almost every person living on the island. Among the company of builders were men in their sixties and seventies, one of whom, Sydney Scott aged seventy-eight, had worked during the 1937 disaster as a young man. Another, John Tulloch, Senness, in his teens at the time, had helped to control the many native sheep that came inland from time to time. Sometimes two or three people from the Bird Observatory turned out and enjoyed working with the islanders, as did Trevor Baxter.

Just for the record, and as near as I can estimate, North Ronaldsay on its own built something like 1485 pace (a pace is approximately one metre) of upwards of five-foot dyke, sometimes even higher. This would equal from 3000 to 3500 tons of stone shifted, lifted and built. With the seventeen Naval personnel and working together for eight and a half days, an extra 850 to 900 pace, equalling another 1000 tons or more of stone, was built. On Wednesday, March 17, just one day past seven weeks, and after making use of available fencing generously funded by Orkney Islands Council and Orkney Enterprise, the sheep were at last closed back to their own environment. As I write there still remains the rebuilding and repair of some sheep punds.

Before I complete this saga of the dyke-building I have to thank the Navy, on behalf of the island, for their considerable help. Without their assistance those of us who have worked from day to day would have had to face an extra two weeks or more of building. Though inexperienced at first, there is no doubt that the contribution of these young men, helping as they did and taking an interest in our dyke, was entirely commendable.

As we all worked together, one familiar Naval saying often heard was the call 'Two to six!' This was said when two or three men placed a heavy stone. One fresh and windy day at Nouster, this expression was explained to me. A group of us stood round the dyke, and using stone on stone I drew a diagram for explanation under the guidance and enlightenment of that soldier of fortune, a Navy man named Andy Gardener. On the old sailing ships the cannon on its carriage was manned by a gun crew of eight. They numbered 1-2-3-4 on the left and 5-6-7-8 on the right. On the recoil, the cannon moved back. The order was then given 'Two to six!' and gun crew numbers two and six heaved on a rope through a pulley which brought the cannon back for action.

In order to show the island's appreciation for the Navy's contribution, and also to give these young men both from England and Scotland a chance to meet the folk of North Ronaldsay, two functions were organised. On Saturday, March 13 a dance was arranged on a night when the wind was down and an almost full moon shone through a hazy sky. There, in a hall lit up by a long garland of coloured lights, three accordions provided lively music for the dance, with Lottie and Ann Tulloch playing away all night long. Through the evening, tea and the very grandest assortment of baking and sandwiches were served, specially prepared by most of the island's women. Among the seventy or so islanders and Navy personnel was Robin F. Jones, Captain of Fleet Maintenance from the Fleet Engineering Centre, HM Naval Base Rosyth, and his wife. The dance was a magnificent success with the MC duties being shared between a Navy man and an islander. Shortly after 2am the long night came to a close with the singing of 'Auld Lang Syne'. Following resounding cheers, short speeches were given by John Swanney on behalf of the island and Midshipman Robbie Thompson on behalf of the Navy.

The second of these two nights organised for the Navy took place at the end of their work on the island, at a drinks party given by those islanders who had worked on the dyke repairs. There, with taped background music by Jimmy Shand, a very splendid exchange took place between the combined workforce and those islanders and friends who appreciated the Navy's help.

Midsummer Memories from the Past
July 8, 1993

In May, on a day when a cool wind blew freshly from the north and a brilliant sun shone down with considerable strength, I took a fancy to retrace an old often-trod walk down to the West Banks.

A sea of the deepest blue was all a-dazzle with little wind-broken wave tops, and within a few minutes I was picking my way down into Riff Geo. There sea-thrown stones were dried and whitened by days of sun and wind. Below and past the arch which connects the dark walls of the geo, the incoming tide blackened stone and rock as the water crept in, and in many clear pools and trinks coloured seaweeds swirled this way and that.

In well-remembered cracks and crevices, often examined in the past for some of the great numbers of synthetic Russian corks that came ashore and were used for corking and buoy-heading creel ropes, my roving eyes picked out two old corks which I prised away from their rock prison.

And so away I went on that old cork-finding route, moving quickly north. Up and down the familiar rock formations I went, retracing steps of nearly thirty years ago with something of the old excitement I used to feel, seeing in flashes of memory exact positions of many paintings executed over the years, and often recalling actual pictures. On I went, investigating great cracks, inlets and geos, which were of old sure traps for corks and drift. There was Antabreck Geo, Verracott Geo, South Himera Geo, geos which must date back to the Ice Age and so remain ancient and mysterious, and where only the sea and sky hold sway.

Before entering North Himera Geo – the cave geo – I stopped for a minute and drank a draught of cold, fresh water from a nearby rock spring we know. Himera is a classic North Ronaldsay geo, one I have painted many times and from many different angles – even from within the cave itself. There is something timeless about its atmosphere and unusual construction. The cave can be approached from the geo proper where it hides very cleverly round a corner, or by climbing down the sides of the geo. And so for a short time I sat within its entrance catching an angle of sun and sheltering from the north wind.

There I thought for a bit. I remembered a cousin of mine who lost her pearl necklace in the geo one summer long past, but it was found again shortly afterwards in a rocky pool, to be worn once more. Then, at the time of the press gangs it was said that some North Ronaldsay men hid in the cave and so escaped. Do their ghosts still come here, I wonder? Beyond the dark rock in the geo's centre, the sea sparkled. Passing this rock it relentlessly moved in, to eventually fill the geo. The cave in which I sat seemed like a giant seashell, catching and forever holding the sound of the wind and the great rolling ocean.

In my last letter I gave an account of the sheep dyke building and the Navy's participation. Among the helpers still to be mentioned are Captain R. F. Jones from HM Naval Base Rosyth, whose assistance guaranteed the success of the Navy's venture, and who enthusiastically got down to dyke building one fresh and sunny day at Ryas Geo. Then there were Peter Donnelly, Andrew Cowe and that ever-helpful young fellow in all things pertaining to North Ronaldsay, his son James. They worked for a few days, as did a professional dyker, Duncan Mills, the Bird Observatory warden Alison Duncan and L. Shields from Kirkwall. Then there were the Ogilvies, newcomers to the island, with Anne cooking for the Navy, and Sidney (a sheep owner) helping commendably with the rebuilding.

Working together with fellow islanders, friends and helpers, remains, as long as we can manage it, an enjoyable occasion. It was good to see some of the younger generation, such as James and Alison, sharing in that experience.

Well, even a prince came to see our sheep and sea dyke, and he was entertained in the New Community Centre, specially decorated with many examples of island work, plus a display by the school. Thanks must go to all those who helped prepare and lay out the magnificent choice of food, so grandly presented, and for all the work carried out on a voluntary basis. I wonder what the old sheepmen would have thought if they were still alive. I think, had they sampled a few drams of the ten-year-old malt whisky, very kindly donated by the Highland Park Distillery, they would have had quite a lot to say.

After Prince Charles' visit, seven Navy men came back and worked mainly on their own in quite glorious weather, when the island was all alive with land work, calving and other spring chores. Before they left, the Navy men (under Midshipman Matt Reid) were treated to a farewell drinks party.

Since then time has flown. Island creel boats are once again trying to work in waters already harrowed weeks before by the much larger boats which come over from the neighbouring islands. Even still, as I write, the North Ronaldsay boats are having to compete with hundreds of creels, set to catch everything which might be moving inshore, where the main local fishing grounds have always been fished by our small open boats. Otherwise, island work keeps moving along, as does the year. Nick and Louise are again helping to build – this time some remaining pund dyke, working with local folk who have the time.

The North Ronaldsay and Papa Westray schools have recently been across to the Mainland on two trips under the supervision of Liz and Trevor Baxter and Christine Hopkins. During the first three-day stay they visited Kirkwall Grammar School and learned how the telecentre's whiteboard communication system worked. Glaitness Primary School was also visited. Next day saw everybody learning about Orkney's past at Kirbuster Farm Museum. Doehouse farm was next on the list. The children enjoyed feeding some of the many animals living there, plus seeing how the hair of the Angora rabbit could be spun. Then followed next day a visit to Happy Valley, meeting the creator of that marvelous garden area, Edwin Harrold. At Fursbreck Pottery the young visitors were allowed to model objects in clay and learned how the kiln worked. Finally on their last day, Pickford's travel agents and the Bank of Scotland were seen – tying up with this term's European project. At both places the children were presented with little presents to help them with their project.

Their second adventure at the beginning of June had care assistant Evelyn Scott assisting the group. First, they had a great time at the Orkney Farm Park, seeing some of the rare breeds looked after there, a special highlight being feeding the ducks. Then at the Dounby school, children from that area were met, followed by lunch served in the school. And so on to Stromness where the children participated in the 'It's a Knockout' competition.

Once back in Kirkwall, the next port of call was Shapinsay, where the castle and its gardens were explored. Then, rounding off their memorable few days, a great time was spent having fun in the Brandyquoy Play Park. During both trips to the Mainland a lot of swimming was managed, with certificates being awarded to each pupil.

All of this is far removed from my schooldays. It is marvellous that such opportunities exist and that our teachers are prepared to give so much of their time and experience. Without Loganair a very different state of affairs would exist.

Otherwise, social activities are quite quiet apart from a rather grand little house party at South Gravity, given by Albert Scott and Louise Barker. Everyone who cared to go was welcome, and a great selection of food was available throughout the evening. Later, Eightsome Reels, a Scotch Reel and the Highland Shottische were danced. Well, it was a memorable night with very lively discussion on sheep, birds, dykes and many other subjects under the sun. And talking about the sun, it was just clearing the horizon when I left about three-thirty in the morning. Its low angle made the island's grass appear the very deepest dark green and moving west. Just for a second or two as I watched, the brilliant disc of the sun blazed momentarily, ninety-three million miles away, behind the lighthouse – its diameter almost equal to the tower's height at that distance. As I walked on, hundreds of dandelions in seed shone like orange candles as the sun showed its light from behind, and further west the short blades of a newly reseeded grass field picked up the gold-orange beams of the sun like little tongues of flame, which lit and died as I passed the angle of reflection. All the while the air was full of the skylark's song.

Last year April was drawing to a close when I took a walk down to Ancum Loch. At that time the marsh marigolds were just about to colour the loch edge like yellow gold. This year I waited a bit longer until the marshy areas were all ablaze and shining beautiful. Hardly any wind stirred except for cool, light breezes, which came and went from a northerly direction. Across a pale sky, purple-grey clouds stretched in long banks and tumbling, broken formations. Between circles and patches of sword-like segs, various mosses and marsh plants carpeted the soft ground. As I walked I picked my way very carefully, remembering warnings about insinks. Disturbed small flies darted this way and that, stopping when I did to alight briefly with folded wings and long bent legs. On the loch, two dignified swans sailed slowly in different directions studying the water carefully, occasionally plunging their heads below the surface. The very stillness of the air gave full volume to the loch birds that called continually – teewup (lapwing), shelder (oystercatcher), whaup (curlew), gulls, and coots. Every now and again the horse-gawk (snipe), flying fast, whirled and drummed away as he performed his familiar diving patterns, and further afield the skylarks sang long, marvelous, complicated songs.

Soon my wandering footsteps took me to the east, and once two graceful pickie-ternos (terns) passed over, clipping their way through the evening sky. In a more northeasterly direction the tall, banded 139-foot lighthouse rose gracefully skywards, and a little further east the Old Lighthouse stood in her own elegance. Behind her much lower tower (lit in 1789) and thirty miles or so further east still, the Fair Isle appeared, clear and blue, across the deep waters.

Near the loch stands the old farmhouse of Sangar, now in the process of being renovated by a young island couple. On a nostalgic impulse I ventured into the interior and stood in the area where the kitchen had been. Once long ago I modelled a portrait of Alec Swanney, who lived there with his sister Bella. He was in his nineties then but had earlier worked the farm on returning from his pioneering days from Canada.

On the north wall remains part of the kitchen stove, which reminded me of one time when I was making a prearranged New Year visit. Part of my supper waited in the stove's oven, and when the plate of pudding and custard was placed before me, I noticed a sprinkling of soot on the dish. Bella's stove and eyesight were not too good by then – but I tell the little story with no disrespect, nor did the soot bother me unduly (soot actually is an antiseptic). One has, many a time, to turn a blind eye to such minor incidents. I may say my supper was most tasty and enjoyable as was the 'discoorse' as we sat comfortably at the fireside,

More than sixty years before, when Bella was young, she had worked as a professional cook in a grand house in London, and my supper table on that same night was beautifully laid out with napkins, lace table cover, and china. I remember she told me how, when on holiday from the south, she had sometimes sailed by steamer from London up the east coast of England and Scotland, across the Pentland, then from Kirkwall to Sanday, and from there, by sailboat to North Ronaldsay.

I wonder, if she were still alive, what she would now think of the island's connections, with its air service of six days per week, twice a day, with a separate freight plane every Tuesday. All this in addition to a weekly steamer on Fridays with a back-up system on a Sunday. And what, I wonder, would she have thought about the recent very substantial subsidised air service to residents living on the island – which can combine with the steamer if so wished. And if all of that is insufficient, well, it's still possible to fly the thirty miles from North Ronaldsay to Kirkwall for £22 return.

As I finish this letter, tomorrow will be the longest day. The wind is in the northwest, and ever since Beltane, when it was northeast, his wanderings have (according to the old saying) mostly been from those northerly points of the compass. The sky is overcast, and dark purple-grey clouds are rolling towards the southeast. Nearer the horizon, the last faint mauve colours of an unseen sunset stretch in narrow brush strokes so very far away. But the night is cold and the sea, dark blue and black, is sounding with a touch of menace. I just wonder what the wind and weather will do over the rest of the summer.

Fleeting Memories of an Island Summer Past
October 14, 1993

Not so very long ago I borrowed an old Parlophone 78 rpm record in excellent condition, and which featured Jimmy Shand and his band, recorded over forty years ago. Listening to that band playing a Scottish waltz immediately reminded me of the rural cinema shows of the late Forties and Fifties in North Ronaldsay when, before the show and between reels, such performers as Jimmy Shand, Bobby MacLeod, Robert Wilson and others entertained the audience on record.

In the summertime, pinholes of light coming through small chinks in the wartime felt window blinds would show like little searchlights, throwing the light from the late evening sun across the Old Hall. Some of these films remain as acknowledged cinema classics, films such as *Great Expectations*, *A Tale of Two Cities*, *The Cruel Sea*, *Whisky Galore* and many others of that era. For me at least, the early Jimmy Shand Band's records somehow recapture those fleeting years and early memories of North Ronaldsay.

My last letter to *The Orcadian* was finished on Midsummer's Day. I meant to write this account some time ago, and in order to change my format a bit, I set off one day with my two nieces for a pony and cart ride. So away we went, me with a notebook to record our little journey, and to remember the various activities over the summer as we travelled along to the clip-clop of Jane's two Shetland ponies. The most of this letter, then, is a combination of my notebook, diary and memory, and the assistance of my travelling companion, Ingrid.

We began riding north one fresh day early in September. Teewups called, and a lark was singing as we passed the very old farm of Verracott, standing rather sad and lonely to the west. The sea, as always, was sounding across the short land distances, and on Ancum Loch swans swam. As we passed along the road sow thistles stood tall and yellow, and wonderful clusters of purple blue vetches were a pleasure to see.

Still travelling north, we remembered the first dance of the summer held in the Memorial Hall, and organised by this year's two wardens, Alison Muir and Ingrid Tulloch. A video of Prince Charles' visit to the island began the evening, followed by tea, sandwiches and homebakes. Lottie and Ann

Tulloch played for rather a swinging dance which lasted until between 2am and 3am on that summer morning.

At the dance were four generations directly descended from Nether Linnay. Both wardens had a busy season, with 200 attendances some weeks as holidaymakers and workers from the Prince's Trust added to the numbers.

Continuing our journey, on our east side we passed the loch rippling in the wind. Coots and oystercatchers called, and high in a silver-grey sky we could hear terns crying as they flew past. We turned east at the Turn o' Ancum, then north up and round the Brae o' Breck. There the remains of two small dwellings – Nether and Upper Breck – stand on their high vantage points. Once, long ago, William Tulloch, one of the many island weavers, worked at Upper Breck. Two of his sons went to sea. One, William, as a deep-sea captain and the other, John Tulloch MBE, served as bosun for many years on one of the Northern Lighthouse Board's ships, *Pole Star*.

As we bounced along on the uneven ground, first north then east, my writing looked as if I had been at the whisky bottle. Then from Quoybanks and back once more past Nether Breck from where, I am told, a John Cutt farmed on the Canadian Prairies, crossing the Atlantic three times before returning to end his days on the island. To the northeast the thin black line of Seal Skerry broke through the grey sea, and on the far horizon a white ship stood high against the sky. To our right and left among thistles, curly doddies and withering grass, little clusters of forget-me-nots and purple-blue violets were to be seen on Sanders' mixed fields.

Near Westness we could see a part of the sheep dyke where the Prince's Trust workers had been. Over their short spell on the island they had worked from 9am till 5pm with only short breaks on location. On the night of their arrival, a concert and dance were organised for the school, under the head teacher Liz Baxter's direction, and held in the New Community Centre. A visiting teacher from Graemsay, Irene Mathieson, performed a well-received selection of songs. After the concert a magnificent choice of food was available to the 100 or more islanders and visitors who attended the function.

Amongst the company were, interestingly, eleven teachers. Five live on the island. Two were from the island – home on holiday – and the remaining four were visiting teachers, one of whom was Jean Swanney who is well remembered as having taught on the island for some years.

Total monies collected for the school funds amounted to the spectacular sum of £261. Part of this was realised from the raffle: a bottle of wine and a box of chocolates donated by Liz and Trevor Baxter, a bottle of whisky donated on behalf of the Prince's Trust workers by the team leader PC Sheena Melvin, an anonymous £5 donation and finally, a print by Louise Barker, were all given for the occasion. Ann and Lottie again were the accordionists, and in the early hours of a moonlit morning a most enjoyable dance came to an end.

Returning to the Ancum turn and riding south, Westray could be seen, blue and elegant on the western ocean. A cool wind still blew, and the sky above the two Westrays was a silvery grey streaked with pale yellow. For a moment, one short burst of sunlight flashed earthwards through rifts in a cloudy sky. Clippety-clop went the eight little feet of the ponies down the Ancum brae, and as we rode we thought about other events which had been through the summer.

A Spanish sparrow had attracted two to three hundred twitchers to the island. Then there was the punding and clipping of the native sheep, and earlier, a farewell party for the Prince's Trust's fourteen workers. For a week the children on the island enjoyed the experience of the bouncy castle (a large inflatable), and as I had told a story about lost pearls in my last letter, Eline Steen, home on holiday from Australia, once more retraced her steps down into Himera Geo where her pearls, some forty or more years before, were lost, submerged by the sea, and miraculously found again.

During the Science Festival, the North Ronaldsay school, along with their Papa Westray colleagues, were off to take advantage of the occasion. A book exhibition was seen at the library (and books chosen for school reading). Two swimming classes were managed, and visits were made to the Wireless Museum, South Ronaldsay, the Fossil and Vintage Centre, Soulisquoy Printers and the visiting planetarium. Apart from seeing the Kirkwall City Pipe Band, a steam engine, and vintage cars in Kirkwall, a newly released video was also watched along with a visit to a performance at the Arts Centre. I should think that Liz and Trevor Baxter, Chris Hopkins and Evelyn Scott must have had their hands full for a few days.

Shortly we passed the War Memorial, then the shop and the Memorial Hall where a grand tarring day of this felt-covered building had ended with a dram, sandwiches and tea (attended to by Winnie Scott). Passing the Old Hall reminded us of the last summer dance held on August 20. It began with a short performance by the young people from Holland House, whose great-grandmother, Mrs Dax from France, aged almost 100, was there to hear them and enjoy the dance. Refreshments and tea followed, and then to the music of Lottie and Ann and a visiting accordionist, Roddy Watt (on holiday at Holland House), a very successful dance was enjoyed with three of Wilma Taylor's dances being performed – the Barley Bree, Seven Step Polka and a Barn Dance. Throughout the proceedings at the three dances James Cowe had helped with raffles, decorating and the cleaning-up. John Swanney, John Payne and Ian Deyell had also helped with MC work and raffle presentations.

On we rode past Holland's gardens where sycamore, fuchsia, New Zealand flax and escallonia made a splendid display. Along the roadways during our ride we had seen a number of flowers and plants such as coltsfoot, tansy, the moon or oxeye daisy or marguerite, greater knapweed, silverweed, common horsetail, goosegrass, yarrow, wild chamomile, devil's bit-scabious, what looked like common cat's ear and even still, bird's-foot trefoil. (Some of these, I may say, identified with assistance.) Well, our pony ride had taken about forty-five minutes, during which time we had covered between five and six miles.

A month or more has passed since that journey, and the small amount of crop now grown on the island has been more or less cut and stooked during some marvelous Indian Summer days. Three other events I will cover briefly.

During the Science Festival an illustrated and most interesting talk was given by Paul and Alison Newman on 'Old Orkney Farm Buildings'. On October 1 Dr Kevin Woodbridge gave an illustrated talk on 'Wind and Solar Power in North Ronaldsay' (Aberdeen University/OIC illustrated lectures). Refreshments were served on both occasions. Then on October 6 the school was open for a coffee afternoon/character day, when anyone was welcome to go along and listen to the pupils (who were dressed up as story characters) reading from their favourite books. This was altogether an enjoyable and interesting experience. A very grand feast of homebakes was available during an interlude.

I am finishing this letter to the sound of the northeast wind. Mists of drizzle are driving across the island. Along the exposed coast a line of white, broken sea is smoking away behind Breck and on past the two lighthouses. Days earlier, by contrast, the Merry Dancers had rippled in ever-changing colours of white and green across the northern sky. But the shimmering lights were the heralds of a southeaster, which came shortly afterwards and drove many creels ashore, damaged and tangled. In the far north the Greenland Eskimos of old used to think that those northern lights were the souls of their ancestors, playing at ball in heaven. This seems to me as fine and poetic a belief for those ghostly displays as ever one can imagine.

Celebration as the Harvest is Safely Gathered
December 2, 1993

Yesterday, November 16, a very strange sky appeared in the mirking of a mild and windy day. A great triangle of hazy purplish cloud stretched north in one long bank and then continued south to almost cover the late afternoon sky. But between these long blankets of cloud and dominating the southwest, another great triangle of pale, wintry blue sky shone with a marvellous luminous light. Across this space small clouds, scattered in little groups, still retained the fading orange and pink of the sun's dying rays.

Somehow, this combination of strange sky, misty colours and a fresh southwesterly wind blowing the remains of the summer's plants and grasses hither and thither seemed rather sad. It brought a mixture of memories of the passing days and a realisation that this year of 1993 was, like the November day, coming to an end.

Not long ago we celebrated Hallowe'en with fireworks and a truly magnificent bonfire on the Links. Later in the Community Centre Winnie Scott's tasty soup and baked potatoes were served, with assorted fillings prepared by various folk. Through the evening some of the school children, dressed up appropriately for Hallowe'en, ladled up glasses of their witch's brew from a sinister black pot which, despite the name, was actually very tasty. Dooking for apples followed, adding to the enjoyment of the celebrations.

The following night, November 6, ladies from the North Ronaldsay Lifeboat Guild organised a video show and sale. Raffle items donated by the president, Isobel Muir, and the secretary, Sheila Deyell, added to a fine total collection of £206.40 for the RNLI. Tea and homebakes, nicely served on tables, completed a very successful occasion.

A little before those two events Stromness Books and Prints, who were invited to send books to the school, very kindly gifted £50 worth of books for the school, and Red House Books donated their profits of £96.23 to the Malcolm Sargent Cancer Fund – having sold books amounting to £272. Their donation plus £104 collected from the island gave a total of £200 for the cancer fund. This very successful affair was organised by Liz Baxter in connection with Children's Book Week, with help from parents and school staff.

And so we come to the Harvest Home held in the Memorial Hall on November 12. Over eighty attended the function with many Ronaldsay-connected folk coming out specially for the occasion. Loganair once again helped to bring everything together, and Peter Donnelly's photographs should convey something of the atmosphere of what was indeed a very splendid and memorable night.

Well after 8pm everybody was welcomed as they sat in the flickering light of candle and barn lantern. The Community Association's guests this year were Willie Tulloch and his wife Jenny; Robin Anderson, accordionist, and his wife Muriel; Raymond Sinclair, singer, and his wife Eileen; our man at the mart for many years, Gordon Muir; and Wilma Taylor who had previously been our dancing teacher. Following the introductions and thanks extended to all who had helped with every aspect connected with this highlight of the year, John Cutt once again said the grace.

After a splendid supper of native mutton, clapshot, cider, cheesecake, tea and homebakes (with whisky for the toast) our guest speaker, a North Ronaldsay man, Willie Tulloch (formerly Upper Linnay), returning with his wife Jenny for a few days on the island, rose to propose the toast to the harvest. His speech was quite admirable, witty and amusing. He reflected on days past and present. Days when there were more people and fewer empty houses, and when often there was friendly rivalry between neighbours to see who would start or finish first, the main work of the changing seasons.

He talked about when there were far more crops to be seen, remembering especially the red poppies that grew on Sander's cultivated fields. Finally, he proposed two toasts, one to the people who had come to the island and secondly the main toast of the night, to the Harvest Home.

Then followed a flurry of activity as tables were cleared and carried outside through the north door. Dishes were washed, Slipperine applied to the floor, and after two introductory songs by our guest singer, Raymond Sinclair, the dance was off to a flying start. Robin Anderson led the playing with Lottie and Ann Tulloch supporting. David Cursiter from time to time returned to playing drums and Sinclair Scott played the pipes for one of the Eightsome Reels.

Dance followed dance, with Raymond often singing along with the band and helping John Swanney with MC duties. Through the night, tea and more of the wonderful selection of homebakes and sandwiches were served. Two bottles of whisky were raffled, one from Councillor Howie Firth (who intended to drink a toast to our Harvest Home from his fireside) and another from Anne and Sid Ogilvie. Ian Deyell supervised the raffle, with Mary

Thomson, Nether Linnay, picking the winning tickets, which altogether brought in almost £60 for the association's funds.

As the dance continued time seemed to fly, catching the company unawares. And so, between three and four in the early morning, the words of 'Auld Lang Syne' finally sounded through the Old Hall.

Again, on behalf of the association, I must thank all those who helped in any way with the days and nights of preparations for the Harvest Home. The names are too many to mention (apart from the willing young helpers that I should – James Cowe, Marion Muir, Geira Bews, Wendy Deyell and Christopher Baxter) but there were those who supplied the five native sheep, the neeps and tatties, serving the tables, preparing the food and cooking the mutton, looking after the lanterns, accommodating and attending to the guests, the players and singer already mentioned, the three gallant musketeers from the Bird Observatory who didn't need to help but did so with a will, and all those other helpers whose unseen chores, when all put together, created the North Ronaldsay Harvest Home.

When I finally left the hall in the darkness of the night, the sky was alive with brilliant winter stars, and the Milky Way stretched far across the heavens. Making my way home I thought about Willie o' Linnay's speech, and how he had so enjoyably woven the many aspects of life on the island into his discourse. I too remembered those past years, when North Ronaldsay's then extensive fields of oats and corn waved bravely, golden and ochre, ripening in the sun and hairst winds.

I recall when more folk worked longer and harder to save their all-sustaining crops. When the leading of the sheaves was carried out sometimes by the light of the moon, or in glorious autumn days, or between pelts of hail and rain. During windy weather sometimes heavy weights had to be laid on the weather side of stacks as builders fought to reach the top. And I remember when those who had finished leading would gladly help the neediest with urgency and pleasure.

Then I think of other great times – at Holland farm, for example – when many of us of varying ages went to help build stacks on Ronaldsay's largest farm. After darkness had fallen on the hairst fields, we looked forward to the 'lightsome' suppers in Holland farm house or Trebb. Suitable refreshments got the company in good fettle and helped to make some unforgettable nights. I am talking of course of twenty to thirty years and more ago, and many of those helpers are now, sadly, long since gone.

But I also remember, as we all still do, when our 'green and pleasant land' was as free and accessible as the winds that come from all airts. When one could walk the scattered fields and little hills and dales without a care, to work, play or visit, or simply to wander here and there for the pleasure of striding across the land upon which we had been brought up, lived and worked on and upon which our forebears had lived their lives, passing on the land from generation to generation.

Where our history and heritage, spanning the centuries, still stands to be seen in enduring stone is to be respected and remembered. Beneath the ground round those ancient sites, many of our ancestors must lie, and I like to think that if they exist in some unexplained form in this universe of ours or beyond, they will still return from time to time if they can, to walk unhindered over the island and to see once more their homes of long ago.

But I close by mentioning, like Willie, the red poppies that grew in many a field in those old hairst days. This flower once familiar in this island became eighty or so years ago, a symbol of remembrance and sacrifice of the Great War. The anniversary of its ending, seventy-five years ago, fell on the day before our Harvest Home.

A Summer Sky and a Frozen Loch on Christmas Day
January 13, 1994

Recently when in Kirkwall, I visited the grave of the distinguished explorer Dr John Rae, of the Hall of Clestrain, Orphir, who made four epic journeys to the Arctic between 1846 and 1854. 1993 was the centenary of John Rae's death, and was marked by the publication of a splendid book, *No Ordinary Journey* and a fine exhibition celebrating his life which was seen in Canada, Edinburgh and the Tankerness House Museum in Kirkwall.

By reading the book and having visited the exhibition, I learned more about this remarkable man, John Rae, whose success was in no small way due, as he readily acknowledged, to his understanding and adoption of many of the Indigenous Indian and Inuit ways. They were, after all, people who had mastered the art of travel and survival in the vast and inhospitable areas of northern Canada. Rae respected and admired these native peoples, and they reciprocated in similar fashion.

How marvellous it would be for Orkney if his old home at the Hall of Clestrain was restored, as it should be, to house material collected by Rae and items of equipment used by him, along with an 'explanatory' exhibition to celebrate the life of one of the Arctic's great explorers.

But to get back from the Arctic to North Ronaldsay, what have we been up to since the Harvest Home? Well, there has been some punding, where those of us who understand something of the old Orcadian communal system of work were there to carry out various obligations and related duties. Then the North Ronaldsay primary school, along with their colleagues from Graemsay and Papa Westray, spent a weekend in Kirkwall seeing the Christmas pantomime *Aladdin*, visiting exhibitions, attending seasonal parties and even meeting Santa.

The school sale of work (covered in *The Orcadian*, December 16) finally realised a very generous sum of almost £270 for Children in Need, and later about £100 was donated for the children's Christmas party on the island.

Our school meals Christmas dinner again brought out another good attendance, with Winnie Scott (school cook) assisted by Anne Ogilvie, cooking a splendid meal. After the dinner the school pupils, along with two pre-school children, entertained everybody with their presentation of the Christmas story, and singing carols both modem and traditional quite beautifully to the accompaniment of Alison Bardgett.

On the evening of December 1, the school Christmas concert took place in the New Community Centre, and very good it was considering the few pupils available. Much work had gone into the costumes and stage scenery by staff and pupils alike, but particularly by Evelyn Scott (care assistant) who used her artistic talents to good effect. For an hour or so a fine turnout was well entertained to mime and song as the children performed *Doo Bear and The Night Before Christmas*. Into the production was woven, quite cleverly, some topical and amusing up-to-date island lore. Kenneth Cutt, Gerbo, kindly videoed the concert. At the end of the programme a second round of applause was called for everyone involved, but particularly for the young actors who had performed so magnificently. Alison Bardgett was thanked again for her keyboard accompaniment and presented with a beautiful hamper of fruit by the school and staff. Other gifts were presented to all the children present on behalf of Mrs Mackenzie, Garso. Finally, the head teacher, Liz Baxter, whose inspiration and hard work marks the success of all her endeavours, received just praise and applause.

After tea, sandwiches and cake, a lightsome little dance got under way, improving as the night advanced. More refreshments were served late in the evening. James Cowe attended to the sale of raffle tickets offered for the Community Association's bottle of whisky and Liz and Trevor Baxter's bottle of wine and box of biscuits. Arranging the draw was Ian Deyell who invited the two eldest ladies present, Mary Thomson, Nether Linnay, and Bethia Scott, Antabreck, both aged eighty-two, to pick the winning tickets. Lottie and Ann, our ever-faithful accordionists, provided the dance music, with Alison Bardgett on keyboard, until about 3am when the last dance for 1993 came to an end. After the singing of 'Auld Lang Syne', Liz Baxter was carried shoulder-high. The raffle plus donations amounted to £131.10 which will go towards the purchase of playground equipment.

And so we came to Christmas Eve when the association's children's party was held in the Community Centre. Tea, sandwiches, cakes and trifle were served after the afternoon's games and dancing. Finally Santa arrived, escorted by his ever-faithful and experienced attendant, Winnie Scott, to hand out a gift and fruit to every child present. After final goodbyes Santa disappeared for another year.

Next day was Christmas Day and its splendour was exceeded only by the memorable perfection of the following day. Hardly a breath of wind stirred at all, and icy roads shone like polished glass in the sun of the winter's afternoon. Indeed, so magnificent was the day that I decided to go on a meandering walk across the island.

The time was 12.20pm when I set off under an almost summer sky. Each footstep cracked on the frozen grass and crisp snow-sprinkled fields. In the western sky the lowering sun shone with a blaze of yellow gold. When its dazzling face was glanced at momentarily, it would leave multiple little red suns glowing away whenever I happened to close my eyes.

A slight easterly land sea, with its breaking shore waves, sounded sharply over the frosty air, but otherwise all was still – save for the sound of my footsteps, an occasional calling bird, and a faint sea murmur from the west.

Ancum Loch, in contrast to spring and summer, was almost frozen across, but in a small area of open water I counted eight swans moving elegantly. Further away and standing quite still on the ice, a number of coots seemed mesmerised by the unusual change in their familiar surroundings. As I walked near the loch edge little pools imprisoned plants and mosses in green. Black ice cracked under my weight like pistol shots in the still air sending a flock of wild ducks whirring away.

A little above the New Lighthouse which, along with the landscape, was catching the full-coloured glory of the setting sun, the rising moon, just clearing some purplish cloud, appeared translucent and ghostly, while further east the Fair Isle's high hills were snow-capped and crystal clear.

Very soon, walking alongside the Stripe o' Sangar, I reached the sheep dyke, which borders the Links, and upon which still leans the remains of a wooden dyke ladder used by the laird, William Traill, and his golfing friends – maybe more than 100 years ago. Further south in summers past, kettles of hot tea made at North Gravity were taken over the same dyke near the farm for the grand picnics that were often held on the green and springy links.

Anyway, over the dyke I went, where my sudden appearance disturbed a golden plover, and where the water coming from Ancum Loch runs bubbling and tinkling under a gap in the dyke. From there it continues its journey over stones, under a little flagstone bridge, and eventually to the sea. Sandsheen, a winter loch nearby, was a sheet of ice, which shone very brilliantly when its surface was between me and the gold of the western sky. But not long afterwards the sun disappeared, leaving little drifts of low cloud glowing bright yellow and orange, while in the east the moon was becoming brighter and higher in the sky.

Once below the smooth sea-pounded stones of Linklet Ayre – fast becoming dark as its high bank became silhouetted against the intense, bright afterglow of the setting sun – isolated pools of water took on an inky appearance, whilst to seaward, long lines of three to four feet high waves advanced menacingly, darkening to black and green before breaking with small crashes of white on Linklet's sandy shore.

Sometimes I stood still in the incoming water as it rushed past and then back in rope-like, swirling rivulets. It gave the rather unsteadying illusion that I was still moving, and moving very fast. The moon by now was becoming quite brilliant, with her beams dancing on the pale blue and green sea. Two seals swimming inshore followed me during the remainder of my Linklet Bay walk, their shining black heads reflecting the moonlight from time to time.

From my notebook I see that I completed my wanderings at exactly 4.14pm – just short of four hours, in which the sun and moon, and the elements of sea, water, snow and ice had been seen in the sort of splendour that will not often be repeated.

Hogmanay passed quietly enough with a wonderful night of moonlight, stars, and magical, sparkling frost. While celebrating the first of the New Year, it was particularly interesting to be reminded that in the *Old Statistical Account of 1794* the Rev. William Clouston, minister of Cross and Burness and North Ronaldsay, says that he 'has seen sixty of the inhabitants assembled there on the first day of the year and dancing with moonlight.'

Some visitors from 'sooth' who had been taking the trouble to learn something of North Ronaldsay's history, noticed this information, and since they were first-footing not an hour into the New Year, suggested that such an event might be attempted, especially since it seemed that it could be 200 years to the day when first this activity had been recorded. Well, next year, if we are all spared, perhaps we should revive this mysterious tradition – even if only for the sheer fun of it all.

By way of possible compensation though, a night or two later those same friendly 'sooth' folk, namely Liz Forgan and Laurie and Cathy Taylor, instead of dancing round the Standing Stone, had to dance round Neven's renovated, comfortable byre in front of a magnificent fire. There they learned a Seven Step Polka and the Scotch Reel.

This procedure, carried out to the music of an old 78 record of Bobby MacLeod, was watched by the well-known underwater archaeologist Rex Cowan (another friendly visitor) who, despite his recent broadcast in which he talked about his dancing days in New York, viewed the proceedings with something of a disinterested eye. But warming later to such hilarious goings-on, his look became one of surprised approval – and very appropriately too, since had the house's previous owner, Willie o' Neven, been there in full swing, he would have given the dancers many an encouraging nod, and certainly his eyes would have been all a-twinkle like the bright stars in the winter sky far above the flagstone roof of Neven.

Old Farming Practices Survive Centuries
July 21, 1994

I am writing the beginning of this letter from Aberdeen, where I find myself staying unexpectedly for a few days.

On my various journeys up and down streets (in a residential area of the city) private house gardens, which come down to the dyked pavements, are ablaze with colour. All sorts of flowers, shrubs and trees please the eye, and marvellous scents – emanating from the many and varied gardens – pervade the warm, light air.

But to be in Aberdeen at this time of year is something of a coincidence and rather nostalgic, for exactly thirty-two years ago I was finally taking my leave of Gray's School of Art and from the granite city where, apart from holidays, I had lived for five years.

My memories of those far-off days centre mainly round the sculpture department of the school, where I worked for three of those years. The sculpture studios were always alive with sound and activity. All sorts of work was in progress: life-size figures, portraits, relief panels, etc., being modelled in clay to be cast later in plaster of Paris; the chipping out of those casts; letter cutting in granite, marble or slate; stone carving – mostly sandstone, but also soapstone, serpentine and a soft building material called Siporex, which allowed carving experience on a large scale in a short time.

Then, every week for a day there was the rattle of air-powered carving tools, when apprentices from the various Aberdeen granite firms received instruction in relief work. This insight into the sculptural aspect of monumental work added to their five years' apprenticeship in the trade colleges.

Today there is hardly any Aberdeen granite left (most granites are imported), and lettering is managed by computers and sand-blasting. Proper V-cut letters can be got, but at a price.

In the general sculpture studios, first and second year students came and went. (In the first two years all subjects were covered – drawing, painting, design, sculpture, metal work, jewellery, ceramics, anatomy and the history of art.) I remember the special smell of the sculpture studios – a sort of stony/earthy smell which came from a combination of clay, plaster of Paris and stone. Very often this would be most noticeable just after spraying the clay pieces to keep them moist. The water falling on dust-strewn floors seems to combine those smells just as, in the same way, rain on a warm day releases the scent of stone and ground.

Anyhow, this being what used to be called diploma time, I managed to see the students' graduate exhibitions – not in the old School of Art but in the new building just outside the centre of Aberdeen. I will very briefly describe one piece of sculpture and one painting – for both reflect the general impression of the work for me – apart from subjects which come under 'design'. They still demand skill and craftsmanship.

The example of sculpture which I chose consisted of a large plastic bin (about four feet deep) full of black oil. It bubbled merrily away, and at its base the caption said something like 'Beware of boiling oil'. The painting which I saw, like most, lacked design or colour, and pieces of it (bits of painted cardboard glued to the surface) were, here and there, in the process of leaving the painting altogether. Among piles of work-sketches, carelessly presented, were word-processed and laser-printed 'Theses'. They looked professional, and no doubt, had I had the time to read them, all might have been revealed. Well, I wonder!

Once, some time ago, Gray's School of Art had a reputation for excelling, not least in the sculpture department where the outstanding lecturer and teacher Leo A. Clegg taught his students the craft of sculpture and the meaning of art. Art he equated with life – 'for artistry is to be found in the many works of man!'

Aberdeen is also known as the Silver City because of the silvery-grey granite with which it is built. But walking down the street on my last day I could see another reason for this description, for in the bright morning sun, thousands of minute micas contained within the granite flashed from pavement and building as my moving steps caught the sun's angle of reflection.

These magical pinpoints of shining light reminded me at once of Christmas and New Year, when I wrote my last letter from North Ronaldsay. At that time the island was white with a scattering of snow, and the cold crystals sparkled like fairy lights in the moonlit nights.

Since that time, not much of great significance has taken place. For a day or two, men from Linklestoon (and other toonships in their areas) built up allocated dyke which had been damaged with winter winds. I should explain that there are six toonships and that the twelve to thirteen mile sheep dyke, which keeps the sheep on the foreshore, is divided into complicated mixed sections, apportioned fairly, or as near as possible, by the old sheep men long ago.

On that day of rebuilding it seemed to me that little books could be written about each toonship's dykes and the stories connected with their upkeep. It is exactly when such communal work takes place that many of those stories are remembered, often brought to mind when working along those areas. A stone here, a mark there, a carved name on a stone weathering the years, with the carver long gone. The reason for a brig over a small stream, a disputed toonship dyke end, a reason for this, a reason for that. One story leads to another and sets the memory alight – the day war broke out and when it ended. Two of our small company were in fact veterans of the 1939–45 war. One, Alfie Swanney (ex-RAF), was in sharp and sparkling form expounding on some of those headings above. The other, Willie Muir (ex-RN), added to those memories of past days and the great characters who lived then.

In Easter we had a show of films from the Scottish Film Library, one of which was about St Kilda. This was followed by a little dram, tea and cake, but a planned practice dance proved a touch disappointing. Still, a few of us danced away to the music of mostly old 78s.

I meant, but never managed, to write my North Ronaldsay letter long ago. From time to time, many ideas to write about would cross my mind. I could, for example, have told Alfie's stories and must yet do one day, along with many others – but I shall have to write them down word for word. They are after all part of the island's history. I cannot remember who said that 'A country that forgets its past is dead.' Kevin Crossley-Holland, in his book *Pieces of Land*, talks about 'the heart of an island' which, he indicates, resides within a community which has its roots firmly held in the island's history, lore and its unending war with the elements.

How often today is the scythe used? Not many times I think, yet the humble scythe can manage great work. It could even cut a few weeds if folk bothered. At the turn of the century for instance, three men working in Stronsay during the hairst time cut nine acres of oats in a day. One of those men came from North Ronaldsay – a Willie Muir, Waterhouse, who was over six feet tall and had a reputation for being a great scyther. The other two were Stronsay and Eday men. In North Ronaldsay sixty or more years ago a man and his wife cut, bound and stooked three quarters of an acre in a day. It agrees with a similar achievement by two men who completed the work in six hours without stopping.

This year for interest I timed myself when sowing by hand, but only having one person to fill my 'saaing cubbie' at one end of the field, it took about thirty-five minutes to sow two and a half acres of oats. Once I remember sowing three acres in about thirty minutes, but on that occasion, two fillers kept my cubbie full so that I barely stopped. At that rate it would be possible to cover six acres in a bit over the hour.

Well, it's still fun and very satisfying to work in this way, and to realise that, as we approach the year 2000, the earliest farmers of many thousands of years ago sowed by hand in exactly the same way. But such activities are probably not practical, nor can they continue, although in many Third World countries very little mechanisation exists at all.

I have to say though, that there are not many jobs of such a nature which bring one nearer the land and the traditional ways, or which are better enjoyed. Imagine for a moment a day in spring when the sun is strong and bright. The sea will be brilliantly blue with white wave crests dazzling the eye. Above harrowed fields white maas and black-headed gulls will be calling and wheeling, and for sure skylarks will be singing. Maybe the wind will be blowing fresh and sharp from the north, with just enough of a side angle to make sowing easy, and sometimes when eyelids close protectively against a stray chaff or two, the eye will hold for a moment the splendid vision. A vision of countless hand-thrown seeds falling earthwards, but stopped for an instant in time against the wind and the blue sky.

Heritage Trust Launch Appeal for Memorial Hall

August 11, 1994

The North Ronaldsay Heritage Trust have launched their appeal for the Memorial Hall.

Almost four and a half years have passed since I wrote my first letter to *The Orcadian* which began with a short account of the first of a number of functions held in the Memorial Hall to mark the 70th anniversary of its erection. In that brief article I wrote: 'All islanders living in North Ronaldsay and elsewhere will always have happy memories of the Old Hall and many have expressed a wish that the building should be looked after.'

That duty and obligation had actually been covered in the constitution of the North Ronaldsay Community Association, where a clause existed, stating: 'To secure the maintenance and management of the North Ronaldsay Hall for activities promoted by the association in furtherance of the above objects, or any of them.' This clause was inserted after the New Community Centre was opened in 1981, and it was put there by those islanders who understood the significance of the building and in agreement with the education authority at that time.

In 1990, after the hall had suffered storm damage the year before, various decisions were taken about its future, one of which was the setting up of a trust. It was an idea conceived by a number of islanders, and which was put to and accepted by the island. The trust's first duty was to maintain the hall as a continuing memorial to those islanders who had served and died during the 1914–18 Great War.

And so on Friday, July 29 at 8pm, with the help of many people, an evening was arranged to launch the appeal for the Memorial Hall. In a short introduction, everyone was welcomed with a special mention made of a number of guests. There were Elaine Batchelor representing the Clydesdale Bank, who had very kindly given considerable financial help with the production of the appeal leaflet; Amy Collop and Sarah McFadyen, two fiddlers from Hoy; and ten volunteers from the Prince's Trust, who were on the island to help rebuild some of the remaining 1993 storm-damaged sheep dyke.

Duncan Robertson, laird of the island and a trustee of the NRHT (the North Ronaldsay Heritage Trust) was then asked to explain something of the history of the Memorial Hall and the Trust. I should mention that his grandfather William Henry Traill bought the building to be used as a community hall for ex-servicemen and the people of North Ronaldsay in 1920, and that Duncan had very kindly gifted the hall and its surrounding ground to the NRHT. In a short speech, the laird gave an account of the Memorial Hall and the Heritage Trust, commenting on the importance of each generation to remember its past, and to retain its best traditions.

Duncan was then thanked for his speech and kind remarks before the beginning of a slideshow of Dr Garvie's outstanding photographs taken over sixty years ago. Dr Garvie was the medical practitioner on the island from 1930 until just after the last war. During that time living in the island she took hundreds of photographs, and they are a unique record of North Ronaldsay at that time.

Many of Dr Garvie's photographs will be used along with others, including maps and text, to describe North Ronaldsay's long history and way of life. The initial idea is that this extensive display will constitute an information/interpretation centre within the main hall. A proposed extension with improved amenities will also incorporate a storage area (for items like display stands), allowing the main hall to be used for Harvest Homes, occasional dances and whatever purposes meet the aims of the trust.

At the end of the slideshow Howie Firth, who had hired a boat specially from Sanday, was invited to say a few words and conclude the first part of the evening. Howie did so in his usual inimitable style, mentioning his trip across the North Ronaldsay Firth for the function and telling of an earlier crossing, some years ago, when he first visited the island. Howie also, like the previous speaker, mentioned the importance of history and tradition. Concluding his short speech, he presented a very generous donation, along with a number of books to be sold for the trust.

Over the past almost four years, including this function and since, many generous donations have been received for the Memorial Hall, and this official launching of the appeal concentrates our efforts in raising the considerable sums required to carry out the proposed development of the building.

All the many folk, both young and old, including the community official wardens, Alison Muir and Ingrid Tulloch, who have been attending to the Community Centre's facilities through the summer, were thanked for their enthusiastic assistance – for without such help and communal effort the evening and many others would never be possible.

Without a moment's delay, upwards of 120 people then turned their attention to the dance. The hall itself was appropriately decorated both inside and out with flags and bunting (kindly supplied by Orkney Islands Council) chosen to symbolise the origins and connections with the Great War. Outside, the Union Jack flew high on the south gable end and the Saltire flag on the north. Gaily-coloured bunting rippled from pole to pole and across the road, making the Old Hall look like a ship sailing in an imagined sea of time and memory.

Then the dance began with one very long Strip the Willow. Three-quarters of the stage had earlier been manhandled outside and into the Sugar Hoose. Many dances followed with John Swanney acting as MC. Up and down went the bows of the two fiddlers from Hoy while ten North Ronaldsay fingers flew over the accordion keys, as did Howie Firth's over the recorder. At one time Sydney Scott, who had played at many great dances and weddings, exchanged tunes in a short interlude with Amy and Sarah. Tea, sandwiches and a marvellous selection of homebakes put new energy into the crowd as they swung back into the dance – Dashing White Sergeant, Gay Gordons, more Strip the Willow and then a swinging Eightsome Reel with two other trustees, Howie Firth and Bessie Muir, dancing with huge energy in the heat of the night. Bessie, like Howie, had made sure of her attendance at the Old Hall filled with memories of the past.

During all this activity Christopher Baxter and Sam Taylor attended to a raffle for the trust, which brought in £36, adding to the door and donations amounting to over £500.

On went the dance. Sometimes older, more experienced dancers whirled away to the music on the floor, now taking on a silvery sheen, but evident was the feeling of life generated by the many younger people enjoying themselves with amusing abandon, and it must be said with some unorthodox steps. Even it was reported that a pair of dancing shoes danced away into the night. Backwards and forwards went the dance, but missing from the stage was the swinging accordion of Ronnie whose return to health we hoped for. Heuchs, yells and hand-clapping sounded in Eightsome Reel and Strip the Willows until at last between 2 and 3am, the long evening was brought to a close with the singing of 'Auld Lang Syne'. Soup followed to complete a very memorable occasion.

Outside the hall the two main flags flew, rippling against a cloudy sky, their colours temporarily subdued but still identifiable in the darkish night. They seemed somehow to be like the Great War, in which island men and women had served and died – faded memories of history and a lost generation.

But looking at the flags again, and a dying moon in the east, an image of Dr Garvie's last photograph which we had seen came to mind. It was a particularly suitable view for her to have chosen to end her original lantern slideshow of long ago, for it caught an instant in time – a crowd of men, women and children attending a Remembrance Day service at the War Memorial in 1934.

It summed up the meaning of the Memorial Hall for there was a representative group of islanders remembering the sacrifice and suffering of so many thousands of that wartime generation, who had died for so-called civilisation.

Cavalier Creel Boats
December 1, 1994

Here I am, with one hundred and one jobs waiting to be done, writing another letter from North Ronaldsay. Time has flown faster than ever since I gave an account of our last event, almost four months ago when we launched the ongoing appeal for the North Ronaldsay Heritage Trust.

November is a time of year when the island colours have lost most of their sparkle and warmth, yet skies and sunsets compensate partly, from time to time, with spectacular and colourful displays. A few days ago I watched for a while a marvellous sunset. A light, almost warm wind blew from the southwest, where the sun had just disappeared from view. The wind's direction carried the sound of crashing waves clearly above the continuous pounding of a heavy west sea. Sometimes white spray from breaking seas would be thrown high above the seaward side of the Dew Park as waves exploded against unyielding lines of black rock.

Above this turbulent sea, the sky was a fiery yellow-orange, glowing intensely against the darkening land and silhouetted dykes. North from the setting sun's background, great layers of purple cloud stretched in long lines, each cloud edge glowed orange-red, while scattered single clouds, dark against the bright sky, displayed the same radiant edges. Along the line of the horizon the high hills of Westray, Eday and further Rousay, became less and less visible, eventually merging with the misty blue and purple of the fading night sky. As I was watching this changing scene, a blackbird flew banking and speeding along dykes, then up and over a near rooftop with a chic-tic-tic-tic.

On looking through my diary and consulting with better memories than my own, here goes for our news. In early August I see that we were busy with punding and hay. Later, on August 19, a concert and dance was held in the Memorial Hall, when over seventy folk were present at this successful occasion. Head teacher Liz Baxter and her husband Trevor worked very hard to make the concert a most enjoyable one. The itinerant music teacher, Louise McLean, helped initially with music guidance. North Ronaldsay pupils Chris and Emily Baxter, Lorna Tulloch and Kirsten Payne sang beautifully, with individual performances with Chris on fiddle and Emily, Lorna and Kirsten on recorders and percussion. Ann Tulloch, keyboard, and Trevor Baxter, guitar, accompanied the singing as did Luke Woodbridge, guitar, with his sister Meike playing the flute.

In addition, the two community wardens, Alison Muir and Ingrid Tulloch (organisers of the event), Wendy Deyell, Marion Muir, Caroline Williams and her three young daughters, Kate, Jessica and Alice, added their voices to the most enjoyable singing. Kate, Jessica and Alice also played musical instruments. It was good to hear among the many and varied tunes a selection of the old Scottish songs.

One song learned was rather special as it will always be associated, by me and others, with the great Hogmanay and New Year nights of years past. It was the sad sea song 'The Bride's Lament'. Among the audience was the 100-year-old Mrs Dax, grandmother of Kate, Jessica and Alice, all on holiday at Holland House. A good and lively dance followed with three local accordions providing the music and John Swanney acting as MC.

Missing from the occasion (and a planned punding) was a unit from children's BBC TV, who lost a little confidence and withdrew at the last minute. Arrangements for dealing with the formidable North Ronaldsay sheep proved a shade too daunting for the London organisers. Initial disappointment felt by the children was soon forgotten with the success of their performance and the flurry of the dance.

From September 9–12, the North Ronaldsay school pupils, along with Papa Westray, were away to the Mainland where they took full advantage of the Orkney Science Festival, visiting various venues, including an exhibition in Stromness called *North Ronaldsay, an Island Experience*. As part of the same festival, back in North Ronaldsay on September 12, Iain Sutherland from Wick gave a most fascinating talk on herring fishing. A very good attendance enjoyed tea to round off the evening.

As September spent, harvest work was begun and almost completed in marvellous weather. Then in early October Stromness Books and Prints, who were invited to the island by the North Ronaldsay school, sent out a great selection of books. Duncan McLean, living in Stromness and fast becoming well known as a writer, set up the exhibition and supervised over the weekend. The opening of the book show coincided with a 16mm film show, when the Northern Lighthouse Board's film *Northern Lights* was shown.

Lighthouse keeper Alastair Henderson had very kindly procured the film, and subsequently presented the island with a video copy. A very good attendance of about fifty people enjoyed the film, which contained footage of our own lighthouse shot in the early 1960s. Tea was served, and while some folk browsed through the books, others got in a little dance practice.

Among the dancers was Marie Linklater, formerly from Nether Linnay and home on holiday with her husband. She very much enjoyed our little dance and learned with amusement the Seven Step Polka – a dance once performed by her grandmother, the great island storyteller Annie o' Bewan. Marie said how she remembered her grandmother calling the dance the 'Seven Stepped Polkie'.

And so October marched on. At the school some of us enjoyed listening to pupils reading from their favourite books, this being Readathon week when the school concentrates on books and reading. A great selection of homebakes made by pupils, staff and parents was served with tea during an interlude. £160 was collected for the Malcolm Sargent Cancer Fund.

Then on October 18 a strengthening southerly wind developed into a southeaster, which for some days pounded the east side of North Ronaldsay, eventually driving creels ashore and scattering others in deeper water. This almost yearly occurrence more or less ended the lobster fishing season – a season where the island's open fishing boats have had to endure the most sustained, unyielding and ruthless overfishing yet experienced on our traditional inshore grounds.

Five large boats from neighbouring islands worked thousands of creels before, through and after our short season, fishing quite indiscriminately, often setting over and inside the local boat's single creels. It's sad to see how our neighbouring island fishermen can be so uncaring about other toilers of the sea – North Ronaldsay fishermen who have to work from small open boats, without a harbour, in the treacherous waters round the island shores.

Are those crews or boat owners members of the Orkney Fisheries Association? And if so, what sort of principles, guidance or conservation policy exists within that organisation? It is becoming clear that if this sort of cavalier and selfish behaviour continues, it will ruin our inshore lobster fishing, practiced by generations of North Ronaldsay boatmen.

November 5, Hallowe'en and bonfire night combined: a spectacular bonfire with a fireworks display would have sorted out any lurking, unpleasant spirits left over from October 31. In the Community Centre later the grandest feast was ready for a good attendance of young and old, with baked potatoes and hot soup prepared by Winnie Scott. Also available were all sorts of fillings, cakes and a witch's brew. Dooking for apples completed a very pleasant evening.

At our next couple of communal punds, five magnificent specimens of native sheep were caught and kindly donated for the main function of North Ronaldsay's year, the Harvest Home.

It's interesting to ask and learn about how island social occasions used to be conducted in the past. In the 1930s for example, (before that time is another story) well over 100 folk would have attended the Harvest Home – in fact, a figure of 180 was apparently once noted in the Memorial Hall. That is double our average number nowadays of eighty, plus another twenty – no need of heating, and indeed in those days it was unusual to have any. Howie Firth tells me that there is a calculation of 100 watts of heat given off by a person. No wonder, as the night wore on, that the opening of windows was more necessary than any heaters.

The hall would have been packed, women on one side, men on the other, with the lower end of the building five or six rows of men deep, while outside from time to time half bottles of whisky would have been sampled (no alcohol was allowed within the hall).

Folk walked from near and far to attend such functions, arranged if possible when it was moonlight, for obvious reasons. Cups, knives and forks were marked with distinguishing threads. Plates were more easily remembered by their owners. Water was carried from a well some 100 yards or so away, with Primus stoves used for heating and cooking, and Tilley lamps provided light. Music for dancing was mostly the fiddle, but also the button-key melodeon, and later the accordion. Clapshot was the main vegetable dish, with many folk supplying a cooked hen or even tins of corned beef when available. Seldom in the early days could the island afford or spare the native sheep.

Decoration of the hall was less extensive than today, though evergreens and oat sheaves were used – but there was no need for anything more. Every person there knew about seed time and harvest, having endured long, hard days of work in good and not-so-good weather. Sheaves, stooks, stacks and simmans were part of their daily lives, and through the winter months the continuing cycle of work went on, until on a spring day the seed was once more scattered on ploughed fields. For all that and more, folk got together to thankfully celebrate completion of the year's harvest.

And so, like in the days of old, on as it happened the night of a full moon – November 18 – the Harvest Home took place. The guests this year were the speaker, Jim Anderson, Director of Education, and his wife; Tom Fleming, from the Department of Agriculture and Fisheries, and his wife; Howie Firth; Andy Leonard, our accordionist from Stromness – an ex-*Pole Star* man; and a young fiddler from South Ronaldsay, Sarah Thomson.

After kind words of welcome, followed by acknowledgements and thanks to all the many people who had contributed in one way or another to this special occasion, Alison Bardgett was asked to say the grace. On the tables were displays of red carnations, and round each home-made candle holder the schoolchildren had created pleated straw decorations as their contribution to the hall display. Earlier during the harvest operations they had also taken part in the actual stooking of sheaves in the last field to be harvested

Once the homely supper was finished, Jim Anderson was asked to make a speech and to propose the toast to the harvest. Resplendent in kilt, and with his polished belt buckle reflecting the flickering lights of candle and lantern, the speaker rose to entertain the company with a most enjoyable speech. Amusing stories were told and an account given of his own experiences with harvest work in Fife over forty years ago. Jim Anderson concluded his discourse with a fine performance of the old Scottish song 'John Grumlie' with his own guitar accompaniment, before asking all present to raise their glasses in a toast to the Harvest Home.

The dance which followed kept splendid momentum to the lively playing of Andy Leonard, accompanied on second accordion by Ann Tulloch, Howie Firth with his recorder and Sarah Thomson on fiddle. Sinclair Scott piped his way through a lightsome Eightsome Reel. On went the dance with more servings of native mutton, tea and homebakes. Marion Muir attended to the raffle taken for a bottle of whisky, donated by Isobel Muir, a grand cake made by May and Kirsten Payne and a box of chocolates from Alison Muir. Ian Deyell sorted out the draw, inviting Jim Anderson, Tom Fleming and Andy Leonard to pick the winning tickets. John Swanney acted as a very competent MC.

At about 3am 'Auld Lang Syne' was sung with Burns' familiar words echoing round the hall. Finally, hot soup was served. And so the North Ronaldsay Harvest Home came to end, passing on through time, its sounds and music picked up by the November winds and carried far away.

'May most of your dreams come true, and let us hold the hand of the past'

January 12, 1995

For a while I've been wondering how I should begin this letter and how I could cover our most recent goings-on. Well, for one thing, the November winds that were blowing when I last wrote, and which as I said blew away the sounds and music of one of our grandest Harvest Homes, have become January winds – and fiercely cold, wild and stormy they have been.

Down they have swept from the North Pole – backing a little to the west, but bringing sharp, rattling hail and snow flurries, to make Hogmanay and New Year's night daunting for first-footing, or indeed anything else.

I must tell you as I write, that I am listening to a tape I recorded of one of the many 'Rhoda's 78s' programmes that travelled down over the airwaves from Shetland. Hearing those tapes now and again gives me much pleasure, as does the voice of Rhoda Bulter, poet, writer, broadcaster and defender of all things truly Shetland.

Alas, that great lady from the northern islands died last July. Many of her 78 rpm records are familiar to me and bring back memories of past days and times. Just a minute or two ago I, or anybody else, could have been heuching and dancing to the swinging music of Bobby MacLeod and his Scottish dance band, and funnily enough, as I continue to write, the Mansfield Singers' recording of 'Bonnie Gallowa' is playing.

Now, that song was always sung on Hogmanay or New Year's night by Johnny o' Waterhouse (John Muir), and hearing it immediately reminds me of those very different nights thirty-three years and more ago. In January of 1993 I wrote at some length about how we used to celebrate the last night of the year and New Year's night.

Would it be possible to recreate those nights, I wonder? I fear not. For one thing Hogmanay was celebrated exclusively by the men of the toonships, and on their own toon they stayed to visit each neighbouring farm. This was done as a company, following an accustomed route. Many of the older men were veterans of the First Great War, some having endured the horrors of trench warfare, or had served on the Northern Patrols and elsewhere. Of that company of men that I mostly remember on Linklestoon (Linklet's Toon) only five of us remain in the district today.

As young boys or men we respected those older members and listened to their 'discoorse'. Not until the last years was there any TV, and as with the wireless before, neither were watched or listened to for very long, apart from taking in the New Year and hearing the chimes of Big Ben as the old year finally died. Much of the 'discoorse' on that night was about the land and sea and the past year's ups and downs. How, for example, were the animals in their byres coming on this winter, or what sort of crop was in the yard? Had it been a good or bad year on land or sea?

Stories old and new would have been exchanged, and sprinkled here and there would be gossip and good-natured banter, along with a song or two. And those songs would very often have been connected with the sea – or maybe a wartime song. Of course, there were also contemporary songs but I think, for me at least, the older songs had more substance than many of those we hear today. I suppose each generation will make the same criticism, and only the test of time will sort out those that endure through the years.

The truth is that the way of life even thirty years ago has completely changed, as have attitudes to a great extent. Many of the old stories, songs and customs are unknown to the new generations. Harvest, for example, is but a fast-fading memory of its former toil, help and companionship. In so many ways those values, ways of life and shared work were largely responsible for holding a community together. It was an era where the inevitable little dispute had to be set aside among people who depended upon one another more so than today.

But to get back to Hogmanay, once the mill stopped working in the early 1960s, the home-brewed ale could no longer be made, and so the old ways of celebrating Hogmanay and the New Year came to an end.

I've been playing recorded tapes during all of my writing, and by way of a warming diversion, my feet have just finished flying around the floor to Jimmy Shand's band. He was playing 'She'll Be Coming Round the Mountain', 'Can I Sleep in Your Barn', and 'Hand Me Down My Walking Cane'. I'm playing those old tunes because they stand the test of time, and because many of the songs used to be sung on New Year's night when the company made their 'merry way' round their neighbours' houses.

Now then, it's time to sweep through our social events, which I will do in a slightly extended diary form.

Before Christmas: Howie Firth Talk. Subject, 'Folklore' by Walter Traill Dennison – mermaids etc. Good attendance and a most enjoyable and interesting evening. Tea etc. Howie very kindly donated four books for a raffle (Children's Christmas Party). Total collected plus donations – £100 or so. Howie booked for a return visit – January.

December 16: Liz Baxter's school Christmas concert. Principal actors: Christopher and Emily Baxter, Kirsten Payne and Lorna Tulloch. Supporting actors: Louis and Joni Craigie. Accompanying player: itinerant music teacher Louise McLean. Presentation: *The Dream Maker*, cleverly adapted in parts to poke fun at certain worthies and island happenings. Artistic scenery: Evelyn and pupils. Result: an amazing display of confidence, originality and enjoyment, all accomplished with a few days' intensive practice. At the end of the performance Louise McLean was presented with a shawl (knitted in North Ronaldsay wool) by head teacher Liz Baxter on behalf of the school and staff. Children were presented with boxes of chocolates sent by Liz Forgan. Attendance: most of the island. Dance was lively and as good as it could be. Tea, sandwiches etc., were served. Raffle, door and bar resulted in £129.25 for school funds.

Christmas Dinner: School Meals. Splendid cooking by Winnie Scott, assisted by Anne Ogilvie. Sixty or so attended and enjoyed a wonderful meal. Christmas carols were sung by school pupils and staff, accompanied by Ann Tulloch on piano, which brought much enjoyment.

Children's Christmas Party, December 24: fairy lights, Christmas tree, games, tea, homebakes, fruit and jelly, Christmas crackers and Santa. Winnie was there to guide and control a very jolly Father Christmas.

Last dance 1994: run by the North Ronaldsay Ladies Lifeboat Guild. President Isobel Muir introduced Martin Gray who began the evening with his spectacular and beautiful slides taken in Spitsbergen. Martin gave a most interesting account of a wildlife tour on which he acted as assistant leader. The dance was another very lively and successful affair. Ian Deyell organised additional games. Paul Jones got folk moving (must keep up this idea). Raffle plus donations for RNLI came to £220. At both dances John Swanney acted as MC. Ian Deyell attended to the raffles. Lottie and Ann played, with Louise McLean and Alison Bardgett helping with the music for the School concert dance.

Other events missed, in sequence: a communal rabbit war has been going on (a concerted effort to control a plague of rabbits). North Ronaldsay School attended the Christmas pantomime in Kirkwall, as did members of the Day Club, with Anne Ogilvie as organiser. A further Day Club gathering was at New Year, at which Alfie Swanney gave an account of his recent visit to Australia and showed a selection of his photographs taken at the time. I've also forgotten to mention a Christmas Carol service conducted by Alison

Bardgett, where the school pupils mimed the Christmas story and sang carols. That's it. If I have missed anything or made any mistakes, I apologise.

Some readers may remember my letter written last January when I quoted from the *Old Statistical Account* of 1794, where a Rev. W. Clouston from Sanday states that he has seen fifty inhabitants of the island dancing by moonlight at the Standing Stone. I went on to mention the possibility, suggested by a history-reading visitor from the 'sooth', Laurie Taylor, that we should repeat that event as it was 200 years on to the day (early on New Year's morning) since it was last reported. Well, as I said, we didn't manage it collectively, but apparently a lone figure was seen doing a 'travelling dance step' round the stone in the moonlight.

It's interesting to speculate whether those islanders 200 years ago sang and danced at the Standing Stone 'for the sheer fun of it all' as we intended, or was this a tradition? There is no mention of whether it was a yearly custom or whether it continued after W. Clouston's visit. It would not, of course, be possible to always dance by moonlight, since year by year the moon phase would be different. Was there still in 1794 some distant link with the original significance of the stone and others in Orkney? Did the full moon (as it virtually was last year) have any bearing on the event? It is thought fairly widely that the stone circles and single stones in Orkney date back to 2000–3000 BC, and that they were in some way used for sophisticated observation of the major celestial bodies.

There is no doubt that those early settlers would have been more in tune with nature and undoubtedly, in common with many ancient civilisations, they would have been particularly interested in the great mystery and splendour of the night skies.

Anyway, leaving most of these speculations aside, and to confuse everything even more, I have just consulted with the Royal Astronomical Observatory in London. I find that there was no moonlight at all on January 1, 1794, although it was the first day of the new moon. So this report by the Rev. W. Clouston requires more consideration, but I'm told that it was common knowledge in North Ronaldsay, not long ago at all, that folk danced at the Standing Stone on New Year's day, and that once the New Lighthouse was built in 1854, people went there to dance instead, and when they got tired of that, apparently, they played football and left the lighthouse altogether – thus having a new ploy for New Year's Day.

But let's get back to the Standing Stone. New Year's day came with no let-up in the arctic weather mentioned. Shortly before darkness began to fall swift decisions were taken, and at the last minute away we went, a small but representative group of imaginative revellers, to pay our respects to those first-footers on our island some 5000 years before.

With a northwesterly wind blowing a full gale, we fought our way across crinkling ice and a snow-powdered field in the direction of the old grey Standing Stone. Great black, menacing clouds were gathering above a dark steel-grey sea, broken every here and there with white disintegrating waves. Into our faces the first flying snowflakes gave warning of yet another snowstorm about to envelop the island. Pausing for a breath and a little shelter in the lee of the enduring stone eventually reached, we all together read a short poem about North Ronaldsay with words, coats and scarfs flying as the speeding wind howled round the stone's edges. Then a bottle of whisky was produced and as the sun goes we drank a fiery toast, followed by a short dance to the sound of the wind and the thunder of the North Sea.

Later, in Neven's contrasting location, we stood in front of Albert's artistically stone-built fireplace, in which a roaring coal fire crackled and burned cheerily. There, with our host Liz Forgan and her guests from last year, Rex, Laurie, and Cathy, and the rest of the intrepid Standing Stone party, all held glasses of white or red wine and prepared to drink to 1995.

As the light from lamp and fire flame flickered through these festive goblets, Rex Cowan proposed a toast for the New Year. It went more or less like this: 'May most of your dreams come true, and let us hold the hand of the past.'

Thinking about the suitability of such a toast, and remembering Bill (William Muir, Scotsha), the islander's passing only a few days into the New Year, I do not think I can do better than close with the same toast to the readers of this letter, wherever and whoever they might be.

Island Remembers Those at War Fifty Years Ago
May 25, 1995

I'm at my letter-writing again, and how shall I begin, I wonder? Well, I planned to answer a critical letter from the south regarding my comments on part of the Rev. William Clouston's report about North Ronaldsay written during the late 18th century. That answer must wait, for I did spend some time in the Orkney Room of the library, reading through the *Statistical Account of Orkney 1796–1798*, and much of fascinating interest was there. It deserves more space than I can afford on this occasion, but I will say that the date 1794, which I quote as being the date of the Account, I saw in Hugh Marwick's *Place-Names of North Ronaldsay*. So more detective work is required, I have decided, before I proceed further.

Let me see, I think I can say that the Rabbit War is in a sort of truce period but not at all finished. Otherwise since the New Year, Howie Firth gave two lectures. One was delivered on Burns Night when the subject was 'Two Romantic Voyages', and use was made from readings taken from the works of Walter Scott, Robert Louis Stevenson and Walter Traill Dennison.

Then in March, Howie talked about 'Ghosts, Folklore and Science'. Both lectures, as a result of Howie's help, brought in money for the Community Association's funds, apart from being most enjoyable. As always, refreshments followed.

The school pupils have been away twice on the Mainland since last I wrote. Once before the end of March when they attended 'Drama Day' along with their colleagues from Papa Westray and Graemsay. Then, as part of their school project 'People Who Help Us', they visited the Balfour Hospital, and later learned something about the work of traffic wardens, including road safety. Another trip saw the pupils attending a puppet show and spending some time with their opposite numbers at the Glaitness primary school.

Dorothy Henderson, Day Club organiser, has been particularly busy, arranging numerous get-togethers for the island's more senior folks and others who like such outings. As well as enjoying Winnie Scott's cooking, attendees enjoyed the opportunity to see and discourse with one another. Various delays have occurred lately, but no doubt Dorothy will be under way again and arranging more meetings.

Shortly after the main spring land work was finished – not, I may say, that such a statement means much when one sees the small amount of cultivated land and compares it with the North Ronaldsay of some years ago. Then, upwards of forty years or more ago, most of the island's fields would have been harrowed and in brown. Anyway, to get back to the subject. After our main sowing was completed (I'm still striding forth with a cubbie, using hand power) I went out on two nights after 12 midnight to see the Merry Dancers, and wonderful they were. Such sights in the sky somehow concentrate the mind on the mystery of the universe, and the meaning of our short existence on this planet.

In the northern sky a great dark cloud stretched, anvil-like, from west to east, behind which a luminous glow of light shone with enough power to allow me to easily see the stones built into our two-storied north barn wall, near which I stood. I remember some of the men who thirty-five years ago helped with the building during a summer long past. Of course, I knew them all, but my father puts me right on these builders and helpers who, in accordance with the old ways, were treated with almost the last of the real North Ronaldsay ale specially brewed for such an occasion. Their names were: Jimmie o' Howar, Willie o' Neven, Alfie and his father Peter o' Gravity, Charlie and Peter o' Greenspot, my uncle Bill from Cruesbreck, Hughie o' Bewan, Johnny o' Linnay and Johnny o' Ancum. Of that company of men, only three remain alive today – Alfie, Peter and Charlie – but if only they could return once again, swift would be their sorting out of our little island's local ups and downs, of that I am very sure.

On my second night a similar sight met my eye. From time to time shafts of greenish white light sped across the sky like searchlights, probing first here and then there. Heavy pounding seas sounded all the time from the west and east. And stars sparkled coldly, some twinkling like coloured jewels so far away that, even travelling at the speed of light, it would take many thousands of years to reach them. At times, sudden shimmers of light would flash across the sky at incredible speed. To the east the warmer lights of a lonely ship flickered, appearing and disappearing between troughs of heavy seas.

If any associations or groups out there have problems decorating their multi-use gymnasium-type community centres – which relatively recently replaced their homely, good-dance-floor halls that served our Orkney communities so well in the past – try this for creating some atmosphere.

(1) Stretch a high tensile wire from end to end and down the centre of the hall at a reasonable height.
(2) Into the wood strapping which normally is fitted round the walls at

about eight feet or so high, screw cup hooks every two or three feet. If no strapping exists, use steel nails for the cement walls. (This, by the way, gives the opportunity for using fishing gut or courlene, which can crisscross the hall at a lower level.)

(3) Now, using stack nets, sling them over the centre wire and take up the ends on the cup hooks, allowing a little slack. If one net is too short use two, or simply knit ones to suit. This arrangement creates a sort of canopy clear of the wall heaters and lowers the high roof area. Into the hanging nets two hundred or more balloons can be thrown, which will concentrate towards the walls, and in addition, other decorations can be hung in the convenient net loops.

(4) Down the centre of the hall, in order to give more substance to this area, construct and hang four or more mobiles (or more clusters of balloons). The mobiles used in North Ronaldsay consisted of a cross from two nine-foot-long, half-inch-wide white plastic strips (DIY double glazing fittings). If not available, use light bamboo rods or thin wood strips, all of which should flex slightly. On these crosses suspend any combination of lightly constructed mobiles.

(5) This leaves four bare walls to be tackled. Break up the space any way you can. For example, cut out ten or more quarter-inch-thick marine plywood circles of sixteen-inch diameter. Then use 400 leaves (forty per circle – diameter eight feet) of New Zealand flax and staple to each board with a centre decoration. If New Zealand flax is a problem, use wire or wooden strips to provide support for alternative ideas, but keeping the flower-like display. On one of the end walls a special feature could be added to suit the occasion.

(6) That leaves lighting. Get rid of the harsh strip illumination and instead use the street festive lighting often seen, i.e. a long flex (join according to wattage) with sockets, into which a controlled lighting system can be made, using coloured bulbs if preferred. Hang round the cup hooks.

I assure you that this creates a real atmosphere and transforms the rather stark appearance of the New Community Centre – typical of all such new community school buildings or separate community halls. Two major drawbacks exist: one is the poor acoustics, and the other is the hard unyielding apology for a dance floor. The latter can only be suffered, and the acoustics, according to a sound engineer, would cost some thousands of pounds with a result of only partial success.

Now then, the decoration system just described is exactly what we used for the wedding of Martin Gray and Evelyn Scott. On April 14 the Rev. Frank Bardgett conducted the marriage ceremony, with his wife Alison acting as organist. Martin and Evelyn were married in the New Kirk, the path to which was strewn with Evelyn's favorite flower, the daffodil. And this yellow spring flower provided the theme for decorations in the kirk and the Community Centre. The mobiles for example, which I got Louise Scott to make – and make them beautifully she did – featured impressive daffodil designs, all handmade, as indeed were all the decorations apart from the balloons.

The groom and best man (James Gray) were in Highland dress, as were the two ushers, Nick Ward and James Cowe. Bridesmaids Fiona Muir and Lorna Tulloch were elegantly dressed in green, and Evelyn wore a beautiful ivory-coloured long dress and looked quite radiant. As the bridal party left the kirk, Sinclair Scott, wearing his Stromness British Legion Pipe Band uniform, piped them on their way.

Back in the Community Centre, a company of an estimated 153 collected, and eventually the bridal party entered the hall. As they proceeded to the top table, Christopher Baxter played appropriate music on his fiddle.

Once the wedding feast was finished with the customary speeches by the groom, best man, and Evelyn's two brothers Albert and John, tables were cleared and photographs taken. Then at last the dance began with the Grand March, for which Sinclair played the bagpipes. Andy Leonard and Lottie and Ann Tulloch, immediately after swung into action with their accordions. And so on sped the night, with the bride and groom circulating with a magnificent bride's cog brew made by Jean Tulloch, back home for the event. Other friends and relations had travelled to North Ronaldsay, with some from the south and one, Wendelin Scott, all the way from the USA. Sinclair did some more piping. Ian Deyell and John Swanney shared the MC duties. And on went the dance until, between three and four in the morning, not that short of a round of the clock, a memorable and special occasion came to a close.

Next day the kirk was again in use, but this time for a sadder and more solemn occasion, for we were attending the funeral service of Ronnie Swanney, whose early and untimely death had been in our minds from time to time during the recent days. But it is the memory of Ronnie and his accordion that remains with those of us who remember his swinging and exhilarating music – seated on the old stage, head back, sometimes with pipe in mouth, playing away back in the days when time was easy, summers seemed grander and more dancing feet carried the day.

Now I come to VE day. On the northern hill of Turrieness a great pile of combustible material, the collection of which was supervised, as always, by John Payne Jnr, stood ready for lighting. Later on in the evening a company of about forty saw John Tulloch, an ex-Highland Regiment man and a veteran of the Burma campaign, light the bonfire. Shortly a magnificent fire developed, throwing its very considerable heat some little distance into the teeth of the north wind, and warming the spectators who stood in the relative shelter of their collected vehicles. Photographs were taken of John Tulloch, who proudly wore his service medals, and of another veteran, Jenny Tulloch, ex-WAAF.

A choice of whisky, vodka, sherry and cider was available and served out in considerable drams in order to counteract the almost winter conditions. Later, hot soup, kept warm on gas cookers fitted up in a covered box trailer, was served. Scottish dance music rang out in the background and was heard as far afield as Upper Linnay – about one-quarter mile away. Eventually a little dance began with wild-looking figures, whose coats and hair flew this way and that, alternately silhouetted and lit by the fierce blaze as they swung into Strip the Willows, polkas, and whatever else fitted the changing music.

And so we celebrated VE day as had been done in North Ronaldsay fifty years to the day before. What has happened in the world since is a disgrace to the memory and endeavour of those who served, and died, in both world wars – and a further disgrace to those world leaders and governments over the years, upon whose shoulders must be placed the suffering, starvation and death which continues in relentless and seemingly endless misery for thousands.

Well, that account of the VE day celebrations completes our activities up to date. The wind is still persistently in the north, and very tiresome and cold it is. Sometimes it even carries flying snowflakes. Yesterday the spring daisies – whose petals shine in the most wonderfully fresh, reddish pink, a colour which never fails to bring me an unexplainable pleasure – danced while frozen hail scattered here and there.

Farewell and Welcome to Head Teacher
September 2, 1995

I'm looking at my last letter, and I read that at that time the wind was persistently in the north. Sometimes it carried little flurries of snow to speckle the ground. And one day I watched a shower of hail dancing and scattering among the spring daisies. In an accompanying photograph, World War II veterans, Janet Tulloch and John Tulloch stand next to our VE Day bonfire. It had been lit by John, who also most recently set a fiery torch to our VJ Day fire – but more of that later.

Well, this has certainly been a summer that equals those we like to remember from the past, and time, it seems, has been flying all the more swiftly. Long ago the poet Virgil wrote, 'It is flying, irretrievable time is flying.' Another poet writes, 'Time was away and somewhere else.' But today, September 4, I am at last, despite the thought of other things, taking time to write another letter from North Ronaldsay.

This day the wind is again in the north, with grey skies, rain and a seemingly rising sea. It's clear that the long, hot days are 'away and somewhere else'. And so is a summer of many events and memorable occasions. Those events on such a night as this stretch a way back into a distance of memory, and I will be within the constraints of time and space, but I will try my best to remember.

As I write, the twilight is creeping in and the wind is shaking our fuchsia trees, scattering many of the scarlet and royal-purple bells on cold, wet brigstones and into grasses quickly losing their summer strength. Purple Monkshood are also being severely battered, and just above them to the east I can still see the white of broken water as the wind spins and lifts the tops of troubled seas. Earlier in the morning those of us who plunged and punched our way by boat, during fishing operations, received many a salty lashing, delivered without ceremony at the exposed low level of our traditional North Ronaldsay praams.

Now then here goes for our main events and activities over the summer. Going back to the Orkney Traditional Folk Festival, who can forget the exciting Irish banjo player, Eamonn Coyne who, along with other artists, entertained us so well? Once he and his banjo got underway, everybody had to shift into at least two higher gears, including local and visiting players. With breathless Irish jigs and reels that at times transformed whatever the dance announced into spectacular high action and unorthodox performances.

No less so was much of the Bird Observatory Opening Dance held in the Memorial Hall. Ann, Lottie, Andy Leonard (from Stromness) and Howie Firth provided toe-tapping music with over 100 people attending. At one point, before our very eyes, Christine Allan, Loganair Passenger Officer (out on holiday with her husband) and myself had to venture forth and master the Seven Step Polka. Howie, having heard of my enthusiastic demonstration steps at the Loganair desk, gleefully announced our leading role on the dance floor. Christine and I tried our best.

Among the crowd a visiting party of Norwegians from Trondheim University sang a short selection of traditional songs, also demonstrating one or two of their local dances. I think they would have, had our valiant MC for the summer, John Swanney, allowed it, danced Strip the Willow all night long. Indeed, so impressed were our northerly friends that if by stroke of troll magic they could have, they said, they would have whisked us all, including the Memorial Hall, off to Norway.

But back to North Ronaldsay. Liz Baxter, head teacher for the past three and a half years, along with Evelyn Gray, made a final trip to the Orkney Mainland with her pupils, visiting among other places, the Longhope Lifeboat Memorial.

The school's Open Day was as always enjoyable, with homebakes etc., held a day before the summer holidays. Once again, the sale of work for the school funds realised a most generous sum of £300.

Parents, pupils and staff had worked hard making the many items for sale. May Payne, for example, had actually made a record fifteen dolls as well as a magnificent rug completed in hand-knitted wool.

For the following night the island had planned a grand farewell concert and dance for the Baxter family. It began with the school presenting a delightful introduction, singing selected songs chosen from an extensive repertoire built up over the years. Trevor Baxter and Owen Tierney provided guitar accompaniment to the children's singing. One song in particular pleased me: 'The Bride's Lament' or 'Song of the Sea', as it was a song from the old days. I had asked Liz and her singers to learn and perform it for last year's summer show.

Immediately after their performance a short speech was made in which Liz Baxter's wonderful record of commitment and dedicated service to the children in her care over the years was acknowledged. Also acknowledged was her husband Trevor's contribution. He had actually begun the first studies for the island's proposed development plan before leaving to work and gain distinction on the Orkney Mainland. He had also helped whenever possible with Liz's memorable Christmas concerts and musical presentations.

Finally, the island's good wishes, appreciation and remembrance were represented by individual presentations to the family. These presentations were made firstly by Kirsten Payne, who gave Liz a gold Burrian Cross necklace. Then Kirsten and Lorna Tulloch jointly presented Liz with a beautiful, inscribed serving tray. Trevor received a Burrian Cross tie tack from Lorna, with Christopher and Emily Baxter accepting signed book tokens from Louis Craigie.

With those pleasant proceedings completed, our invited guests for the evening's entertainment, Hullion (Billy and Ingirid Jolly, Micky Austin and Owen Tierney), took the stage. Their concert of music and song was particularly enjoyable, providing, I may say, a most generous and grand introduction to the occasion.

One song, 'Waltzing Matilda', very appropriately fitted in with Mamie o' Purtabreck's eighth return visit to the island from Australia, where she moved in 1985. A grand dance followed with local players supplying the music and receiving great support from Hullion. Throughout the night Liz and Trevor moved around the hall together, very kindly treating everybody to substantial drams and soft drinks.

And so, the night sped on until at last 'Auld Lang Syne' was sung, bringing this rather special night to a close, but not before Liz and Trevor were carried shoulder-high around the hall to the enjoyment of the applauding company.

Two other dances followed. Both were held in the Memorial Hall, which took over its role as recreation hall during the summer's extensive work being carried out at the New Community Centre. For the first of those dances Dr Kevin Woodbridge gave a very interesting talk on his recent birdwatching trip to Gambia, illustrating the talk with some varied slides. The following dance became a very lively affair, with visitors, islanders and seven volunteer dyke builders from the Prince's Trust enjoying the evening. Before the dance finished, Duncan Robertson of Holland House invited each volunteer to choose a T-shirt as a souvenir of their stay on North Ronaldsay.

Our last dance arranged for VJ Day began on Turrieness Hill where another great bonfire, supervised as always by John Payne Jr, was ready for lighting. To begin the proceedings Duncan Robertson gave a short speech mentioning briefly the history of the war in the Far East and asking the company to remember those of the wartime generation who had not survived.

Duncan then invited John Tulloch of Senness to light the fire. Both men happened to be veterans of the Burma campaign, and each on this commemorative night performed their duties. Then to the sound of dance music, fire blaze and crackle and the more sombre blast of the lighthouse foghorn, a large gathering enjoyed the spectacle – with bar facilities – and the opportunity to dance a little round this unforgettable scene. Not so far from the ever-sounding sea, a grey, damp mist swirled around with the flames of the great fire rippling skywards. The company then made their way to the venue for the evening, the Memorial Hall.

A short speech introduced the evening and included a special welcome to our new teacher, Patricia Thomson, and her husband John. Howie Firth added suitable words of welcome and, on behalf of the island, presented Patricia with a beautiful bouquet of flowers.

Then the dance proper began in earnest, with three accordions, including Howie on the recorder and spoons, providing the music. At least 100 folk enjoyed a great night of entertainment, which included a splendid cake-cutting ceremony. Firstly, John Tulloch, World War II veteran and lighter of both bonfires, cut a special VJ Day cake artistically created by Anne Ogilvie. Then three of the island's 1995 sixty-year-olds – Bessie Muir, Helen Swanney and Oliver Scott – together cut a very large cake, specially designed for them and also for the eighteen-year-olds.

Following the more senior birthday revellers' efforts, five young hands which belonged to the twins Ruth and Gillian Swanney, Wendy Deyell, Alison Muir and the famous young man (with the disappearing dancing shoes) performed their part of the ceremony. A great company enjoyed this entertaining spectacle, which included many former islanders, a number of whom were present for the occasion. One of these was Jenny o' Cavan (sister of Bessie), home on holiday from Australia. Through the night, tea and many generously donated homebakes were available with soup being served at the close of a night surely to be remembered for some time.

For both these and other events, community wardens for the year, Wendy Deyell and Alison Muir, performed sterling duties. For the Village Hall Scheme both wardens supervised for eight weeks the recording of 565 attendances. Many other folk willingly helped whenever required, managing the raffles, baking, making tea, soup and serving. At each of the five major functions both community halls were specially decorated using nets and hundreds of balloons. Also adding to the atmosphere were displays of sweet rocket, New Zealand daisies, and purple-flowered evergreens.

Following on from these events, Jimmy Thomson of Nether Linnay, another islander home on holiday, gave a most interesting slideshow and talk, dealing with his time on Christmas Island in the 1950s while serving in the RAF. It also included a selection of his more recent photographic work.

To complete our activities, last week as part of the Orkney Science Festival, Dr Peter Waddell delivered a fascinating and controversial illustrated talk on 'Secrets of the Wartime Code Breakers', including the Enigma machine. Both of these functions were well attended, with tea to follow.

That's it at least for the main events and not bad for an island of eighty souls. No time as yet to answer my critic from the 'sooth' – though I have, with the help of the Orkney Library, done enough research to do so. No time to talk of the overfishing and the sometimes damaging and potentially dangerous activities of the large-decked creel boats mentioned in an earlier article. No time to talk about silage, hay, communal native sheep punding or the difficult hairst operations – 'Cut green or grey on mid-hairst day' (September 15). Or, so the old saying goes, then what about the rain, the drizzle and the mist – or combinations of all three?

I will, however, tell you that today (September 15), when fishing in our open boats, we saw majestic roller upon roller of westerly 'bod' crash with thundering roar upon Seal Skerry. Often in the final rearing climb of the wave, seals' heads bobbed here and there, seemingly playing a dangerous game but always driving to safety before the final spray-streaming plunge. And sometimes with the boat by chance advantageously positioned, a side view of the breaking wave showed the tunnelled hole just visible for a second or two before the great wave finally turns over, viridian-coloured then brilliantly white as it crashes on the jagged rocks of Seal Skerry.

Well to the seaward side of the half-mile-or-so-land-distant skerry, the height of the breaking wave easily takes the 139-foot-high tower of the lighthouse, situated not far inland on the Brae of Versabreck, quite out of sight. At such times nothing remains to be seen around the boat but the sky and the heaving high swells and deep troughs of the North Sea.

Sometimes great winged gannets sail solemnly on the wind. Today I counted twenty-five flying majestically, north then east. But more often, nearby, streamlined fulmars bank and glide, climb and sweep away, restlessly and endlessly pursuing their destiny.

The Invasion of Local Fishing Grounds
November 23, 1995

This is November 9, with the time about 6.40 in the morning. I awoke earlier with the moonlight streaming in through my west-facing window. Shortly after, I got up. I may say though that by choice it is not usual for me to rise quite so early, but I have. And now I am actually walking outside in a sort of in-between time, a kind of halfway house betwixt the dawn and the lingering night, writing as I go.

To the west in a pale blue sky the moon is still bright, just fading a little on one edge, but shining through white ghosts of seemingly unmoving cloud. To my left and right a few stacks of oats can be seen of the island's now greatly reduced crops. They make a link with the past, when hundreds used to point to the skies of far-away days. Turning now to the east, a rose-coloured dawn stretches along the horizon. A little higher in a luminous sky, dark purple clouds are silhouetted against this curious light. In the western sky, by contrast, the moon whitens those in her proximity. Somehow the moon and the few remaining pinpoints of stars, which still twinkle a little, seem to be more and more out of place as the dawn advances. And as it does I see that a white blanket of frost covers the island.

The lighthouse is still flashing, and east of her elegant tower the Fair Isle is a pale purple-blue. A little further east, the Old Lighthouse's reflection is clearly visible across Linklet Bay, with its surface smooth and flat in the calm frosty air. As yet only light wafts of wind play a little here and a little there, but to the westward a fairly heavy land sea rumbles and crashes.

Now I'm seeing our mire ground. Gone are all the grasses, orchids, ragged robins and the many other plants that I once tried to identify one marvellous summer's day two years or so ago. I mentioned the occasion at this year's Harvest Home, but more on this later if I can fit it in. The moon has just disappeared behind some cloud, and further north I can see grey mists of a shower falling half a mile or more out to sea.

Soon the sun should rise and the lighthouse beam will go out. As I get nearer home, I can hear some starlings mimicking snatches of other birds' songs, and I've just noticed that there is a decided nip in the morning air.

A LETTER FROM NORTH RONALDSAY: 1990–1999

Over the past two years I have written fairly comprehensive reports about our Harvest Home, which is held in the Memorial Hall. This year's celebration is the sixth to be arranged since 1990. I may say that over the years many people, including visitors and guests, have expressed their considerable admiration at the way we manage to create such a grand night. Much of the success is partly related to the suitability and general appeal that the old building generates.

Such encouragement, along with letters of appreciation that we receive, I hope serve to give real satisfaction to all the very many people who contribute to this rather special occasion: the people who gift the native sheep for the supper, those who prepare and cook the mutton, the many folk who make, put up and take down the straw decorations and greenery etc., those who supply the tatties and neeps and those who bake, set tables, arrange heating and do one hundred and one extra jobs.

And let us not forget the musicians, without whom there would be no dancing, nor the many ex-patriots and others who arrive and buckle down to help when asked. For me it is a joy and privilege to do what I can and to be involved with all those many folks who ensure that the North Ronaldsay Harvest Home still goes on at a time when the significance of old hairst ways is fast disappearing.

Our guests this year were the Harvest Home speaker, Colonel Sir Robert Macrae, and Lady Macrae, Loganair's chief pilot, Captain Stuart Linklater, and his wife Hilda, OIC's clerk of works, John Sinclair, and his wife Doreen and the accordionist Andy Leonard. After, Alison Bardgett was asked to say the grace. Following the magnificent supper, a short introduction was made to the speaker mentioning his army career, farming background and his dedicated public service to the people of Orkney, which culminated in his receiving the Freedom of Orkney and a knighthood.

The former Lord Lieutenant of Orkney, Colonel Sir Robert Macrae, then rose to deliver his speech and propose the toast to the harvest. This was a nostalgic return for the former councillor for the island, who spoke of those days in the early Seventies when he attended many community council meetings in the Old Hall. He also mentioned briefly the varied accomplishments of the islanders and the importance of new islanders' acceptance of tradition and island ways, which have survived the passage of time. Bringing his Harvest Home speech to a close, Sir Robert asked those present to toast the harvest.

And so shortly afterwards the dance began, which got better and better as the night progressed, with accordions, pipes and drums providing the music. Through the night a raffle of the association's bottle of whisky and John and Doreen's box of honey and chocolates brought in over £60 for the NRCA funds.

John Swanney acted as MC, and our two local accordionists, Lottie and Ann, played along with Andy Leonard, by now a familiar figure on the old stage. The folk were refreshed periodically with tea, homebakes and native mutton, until between three and four in the morning when cups of hot soup brought the evening to a close.

Now then, the two subjects missed in my last letter. First, let me respond to my critic from the 'sooth' on the issue of the Standing Stone dance. He is absolutely right. I did, without thinking and not enough research, suggest to *The Orcadian* in my letter (January 12, 1995) that the Rev William Clouston's observation (Minister of Cross and Burness and North Ronaldsay 1773–94) of fifty inhabitants dancing round the Standing Stone in the moonlight on New Year's Day was inaccurate.

I based my remarks on Hugh Marwick's work, *Place Names of North Ronaldsay*, where he refers to the *Old Statistical Account* of 1794 (Marwick gives the date 1794) and of Clouston having seen people dancing in the moonlight. I unthinkingly assumed that Clouston saw this in 1794, when I know that there was no moonlight on that particular New Year's Day. But as my critic points out, and as I have subsequently discovered, the *Statistical Account* could have covered his observations over the twenty year period when he must have been visiting North Ronaldsay.

Over that period, of course, there would have been more than one New Year's Day when there was ample moonlight for dancing. I wonder why those dancers danced in the moonlight. Clouston must have been watching them at night or in the early morning when he saw this phenomenon. As for the old New Year's Day, January 13, which was mentioned by my critic as another possible day for moonlight, I would have imagined that the church should have followed the new Gregorian calendar when making an official report! But interestingly enough, on old New Year's Day, 1794, the moon would have been three days short of being full.

By the way, Hugh Marwick also says in his paper that the Puritan clergy of the 17th century frowned severely on practices of ancient superstition, i.e., 'chain dances', old tales, songs, etc. In any case, the idea of dancing round the Standing Stone as of old was all in fun. So let's carry on every year, as we began last New Year's Day. Incidentally, in William Clouston's account of North Ronaldsay, for example, he says that in 1792, 420 lived on the island, of which 211 were males and 209 were females. In many places on the island the sea gains upon the land.

He mentions forty-four farmers, of which forty-three kept a plough. He says, 'There are five weavers, four tailors, and no shoemakers. In 1787 there were 61 houses, in 1791 there were 64.' He mentions 343 arable acres, 249 horses, 256 horned cattle, 1,960 sheep and average of six people to a house. About that time, two-thirds of arable ground were sown to bere and one-third to oats.

In 1615 North Ronaldsay was parochially joined with Stronsay. Later it became joined with 'Cross and Burness' (Sanday). And under the heading of 'sea' only one boat on the island could carry from ten to twelve tons, and twenty-one could carry from one to one and one-half tons. Clouston writes: 'The main fish caught were codling, skate, halibut, but mostly generally caught were the cuithes. Seal were caught in nets and people had been used to eating the young and tender only.' Eating young seals would probably not be acceptable today, but maybe if folk were hungry it would be a different story.

And talking about the sea, indeed (my second subject), take a look at the map of Orkney, pick out the small island of North Ronaldsay and observe the little bays and limited coastline. With this in mind, imagine boats capable of setting thousands of creels, using long 'backropes' to which are attached upwards of a hundred or more, as opposed to the limited numbers that can be managed by open boats with hand-hauled single creels. The backropes ring our island, moving in and out, often over and inside the small single creel drifts of the three Ronaldsay boats. Frequently they trap the local fisherman's creels underwater or sometimes actually cut our marking ropes.

In some instances, where we work in fast tides and deep water (twelve to fifteen fathoms), creels may as a result be lost. Consider the frustration felt by the island fishermen when our traditional grounds are fished to a virtual standstill.

No day is sacred with those large-decked boats. Sunday is the same as any other day to them. They move in and out, shift with the weather, while the small open boats must endure whatever comes. Then there are the fast tideways through which we must sail, where the long uncorked backropes of those boats present significant danger to the local fishermen.

In such situations a small boat may be entangled without warning, and in the powerful tides could be capsized instantly. In addition to the main ebb and flood, there are dangerous eddies, which set up to both these tides, and often those large backrope fishing boats set their creels indiscriminately in these areas where local boats work extensively.

Then imagine those long partially submerged ropes when they are set inshore. There, because of the shallowness of the water, loops of the backrope suddenly rise without design or warning, presenting an extreme danger to the local fishermen who often have to rescue their own inshore creels from the onset of a heavy land sea.

Now that is what we have to endure almost all the limited season that we can fish. This does not even begin to evaluate the financial losses to which local fishermen are subjected in North Ronaldsay and elsewhere when faced with this sort of fishing. I believe that the fishermen working on these large boats in Orkney are asking the OIC for financial assistance to set in motion a program of lobster restocking. They are also, I understand, asking for some form of protection against the possible invasion of Orkney's inshore fishing grounds by non-Orcadian boats.

What about conservation? We practice it, do they? Why have those large boats double or more their fishing drifts – necessity, they say. How long can this sort of fishing continue? Those are some of the questions all OIC councillors should ask themselves and the members of the Orkney Fisheries Association before awarding any financial assistance.

Who are the owners and skippers of these boats? How many creels do they work? What sort of income and lifestyle do they have? Must this necessary part of our income, as well as our lives, be put at risk? I think not, and the sooner this unsatisfactory state of affairs is remedied the better for all concerned.

Well, all of that needed to be said, and it needed to be said for the benefit of people not involved in fishing, who have no idea about such problems. It is also important because those people may be asked to spend public money in relation to lobster restocking and fishing controls.

Now then, I'm at my Harvest Home story. This is how it went. A year or two ago, one hot and beautiful summer's day, tractors were roaring and hammering away in the silage and hay. In a mood of abandonment, I took a couple of books on wildflowers and grasses, intending to try to identify uncommon plants and flowers which grow untouched in an uncultivated piece of miry ground. Eventually, mesmerized and confused by the impossible complexity of identification, lulled by the heat of the sun, and feeling a little guilty about the thought of others working, I said to heck with the lot and shortly fell asleep on a grassy mound.

When I awoke, a bit lost in my mind, I recalled the story of Rip Van Winkle, who after drinking a strong brew supplied by strange little men in the mountains whose game of bowls he had disturbed, fell asleep for twenty years. Well, I wondered if I had suffered such a fate, what sort of island would I have discovered on my waking up? One thing for certain would be my age. I would be seventy-five and I would be wearing a very long beard.

But seriously, what about North Ronaldsay? How many folk would be living then? Given only the present population, certain disturbing conclusions would be very clear. Would more people have come to the island? And what would they be doing for a living? Could we really plan for the future, as we probably should?

What about our history and way of life? Would it finally only be available in books, tape and on film? Does it matter? Can it be taught and handed down? I think I mentioned once before that Kevin Crossley-Holland in his book, *Pieces of Land*, hints clearly at what such an island might be. It would have no tradition, no roots, and therefore no heart or soul. Is this to be the final fate of North Ronaldsay?

I have one other occasion to mention – an Indian summer's day well after the hairst. Remembering an earlier idea of mine, and at the drop of hat, as they say, and before the short warm afternoon became too chilly, I managed to gather swiftly a few likely participants (or, as some might say, 'a few lazy b...s').

Imagine the scene. A table gaily clothed and set out in the middle of a grassy field. Round the table sat a jolly crew, above which was a cloudless sky. Holding down the tablecloth was a modest choice of bottled Highland water, Grouse whisky, ginger wine and Appletise. We drank our first toast to the memory of Mary o' Kirbest (Mary Swanney): others followed. Later, two more passers-by joined the party – by now moved to the shelter of a convenient stack, with table, bottles, seats and all. There we continued discussion on many subjects which were made more cosmopolitan by the interesting views of a most pleasant Japanese lady, Eri Ikawa, who incidentally came back for, and enjoyed, our Harvest Home.

But as I finish this letter, I am remembering our first toast made that Indian summer's day, and I have poured myself a little whisky. Let's all do the same, each remembering one's own late acquaintances.

I'm drinking to the memory of Jean Anne, a brave islander of my generation, Ronnie the accordionist, Mrs Dax, who admired North Ronaldsay greatly, and three friends whose graves I made a point of visiting recently on the Mainland of Orkney: Norman Muir, a great character with whom I shared a desk while at the KGS, Peter Konstam, whose questions kept one on one's toes and Archie Jamieson, who supported my artistic endeavours more than anyone I know. I am also drinking to the memory of all those very many North Ronaldsay folk who have gone since I returned to live here thirty-three sometimes short, sometimes long years ago.

Nurse Janet Tulloch graduation photo, Upper Linnay, c 1905.

Silk embroidered World War I Christmas card (probably made in France).

Willie Tulloch, Seaforth Highlanders, Upper Linnay, NR, killed in action, France, 1918.

Pupils of the NR school, c early 1900s.

Drifters fishing. Such fishing boats were used for mine-sweeping in World War I.

NR Post boat, late 1920s.

Linklestoon men clearing ware road, 1930s. Photo by Dr Garvie.

Father and son (Thomsons), Quoybanks, ploughing with oxen and horse, c 1930s. Photo by Dr Garvie.

Janet Sanderson (née Thomson), South Ness, tramping blankets, 1930s. Photo by Dr Garvie.

NR School Board, 1930s.
Photo by Dr Garvie.

Fresson plane and passengers, 1930s. Photo by Dr Garvie.

Shearing crop, Holland farm, c 1930s.
Photo by Dr Garvie.

SS *Earl Sigurd* leaving NR pier, 1931.
Photo by Dr Garvie.

Tammie Thomson, left-hand side of photo, at the Geo o' Rue pund, 1930s.
Photo by Dr Garvie.

Singling match, 1930s.
Photo by Dr Garvie.

NR shop, wireless station, Post Office.

NR congregation outside UF Church, 1930s. Photo by Dr Garvie.

Willie Thomson, Dennishill, 1930s.
Photo by Dr Garvie.

Viola at Hansie's wheel house, shipwreck, 1939.
Photo 1960 by Ian Scott.

John Scott, North Manse, sowing, 1930s.
Photo by Mary Scott.

Burning tangles to make kelp at Linklet, c 1932. Photo by Dr Garvie.

Kelp burning, Linklet, July, 1932 (Willie o' Gravity). Photo by Dr Garvie.

Men roofing at Trebb using flagstones, 1936. Photo by Dr Garvie.

Roofing work at Trebb, 1937. Photo by Dr Garvie.

NR men rebuilding devastated sheep dyke in 1937. Photo by Dr Garvie.

MV *Mim* wrecked on Reef Dyke, 1939. Photo from Maritime Museum, Norway.

Moshulu in Belfast Lough, September 1938

Full masted sailing ship.
Photo taken from Eric Newby's *The Last Grain Race* (1938).

North Ronaldsay School, c 1940s.

NR folk loading goods on Fresson's plane, 1940s.

Willie Swanney, Verracott, c 1950s.
Photo by David Scott.

Brothers Robert and Willie Swanney 'taekin' Willie's house with simmans (straw rope), 1950s.
Photo by Mary Scott.

1st Kirkwall BB marching in Gilmerton, 1954.

The Linklestoon men on their Hogmanay visiting round on Linklestoon, 1950s–60s.
Drawing by Ian Scott.

NR folk at pier, possibly a family's departure from the island, early 1960s.

North Manse hay-turning team, c 1960s.

Catherine Tulloch, Cruesbreck, 1960s. Photo by Ian Scott.

NR Trip Day, leaving Kirkwall for NR on SS *Earl Thorfinn*, 1960s.

L to R – Hughie Thomson, Tammie Thomson and passenger Eleanor Swanney in the NR post boat, 1970s.

Unveiling Longhope Lifeboat Memorial by HRH Queen Eliabeth, The Queen Mother, 1970.
Photo from *Press & Journal*.

NR School in 1970s.

Repairing roof of Memorial Hall, 1990.
Photo by Janet Tulloch, Scottigar.

John Tulloch, Senness, World War II veteran, being introduced to Prince Charles in 1993.
Photo by Chris Bacon.

Royal Navy personnel helping to rebuild the storm damaged sheep dyke, 1993.

NR men after sheep dyke repairs, 1995.
Photo by Kelvin Scott.

Ann Tulloch and Lottie Tulloch, accordion players, c 1990s.

Memorial Hall, Burns Supper, 1996.

Photo by Jenny Mainland.

Diamond wedding, Sydney Scott and Bethia Scott, 1996.
Photo by Netta Brown.

An event to mark the automation of the NR Lighthouse in 1998.
Photo by Martin Gray.

Harvest Home, 1990s, Memorial Hall. Photo by Ian Scott.

Harvest Home, 1993. Photo by Peter Donnelly.

Memorial Hall, erected 1920.

Making Harvest Home decorations, 1990s. Photo by Peter Donnelly.

Old-fashioned lily (narcissus). Photo by Ian Scott.

Hemera Geo (the cave geo). Photo by Ian Scott.

Sunset, West Beach. Photo by Ian Scott.

NR native sheep on the foreshore.
Photo by Ingrid Tulloch.

Heavy sea, West Beach, NR.
Photo by Ian Scott.

Old Beacon, NR, 2023.
Photo by Ingrid Tulloch.

A Serious Case of Burns is Celebrated
February 8, 1996

> *There was a lad was born in Kyle,*
> *But whatna day o' whatna style,*
> *I doubt it's hardly worth the while*
> *To be sae nice wi' Robin.*
> – Robert Burns

This is the last day in January as I begin this belated letter from Orkney's Ultima Thule. I had meant to put this work behind me away back at the end of the year, but as Robert Burns said, 'The best laid schemes o' Mice an' Men, Gang aft agley'.

Remembering of course that this month is generally thought of as the month of Robert Burns, and especially since this year marks the 200th anniversary of his death, I think it is very appropriate to quote the poet.

My first quotation comes from Burns' poem 'Rantin', Rovin' Robin'. It has been said that there are few of Burns' songs more popular than this one. Anyway, as I step into the time machine of my mind and travel back over the weeks that have passed since my last account, I'm going to try and choose suitable lines from Burns which I will intersperse throughout my letter.

> *Now waving grain, wide o'er the plain,*
> *Delights the weary Farmer...*
> *The sky is blue, the fields in view,*
> *All fading-green and yellow.*

Two Harvest Homes ago, Jim Anderson, Director of Education, (who proposed the toast at our 1994 Harvest Home) talked enthusiastically about a Burns Supper for 1995, but nothing came of that idea. Again, more recently, he reminded us that this was Burns' bicentennial year and that North Ronaldsay should try and organise a celebration in honour of the poet, as they had done on many occasions in the past.

Well, to cut a long story short, a Burns Supper was agreed and organised (I may say with much work and innumerable phone calls). One night, for instance, a number of folk got together and made between 200 and 300 crepe-paper roses.

Orkney Office Supplies printed over a dozen very large photocopies of illustrations from books on Burns. Greenery was very kindly gifted from Sheila Konstam and James Miller and his wife Christine. The Leonards in Kirkwall, with some trouble and help, supplied crepe paper and candles. Now then, put all of that together, including various other ideas. For example, Cathie Mahoney, a BBC programme producer (who had been on holiday at the New Year), suggested the theme of red roses – 'O my Luve's like a red, red rose'.

Till a' the seas gang dry, my dear,
And the rocks melt wi' the sun:
I will love thee still, my dear,
While the sands o' life shall run.

So let's try and imagine the scene on the night of Saturday, January 27, in the Memorial Hall where we held the Burns Supper. Garlands of paper roses crisscrossed the hall from couple to couple. New Zealand flax and greenery adorned the walls and corners, and from the ceiling and walls hung various farming items – riddles, neep baskets and even my famous sowing cubbie (with which, since 1962, I must have sown over forty tons of grain).

All of this was lit by lantern, candle and oil lamp, and Burns' portrait with a lamp on either side, ivy-capped and set against tartan, occupied a prominent position on stage, as did an old-fashioned single-furrow hand plough, such as Burns would have used.

Thou saw the fields laid bare an' wast,
An' weary winter comin fast,
An' cozie here, beneath the blast,
Thou thought to dwell,
Till crash! the cruel coulter past
Out thro' thy cell.

After a short welcome (read in verse with apologies to Burns) which included a special vote of thanks to all those who had helped in any way with the celebration, Sinclair Scott piped in the haggis – 'He screw'd the pipes and gart them skirl, Till roof and rafters a' did dirl' (from 'Tam o' Shanter').

Winnie Scott, stepping to the music, carried the haggis round the hall, finally depositing it before Jim Anderson, who then rose and addressed the Haggis – 'Fair fa' your honest, sonsie face, Great Chieftan o' the Puddin-race!' John Cutt said the 'Selkirk Grace' and without more ado the three-course supper began.

With very substantial drams at the ready, the 'Immortal Memory' was given by Jim Anderson, who traced the life of the poet, illustrating his address with examples of Burns' poetry. Howie Firth gave a fairly serious, but interesting toast to the lasses, with Jenny Mainland setting about bringing Howie down to earth. Finally, Bessie Muir read 'Tam o' Shanter' (to fulfill Mrs Bethia Scott's wish and others'), warming up to the tale as she went along.

To complete a most pleasant and memorable supper, Jim Anderson accompanied the company on keyboard as they sang a selection of Burns songs, such as 'Ye Banks and Braes', 'Comin' Thro' the Rye' and 'A Man's a Man for a' That'.

Then let us pray that come it may,
As come it will for a' that,
That sense and worth, o'er all the earth,
Shall bear the gree, and a' that:
For a' that, and a' that,
It's comin yet for a that,
That man to man, the warld o'er.
Shall brothers be for a' that!

During a pause in the lively dance which followed, with pipes, accordions, spoons, recorder and drumsticks providing varied music, Ella Henderson recited 'To a Mountain Daisy' and Jim Anderson gave us 'To a Calf'.

Between 2 and 3am 'Auld Lang Syne' brought this special Burns Celebration to a close. It had been attended by over sixty folk which included expatriates and visitors, and it was particularly grand to have Liz, Trevor, Emily and Christopher Baxter back for the occasion. And those essential additional people's attendance was made possible by the ever-helpful Bob Tullock and his staff from Loganair. Before the company parted, soup, sandwiches and homebakes were served.

The Wintry West extends his blast,
And hail and rain does blaw;
Or, the stormy North sends driving forth,
The blinding sleet and snaw.

This poem most appropriately takes us back to Yule, and in the time machine of my mind I stop on the second day of the year when we held a slideshow and dance in the New Centre. Over a hundred old photographs, taken in North Ronaldsay as far back as the early 1900s and specially re-photographed as transparencies by Kelvin Scott, were shown.

Again, over sixty folk attended a lightsome little dance in a hall sparkling with Christmas decorations, coloured lights and a gaily-lit tree. Through the night a great selection of sandwiches and homebakes were provided.

New Year's Day, 1795, and Burns writes: 'This is the season of wishes and mine are most fervently offered to you! What a transient business is life! Very lately I was a boy – but t'other day I was a young man, – and I already begin to feel the rigid fibre and stiffening joints of old age coming fast over my frame.'

Well, Hogmanay and New Year's Day were celebrated with much enthusiasm despite fierce weather. On New Year's Day we continued with last year's revival of dancing round the Standing Stone, only this time with about double the company. This entertaining venture was followed by a most enjoyable little party at Neven which finished with an Eightsome Reel.

But hornpipes, jigs, strathspeys, and reels,
Put life and mettle in their heels.

Eightsome Reels and many other dances were also enjoyed at rather a unique barn dance arranged in Antabreck's loft by a few of the island's younger generation. Two accordions, gas heaters, Christmas tinsel and Slipperine made for a very unusual experience – especially so since King Winter ruled outside with a grip of icy iron. Between thirty and forty folk participated, with servings of hot soup to complete an unforgettable night.

But through the evening I could not help remembering one of the three remaining helpers, who had, so many years ago, been at the building of this very loft. His name was Charlie o' Greenspot, who died just before Christmas. His ghost, I'm sure, would have enjoyed the night, for Charlie was a great and lightsome dancer.

Now then, let's speed up my time machine. The school's Christmas dinner was held on December 21. In charge was the cook, Winnie Scott, assisted by Edith Craigie. A magnificent festive dinner was presented by the school and staff.

And still backwards I go, remembering the school Christmas concert held on December 18. With a few pupils of a performing age, head teacher Patricia Thomson arranged this function for an afternoon's presentation. Tea and homebakes were available to complete the entertainment, which was enjoyed by all present. Three other functions remain to be mentioned as I narrow the gap to my last letter.

A whist drive brought in over £100 for the children's Christmas Party. On November 25, the North Ronaldsay Lifeboat Guild raised a most generous sum of £377.90 for the RNLI, and the preceding night over £360 was collected for Children in Need. Both these functions had many and varied items for sale with much time and work being put especially into the Children in Need sale. President of the NRLB Guild, Isobel Muir, presided over the Lifeboat collection, and head teacher Patricia Thomson supervised the Children in Need function. On both nights the usual tea, cakes and biscuits were available.

Finally on November 17, James Thomson, who came specially back to the island for our Harvest Home, gave a most enjoyable slideshow raising over £30 for the North Ronaldsay Community Association and, as with all our communal events, refreshments were served.

My time machine has come to a stop, passing backwards as it has through all sorts of weather and all sorts of events. I've just worked out that the time taken to write over five years of Letters from North Ronaldsay could have produced at least three or four exhibitions. Anyway, here I am finishing another island letter.

Two or three nights ago – one such as I particularly like – the clouds seemed so far away, rippling across the sky like sand patterns left after the passing tide. The wind was down and southerly and the moon shone through those dappled clouds, and through a clearance here and there, against the blue-black velvet of the sky, a lonely star or two glittered with piercing brilliance.

That same night I thought I heard an oystercatcher, but the fast-moving arc of sound was too brief and unheard again for me to be sure. In the northerly direction of the cry, far out to sea, the lights of a passing ship winked as she sailed to an unknown destination.

I've just finished reading *A Stranger on the Bars: The Memoirs of Christian Watt Marshall of Broadsea*, a marvellous book about the days of the herring fishing, which Tam MacPhail (Stromness Books and Prints) recommended. Towards the end of the book, the author says that all those great days and times had passed away like a song – as have all the pleasures I've just been telling you about. But let me finish as I began with Robert Burns, and what better than from 'Tam o' Shanter'.

But pleasures are like poppies spread,
You seize the flower, its bloom is shed;
Or like the snow falls in the river,
A moment white – then melts forever;
Or like the Borealis race,
That flit ere you can point their place;
Or like the rainbow's lovely form
Evanishing amid the storm.
Nae man can tether time or tide.

Epic Boat Trips of Our Schooldays
June 20, 1996

Last night, Monday, June 3, at about 12 o'clock I heard a skylark singing. It was too dark to see this little bird of the sky who I may say sometimes takes a bit of looking for, even on a sunny day. It seemed to me that such a performance so late at night was rather unusual as I can't remember hearing the like before.

I once also heard a lark singing one morning between 2am and 3am when walking home from an island function. I admit that it is not often that I am out walking quite so early but certainly the midnight hour is more familiar. Maybe it simply has to do with being in the right place at the right time or maybe, as is more likely, it's a question of knowing about such things.

As I write I can hear a little wren singing sharply outside the ben window. I never remember wrens much talked about in the past, but now they are very familiar. From time to time I hear the blackbird's song as they are nesting, both here and next door. They have always been around and their song brings back memories from the past.

Last year in the spring there was one who roosted in our front byre, and when the byre was being cleaned out late at night in order to make the morning dieting easier, he would take to singing a few notes from his perch in the corner of the couples. I in my turn, for fun, would attempt to mimic his short line of notes, to which a few seconds later I would be treated to a further snatch of song. By the time morning came he would be away and gone through the open ridge of the byre, but for a while this performance went on, until at last he disappeared.

And thinking for a moment about bird song – I hasten to say that I am no expert on birds whatsoever – why should some sing beautifully and others only call with a limited range of notes? I can, for instance, imagine learning a fair representation of the blackbird's song, but just think of trying to memorise the skylark's. Indeed, I wonder how the young larks manage to pick up such a complication of notes. I think, though, that on listening fairly carefully to the skylark's singing, it contains many variations on a theme rather than a recognised note for note song.

Has the song of different birds remained the same over the centuries? I do remember some years ago hearing on a radio programme that a young bird – maybe there was more than one kind – which had been brought up away from its parents as an experiment, did not manage at all to sing the recognised song of its species. So it would seem that a young bird does in fact memorise the song or call of the parent. I'm sure at least the young blackbird does, as must other birds who have characteristic tunes. As for the sparrow, they do nothing but chatter, but what surprises me is the way in which the tremendous din made by a crowd of them can stop dead in an instant.

Jenny o' Cavan recently gave me a copy of a photograph she took when she was back on the island for our Burns Supper. It shows the Old Hall decorated for the occasion. The photograph is unusual in that it was taken during the day with the westerly sunlight streaming in through the hall's windows. Anyhow, looking at the photograph reminds me that more than four months have passed since I wrote my last letter from North Ronaldsay. It also reminds me that we have had no major community functions for a while.

Last year by contrast the island was entertained by various artistes involved with the Orkney Folk Festival, but this time round the festival organisers were, regrettably, unable to provide us with any musical guests.

Otherwise, Dorothy Henderson's Day Club activities have been in operation in the Community Centre, with badminton taking place most weekends over the winter months. Last night (Tuesday, June 12) though, a most pleasant occasion took place in the Community Centre, when over forty folk attended a farewell to our relief doctor, Dr Linda MacIntyre.

For the past three and a half years, despite a painful and worsening walking condition which has now resulted in her early retirement, she continued to visit and attend to islanders with her usual thoroughness. This commitment and dedication were acknowledged by the island when Linda was presented with a gold Burrian Cross necklace and a generous book token. Following the presentation, tea and a great selection of homebakes was enjoyed, bringing rather a special evening to a close.

Also, I must mention that at a well-attended meeting in February, Howie Firth and Tom Rendall gave a most interesting and entertaining talk, illustrated with slides, on the life and times of John D. Mackay. Mr Mackay taught in the North Ronaldsay School for five years before leaving the island in 1946.

By that time I would have attended the school for one year. In those days the school classroom was divided into two by a sliding partition, making what was known as the Little End and the Big End. Mr Mackay taught in the Big End where the more senior pupils were seated.

I'm actually looking at an old school photograph which must have been taken in 1946. There are I think thirty-six pupils posing for this photo. Today, by contrast, fifty years later, there are only four, with one nursery school child. Of that number only one is of North Ronaldsay parentage. The two teachers who also appear in this photograph are the head teacher Ivy Johnston, who by that time had married locally and was Mrs I. Scott, and of course, John D. Mackay was the other teacher.

My main memories of Mackay stem not from the North Ronaldsay years, but from his teaching days in Sanday, where he moved after leaving the island. At that time and before, and up until the advent of Loganair in 1967, all North Ronaldsay scholars – a word not often used nowadays – who left the island, only got home for holidays at the end of the school term. This meant when there was not a direct steamer we had firstly to sail to Sanday and then continue the journey in the island's post boat across the unpredictable and frequently stormy North Ronaldsay Firth.

This second part of the journey often meant staying overnight in Sanday, and sometimes for more than one night, depending on sailing times and weather conditions. Those stays are particularly memorable for those of us who lived through them. During my time I think there were eight contemporaries including myself who made those fairly unique journeys.

None of us, nor other travellers who experienced those crossings, will ever forget stumbling and slipping over the seaweed-covered black rock with luggage, mail bags, boxes and so on, and then being rowed out to the moored post boat in a small praam.

Nor will any of us ever forget the many rough trips across the firth sailing in an open boat of some twenty-six or twenty-seven ft with a small fore deck and short side decking, with the steersman seated within a separate compartment that housed the inboard engine.

In the open boat, of course, the crew and passengers were exposed to the elements. If the spray was too heavy then an oily tarpaulin was used to provide a raised shelter over the fore part of the boat, but under this protection the smell of oil and engine exhaust fumes caused the inevitable seasickness to which the majority of us succumbed. For that painful performance there was an old galvanised pail, washed out when necessary with a scoop of salt water, or as an alternative we could be sick over the spray-washed gunwales of the boat. Actually, this method was preferable, as the shock of cold water had a reviving effect.

As I've been thinking, remembering and writing about those days which are now a part of history, I cannot but honestly wonder how the new generations of school children and islanders would react today if faced with a similar situation. Perhaps at least there might be a greater understanding of what we used to think was the meaning of island life.

But I have digressed somewhat. I was going to say that during those weather-bound days in Sanday, about which I could write at some length, a visit to John D. Mackay was almost obligatory for all North Ronaldsay scholars, and particularly his former pupils. But his interest and welcome extended to all of us who made those special visits. Nothing could have pleased John D. (as he was sometimes called) as much as those mostly night-time excursions. There he sat in some majesty in his study, the walls of which were lined with row upon row of books with many more spilling over his desk and chairs and even at times taking up floor space, ready to cross-question, argue and talk for as long as his visitors cared to stay.

This is the time of year when the bluebell is in full bloom, and the splendid, elegant, scented lily, with its finely sculptured white petals set off so perfectly by the red-tipped yellow centre. I've got one standing in water at my side as I type. I'm sure that a whole vase of them at such close proximity would be almost intoxicating in some way, with the strength of scent this flower produces.

The very thought reminds me of Ernest Marwick's wonderful essay called 'The Water Meedoo'. In this account he talks about an experience he had in a Meedoo – a marshy valley, which during the summer produced 'bog-hay' as it was called. There one sunny summer day the intense scent of the meedoo-sweet flower, which grew in great profusion, seemed to take control of his senses so that time itself seemed timeless. He experienced the most remarkable sensations, the full result of which was a feeling of being drugged for the rest of the day.

I first read this essay in *An Orkney Anthology*, a magnificent book which contains selected works of Ernest Marwick. I wonder whether John Robertson, who so creditably edited this the first volume, will present us with a second.

I'm off at a tangent again – actually I've just become aware that the wind has got up bravely and is running and rattling all over our slated roof and echoing down the chimney. Through the window I can see at least sixty black-headed gulls all spread out over our Purtabreck shift, as I call it, busily poking away through the grass. In my mind's eye they are suddenly transformed into three or four hundred, rising every now and then in white clouds to settle in tight flocks behind the moving plough or harrows. That vision takes us back to April and the spring work.

April was also the main month of the comet, and on the 10th its appearance overhead was fairly spectacular. Then for a while cloudy nights hid its progress, until finally it could only be seen as a little smudge of light far away in the northwest. By using binoculars, the streaming tail was still clear. On reading about this phenomenon, I learned that the comet's tail stretches for millions of miles. Anyhow, it has disappeared, speeding away on its lonely journey round the sun, and when, if ever, it will come back I imagine nobody knows.

I often wish though that I knew more about the constellations. I'm always tempted to buy just one more book on astronomy in the hope that I can find one that makes it all simple. But really what is required is time, patience, and a bit of study.

When the comet was beginning to fade from view, Venus still remained a brilliant sight in the western sky, and its fairly low aspect allowed the reflected brightness of the planet to make a little luminous path of light across the west sea. Indeed, so bright is this light at certain times that shadows may even be seen.

But what about the stars? Usually they can be viewed best during the dark winter evenings, and yet a couple of months ago there were two or three nights when they seemed as brilliant as ever I've particularly seen them. It had something to do with the black, velvety appearance of the sky – for that quality was also apparent – and on sweeping the heavens with binoculars, the passing stars streaked lines of light across my vision. But even to focus on areas here and there makes one so much more aware of the magnificence and mystery of the cosmos.

They say that man has always dreamed of reaching the stars. Even the nearest one is about four light-years away from the earth. Others are hundreds and some thousands of light-years distant.

I'm trying to think about those unthinkable distances and basing my thinking on the impossible assumption that I could travel at the speed of light – which is 186,000 miles per second. Supposing for a moment that on a fine moonlight night I was to take one fantastic jump to the moon travelling at the speed of light. I would land there in less than two seconds.

If I continued to jump to another moon as far away and so on for one minute's jumping time, I would have travelled the distance of approximately forty moons, and after jumping for one hour I would be 2,400 moons away. Then a day's jumping – twenty-four times 2,400 which is 57,600 – then one year: 365 times 57,600.

One multiplication remains to arrive at approximately the number of moons between North Ronaldsay and the nearest star, and that is by four. Well, the idea of jumping to the moon seemed possible to grasp visually maybe, but now we are having to think of millions of millions of moons and it's time to stop – for me at least – such impossible calculations.

But still, this dream of reaching the stars inspires strange thoughts and a heightening of the mind, and away out there within our galaxy and even beyond, I was just thinking that maybe George Mackay Brown and his writing companion Bessie Skea will have at last mastered the riddle of the universe.

I would like to finish by saying that on St Magnus Day, two North Ronaldsay men sat side by side in Orkney's magnificent cathedral, built in memory of the saintly Earl Magnus. Before the altar rested the remains of a great Orcadian, GMB.

A million light-years beyond the Milky Way
Where Villon and Burns,
Falstaff and slant-eyed Li Po
Order their nectar by turns
(No 'Time, gents' there, no drinker has to pay)
And words immortal gather head and flow.

(From 'Attie Campbell, 1900–1967' in *Following a Lark* by George Mackay Brown)

The Harvest is in for Another Year
October 17, 1996

Ever since my parents' memorable diamond wedding away back in early July, I have been sleeping in one of our westerly-facing attics. I had moved there to make room for some of the guests who attended this 60th wedding anniversary. So pleasant has been the elevation of my sleeping quarters that I've never bothered, as yet, to move back to my old room.

It's been pleasant for various reasons. One is that the wind, when it blows from between the southwest and the north, comes unimpeded in through my little open attic window, swirling and eddying away at face level. It feels almost as if I'm suspended in mid-air, or as near as I can be to sleeping out in the open.

Another reason is that the sound of the sea travels in as freely as the wind. It comes and goes like the surges of the tide, echoing round the room as if it had become a seashell which, as George Mackay Brown says in his 'Shore Songs', 'gives back the innumerable choirs of the sea.'

Away back in June when I was writing my last letter, I had a lily – or more accurately a white narcissus – next to my typewriter. For fun, this time I've picked three autumn flowers: the deep scarlet flower of the fuchsia tree, a sprig of montbretia and the scented honey suckle. Their presence reminds me that the last three months of the year are at hand, and they are also, I fear, about the last of our outside flowers for this season.

Over the summer we have had a few lively and enjoyable events. The first was a concert and dance held during magnificent haymaking weather. The group Hullion – Billy and Ingirid Jolly, Micky Austin, and Andy Cant – gave us a grand concert and also helped with music for the dance. The fifth member of the group, Owen Tierney, was unfortunately unable to come because of haymaking.

A bit later another dance was held, which began with a showing of the classic 1930s film *Man of Aran*, made by Robert Flaherty, and the award-winning documentary, *Bank Ahead*, kindly loaned by Ken Thomson of the Red Cross.

Both these dances were held in the Memorial Hall and both had an attendance of upwards of seventy. The organisation of the two functions was carried out by the wardens for the summer, Alison and Marion Muir.

They completed their activities by arranging a little sports gathering on a fine sunny day on the North Links. Total attendances at the Community

Centre over the eight-week supervised period, including the sports day, amounted to 300.

In the Community Centre there have also been two island functions. One was an outstanding slideshow and talk given by Rosemary Robertson covering her visit to Mongolia. Then more recently, as part of the Orkney Science Festival, Patrick Bailey gave a most interesting lecture entitled 'Living on the Edge'.

Both events were well attended, and in about the middle of October we plan a further talk or slideshow. But the main event of the year will be the Harvest Home, plans for which are already underway.

Earlier in the year a few of us got together, including Heidi Holtan, a Norwegian exchange student at the KGS, and made over 400 feet of simmans. They will replace those we have been using these past six years as Harvest Home decorations. Interestingly, when thrashing the last of our sheaves for this purpose, I discovered that twenty-five sheaves made twelve windlins – one of which would be one meal for a cow. Also, one such windlin made five fathom (thirty ft) of simmans.

Thinking more about harvest, sheaves, stacks and simmans, I'm looking at a book called *Orkney from Old Photographs*, by Gordon Wright. In the section on farming there is a photograph of stacks taiked (thatched) with simmans. They present a wonderful sight, and no wonder, since they won W. G. Rendall, Skaill, in Rendall, first prize and a medal in a stack-building competition held in 1929.

The stacks of Mr Rendall must have held some 600 to 700 sheaves, judging by the height of the two men standing next to the stacks. Those must have been great days indeed, and arguably a return to such times would have many advantages, not least of which would be less weeds to be seen in Orkney generally. And then think of the Harvest Homes. They would become functions of real meaning and enjoyment once again.

Well, that's as may be, but still, I've been doing some estimates on those more old-fashioned farming methods. As to whether the following information will be of interest I know not, however, it should at least be so to the older generations of farmers. They are certainly qualified to question or help with such a diverse subject – maybe I will receive a letter or two.

Beginning with the simmans, I have already worked out that twenty-five sheaves can make twelve windlins, and one windlin can make thirty feet of simmans. Thinking of Mr Rendall's taiked stacks the question is, what length of simman would be required to taik or thatch one stack?

Taking a more average-sized stack of say 500 sheaves, I understand from my father that firstly the stack requires a simman belt placed about three feet high. On an average stack I've measured the length of such a belt to be seven fathom (forty-two ft).

Then at about a one-foot spacing round the belt, simmans stretch up over the top of the stack from side to side, leaving a loop turned through the belt. Each loop was fixed by partly pulling out a handful of the lower stack sheaf ends which was then twisted a few times to make a sort of rope. This rope (called a wouzie locally) came up through each loop with a twisting over-and-under securing movement.

The length of each simman (thirty-three in all) – that is from belt to stack top – was two and half fathom. So adding all of that together, we arrive at approximately ninety fathom of simmans required to taik one stack, and then working back from my estimates on sheaves and windlins, it seems as if about thirty-eight sheaves are needed to make one stack secure against the winter winds. In other words one stack of approximately 500 sheaves would make enough simmans to protect twelve stacks.

Can that be right, I wonder? It seems a lot, but of course much of the simmans so used (at least in early winter) would do the job another year, or maybe more. However, I have no experience of simman durability.

Let's take this subject further by considering the time spent in working one 2.5 acre field in one year: plough, four hours; harrow (four times), three hours; sow (by hand), 0.35; shearing (binder on four sides), 2.45; stooking 1,800 sheaves, 2.30 (300 stooks, half a minute per stook).

Build four stacks: 450 sheaves (one bringing in sheaves, one building, one pitching, at forty-five minutes per stack), three hours. Taking in stack: pitched and built on trailer, forty-five minutes times four stacks, three hours. Pitch and build in barn loft (four stacks), three hours. Thrash with mill for seed and fodder: four stacks at seventy-five minutes per stack, five hours. Total 26.90 hours.

It seems, bearing in mind variables such as type of land, amount of crop and speed of work, that thirty hours would therefore be a fair estimate for the time involved in working one 2.5 acre field sown to oats, including the rolling of the field.

I hope all of that is not as bad as the calculations (in my last letter) about the moon and stars; at least it's a bit more down to earth. Incidentally, a friend of mine calculated that to travel to the nearest star at a possible speed – such as a moon rocket would travel – would take 120,000 years approximately.

Remember, in my last letter I was thinking about the speed of light, which reaches the nearest star in four years. Of course, it's impossible to travel at the speed of light, and the conventional time scale is not much help, so the dream of reaching the stars, or rather reaching a planet such as ours encircling a star, will surely remain a dream.

Talking about dreams, away back in the summer of 1962, just when I had finished my days at art school, I went for a short trip to London before coming back to North Ronaldsay. While on that visit I bought a book of Chinese poems, mostly written as long ago as the 7th or 8th century and some well before.

Dreams are frequently referred to and are often about old friends and acquaintances who have gone to the 'Land of Ghosts'. It's curious and true to think that, as another poet says, only in our dreams do we meet up with those who have gone. And yet the often plausible circumstances and exchanges of the dream are conceived somewhere in the deepness of the mind.

This marvellous little book contains poems on all sorts of subjects – 'On Being Sixty', 'Thinking of the Past', 'Planting Flowers', 'Rain', 'In the Mountains', 'Sailing Homewards'. They are, even after upwards of 2,000 years, as fresh as the day they were written, and despite the passage of time show that people, in many ways, have not changed all that much.

Before I finish this letter I must share some of my recent memories while they are still fresh in my mind. I'm thinking firstly about a 'middling' summer. And yet on the other hand it was remarkably mild, and the work of silage and hay was easy, catching as it did enough combinations of sunny days, wind and blue skies. Easy also were the native sheep pundings, much of which was carried out under bracing winds from the far north.

But what about our Indian summer which seemed as if it would never end? I cannot think of many times when the main of the minimum amount of binder work was carried out in such comfort, when days and nights were as warm as those in the crown of any fine summer. Often I saw spectacular sunsets – even sometimes through turning binder wings, or behind stooks and stacks – and purple islands to the west.

Yet in between all this activity, one fine day a good turnout of folk got down to work and tarred the Memorial Hall. Almost a month has passed since that tarring day, and only a few stacks remain to be built on later-sown fields. But as I write (Sunday, September 29) the Indian summer has gone, blasted away by the equinoctial gales.

Along the roads some tall, dignified and long-legged sow thistles – albeit somewhat tattered – are bobbing their yellow heads in today's strong southwesterly gales, and the three flowers next to my typewriter, even after a few days, are looking better than their relations outside.

Other images remain in my mind. These past nights, for instance, a full moon has been riding stormy skies, sometimes shining brilliantly white when clear of flying cloud. Another day, when helping with others to build corn stacks at Cruesbreck, Nouster Bay danced white and blue, and behind the nearby farm of Howar the North Ronaldsay Firth flashed in long, dazzling sheets of silver in the morning sun.

It's easy to recall such sights and sounds, for they remain easily accessible in the mind. Imagine for instance a sunbeam like a searchlight, streaming through a rift in a cloud and picking out the tall tower of the New Lighthouse, while the rest of the island remains for a time in autumn shadow. Or when out at sea, countless little rainbows appearing and disappearing as the sun strikes the right angle through boat-thrown sea spray. And what about the sight of the sun on a cold easterly morning, when it rises majestic and fiery red from behind heaving seas.

Yesterday in the darkening of the night, a little after 7pm, when returning from a late fishing trip, the moon rose in the east. It remained visible only for a short time before disappearing out of sight behind low cloud, but for that moment it was a strange sight, glowing amber-hued and lantern-like above the dark sea.

I was just thinking at that time about the many creatures that live below its surface, and I would really like to finish with a poem by GMB about one such creature. It comes from his book of poems *The Wreck of the Archangel*, published by John Murray. What lobster fisherman would not be more than happy with such a wonderful description?

Lobster

What are you doing here
Samurai
In the west, in the sunset streams of the west?

How you lord it over those peasants,
The whelks
The mussels and the shrimps and scallops.

*There you clank, in dark blue armour
Along the ocean floor,
With the shadows flowing over you,
Haddock, mackerel,
And the sun the shadow of a big yellow whale.*

Nothing stands in your way, swashbuckler.

*The orchards where you wander
Drop sufficient plunder,
Mercenary in the dark blue coat of mail.*

*Be content, be content far out
With the tides' bounty,
Going from smithy to smithy, in your season
For an ampler riveting.*

*Fold your big thumbs,
Under the trembling silver-blue scales of the moon.*

From America ... for Harvest Home
December 5, 1996

> *There is a spell woven by restless seas,*
> *A secret charm that haunts our Island air,*
> *Holding our hearts and following everywhere*
> *The wandering children of the Orcades;*
> *And still when sleep the prisoned spirit frees,*
> *What dim, void wastes, what strange, dark seas we dare,*
> *Till, where the drear green Isles shine low and fair,*
> *We moor in dreams beside familiar quays.*

This verse is the first one of a poem written by Duncan John Robertson (1860–1941) called 'Sons of the Isles'. It has, in a way, a direct link with North Ronaldsay, since its writer happened to be the grandfather of Duncan J. T. Robertson of Holland House, who returns each summer to the island for a few weeks with his wife Rosemary and their family.

Of course the poem refers to the Orkney Islands, and the sentiments expressed within the poem fit in very suitably with my letter from North Ronaldsay. It also explains, I think, why many former islanders return from time to time – even from the other side of the world – and next year I know that there is a North Ronaldsay man, now in his nineties, who is planning another trip across the Atlantic to the land of his birth.

One of the most enjoyable visits to the island at this time of year which involves a number of former inhabitants, relations, friends and young islanders – even from as far away as Aberdeen – must surely be the visit for the Harvest Home. This year an attendance of ninety people sat down at three long trestle tables for the usual magnificent supper.

Of that number, who all flew with Loganair across the North Ronaldsay Firth – apart from Jimmie o' Nether Linnay, who travelled the old sea road – about one quarter had lived previously on the island or were closely connected through marriage or relationship. Also among the ninety people were a few other friends, with one, Liz Forgan, coming from as far afield as London.

Included in this lesser number were the guests: Councillor Howie Firth, a great supporter of the Harvest Home; Andy Leonard, our favourite accordionist from Stromness; and representing Loganair, without whose interest and support we could never arrange such a great evening, was Captain David Miller, accompanied by his wife Karen.

The fact that each year folk come back to the island for this celebration surely says something about its appeal, and their presence at the function each year revives old times and makes sure, as Burns says, that old acquaintance should not be forgot. It seems that as the words of Duncan Robertson's poem say, 'There is a spell ... a secret charm,' which brings back 'the wandering children of the Orcades.'

And talking about Harvest Homes and the Memorial Hall, it's interesting to note that the first recorded Harvest Home that I can find as having been held in the hall was in 1938. Before that, in fact probably sometime before the erection of the Memorial Hall in 1920, this harvest celebration was called the Muckle Supper. Holland Farm was the venue for those earlier celebrations, and attendance was seemingly by invitation – though many islanders went to help with harvesting at Holland. After the supper, dancing followed in the large barn of Holland House Farm.

Confirmation of the year mentioned comes from the treasurer's book kept by former postmaster and merchant, William Scott, Cavan, who was treasurer from 1920 until his death in 1964. In this fascinating and most important book, which covers the communal activity in North Ronaldsay from 1920–1980, it says, 'Cash for using the hall for Harvest Home, whist drive, in aid of the Balfour Hospital held in Dec 1938.' A sum of £12 was raised.

There are many other very interesting pieces of information, some headings for which read as follows: purchase of lamp and heater oil, and of tar and felt, Burns Suppers, World War II victory celebrations, film shows, concerts and dances, subscriptions from each toonship for use of hall, and so on.

Harvest Homes continued for the next forty-one years in the Memorial Hall, apart from four which are not recorded for the year 1943, '47, '58 and '64. Then from 1981 until 1989 the event was held in the newly opened Community Centre. Ever since, we have held this traditional celebration in the Memorial Hall which has now become synonymous with this event, and which has, for so many islanders, seen the passage of their years, from early childhood, through youth and on to old age.

Coincidentally, and in a similar but deeper vein of thought, a parish minister was recently reported in *The Orcadian* to have said that church buildings are of high importance to local communities, and feelings run high when their future is questioned. Admittedly, he is talking about church buildings – and very true are his comments – but equally what he goes on to say would apply to North Ronaldsay's first community hall, and indeed to many other places and sites which are part of Orkney's heritage.

He says: 'These buildings say something about our history and our identity. They speak of continuity, when all around is changing. Our emotions are bound up in them. We have shared in worship there ... or made our marriage vows there ... They give our community character.'

But before going on to describe this year's Harvest Home, I shall briefly tell you about other events which have been happening since the summer months, when we enjoyed two functions in the New Centre.

A third function took place about the end of October, with a good attendance, when Len Wilson, who was accompanied by his wife Lily, gave a most enjoyable talk on the Hudson's Bay Company fur trade and their fiddle music. The talk was illustrated by an excellent video shot by Len during his recent visit to Canada. Tea and refreshments followed, then at another venue he entertained in full swing on his fiddle.

That event was succeeded by the yearly North Ronaldsay Lifeboat Guild's fund-raising night, and as usual, a most pleasant and successful evening was had. From the sale of RNLI items on display, raffle and donations, an excellent sum of about £500 was raised, with more still to be collected. Tea and homebakes were served at set tables, at the end of which the NRLG president, Isobel Muir, announced the grand total and thanked everybody for their support. Then for the fourth Community Association event held on the second night following the Harvest Home, Dr Kathleen Scott (born in the USA), a distinguished scholar of medieval manuscripts and wife of the Harvest Home speaker, gave a most informative talk illustrated by selected slides.

The talk was entitled 'Depictions of farm and building implements in medieval manuscripts.' This proved to be a completely new subject for most of us. It was particularly interesting from the point of view of old farm implements, quite apart from the artistry and colour to be enjoyed in the photographed manuscripts. Tea and refreshments followed, giving another good audience a chance to ask questions.

On Friday, November 22 came Children in Need Day when the North Ronaldsay School, with headteacher Patricia Thomson as co-ordinator, arranged a sale in aid of the appeal. Parents, staff and friends baked, made or otherwise supplied many varied items for sale. Raffles and competitions added to the fundraising. More than thirty folk who had attended later enjoyed tea and a great selection of homebakes. Over £300 was raised for the appeal.

Well, let me go back in time to November 8 and tell you about our celebrations for the harvest of land and sea. I think, as the poet of my letter, Duncan J. Robertson, said: 'There is a spell woven by restless seas, A secret charm that haunts our island air.'

Indeed, I think there are many spells woven by the memories of harvest and by folk of the past that we remember. I like the idea of the wandering children of the Orcades – I often wish that more of them would return. But one of those wanderers who has frequently come back over the years must be Dr David Scott, an islander formerly from North Manse. Along with his wife, Dr Kathleen Scott, and Jeremy, the youngest of their family of three, Dr Scott came specially across the Atlantic from the USA to be our Harvest Home speaker.

It's not often that we have someone such as the chancellor of one of the largest universities in the United States as a speaker, but David – a distinguished nuclear physicist – holds that eminent position. He is at present chancellor of the University of Massachusetts in Amherst, a university with a student complement of 24,000 and 1,100 lecturers.

With the company seated in the Memorial Hall, a brief introduction was made in which everybody was welcomed, with special acknowledgment given to the many helpers and generous supporters who continue to make this harvest celebration possible. Mention was also made of one of last year's visitors, Eri Ikawa, a most friendly Japanese lady who, in a letter from Japan, asked for her love and best wishes to be given to the people in the most northerly isle of Orkney. John Cutt, Gerbo, followed this introduction by saying the grace.

At the end of the candle and lantern-lit supper, below simmans, buoy heads, crosses and evergreens, and with a tall old-fashioned oil lamp at hand, David rose to make his Harvest Home speech. The theme of his presentation centred round three elements of society as he saw them – change, continuity, and community – the combination of which he considered to be particularly important.

David then proceeded, step by step, to develop this idea, relating his overall concept to North Ronaldsay and its future as the island heads towards the millennium. By moving backwards and forwards in North Ronaldsay's history he speculated on the earliest days, mentioning that not so very long ago the island's population had been as high as 500. He described the great changes in communications and lifestyle over the years, and went on to talk about the personalities and events in North Ronaldsay which had directly influenced his outlook on life and his early wish to become a scientist. But with all those observations he always drew a parallel with the life of the island and his theme – change, continuity, and community. Those three elements he considered vital in the development of any country, university or island.

As an example of continuity, he mentioned the North Ronaldsay Bird Observatory, with its two wind-powered generators – a building situated on the former farm site of Twingness. There, well over forty years before, he recalled how Harry Tulloch, who once made a living at the farm, had preceded this modern development by having his own small wind generator, as indeed had others on the island, long ago.

But as North Ronaldsay moves towards the year 2000 and beyond, David predicted change, in as much as farming the land would no longer provide or sustain a satisfactory standard of life. Instead he seemed sure that a much more sophisticated technology would take over – such as computers, fax machines and so on – when new islanders would come with new ideas. There would be, he thought, some clash of cultures, but emphasised again the importance of the three elements within his theme – change, continuity, and community – and the fusion of the three. This fusion he had seen, and still saw, in North Ronaldsay, and it was there to be experienced, he said, in such functions as the Harvest Home, which he had travelled thousands of miles to attend.

After completing his speech, which he had delivered with humour, style and some foresight, David asked everyone to be upstanding and a toast to the North Ronaldsay Harvest Home.

After those most pleasant and leisurely proceedings everything changed as fast as the weather outside. Down fell the windy rain, out went the long tables and trestles. Ladies clattered through pots, pans and dishes. Carnation displays, lanterns, candles and chairs, all disappeared in a flash, and once our MC John o' Westness had set about his duties (with a liberal dash of Slipperine on the floor), a grand dance took off with fine momentum.

That momentum continued with Andy Leonard and Lottie and Anne Tulloch on accordions, Howie Firth on recorder – or the dance floor, or swinging to the skirl of the pipes played by Loganair pilot David Miller and Sinclair Scott, as they played with twinkling fingers for Eightsome Reels. Fast and furious ebbed and flowed the dance, with Bessie and her team of elegant ladies serving tea, native mutton, sandwiches and homebakes during a welcome break before swinging back into the dance with a Strip the Willow. All of a sudden before anybody realised the time, the morning hour of 4am arrived, and like Cinderella's ball, everything came to an end.

Then with almost the full company still in the hall, the singing of 'Auld Lang Syne' completed one of our most memorable Harvest Homes in recent years. Just before the serving of a very appropriate Norwegian mulled punch, David, our guest speaker, was carried shoulder high to the singing of 'For He's a Jolly Good Fellow.'

Outside, a sudden flurry of snowflakes came swirling on the wind, lit up by car lights against the blackness of the winter's night. Just a little later brilliant stars appeared through snowy clouds. For a moment once I got home, I watched from the shelter of Antabreck, and in a clearing patch of sky, the Plough appeared. I waited for a moment longer and sure enough, as I had hoped, I saw the sparkle of the North Star.

It seems entirely suitable to finish with the second and last verse of Duncan Robertson's evocative poem 'Sons of the Isles'.

Sons of the Isles! though ye may roam afar,
Still on your lips the salt sea spray is stinging,
Still in your hearts the winds of youth are singing;
Though in heavens grown familiar to your eyes
The Southern Cross is gleaming, for old skies
Your hearts are fain, and for the Northern Star.

Will the Angels Play Their Harps for Me?
February 6, 1997

It seems a little out of season to be writing about Yule. But nevertheless I'm going to.

Ernest Marwick reminds us that Yule was an ancient festival, which our Norwegian forefathers took with them to the north of Scotland. It began on December 21 and lasted until January 13 – which of course is Old New Year's Day. When that day arrived all the Yule celebrations and the Yule visits should be completed.

In North Ronaldsay not very long ago, this visiting rule was often referred to by the older folk, and for myself I've made a point of adhering to it. Over the years (some thirty-five or more) many of the islanders I used to go and see are no longer alive, and curiously, but for all that, I am now older than, or at least as old as, those elders I used to visit. The years fly by but the mind travels at a lesser speed.

December 21 was also the winter solstice and generally accepted as being the shortest day of the year in the northern hemisphere, which meant of course that the sun was returning and extending the daylight – albeit ever so slowly – another reason for celebration.

It seemed therefore very appropriate that our long-awaited bonfire and fireworks display should take place on that day – quite apart from the much older custom of lighting bonfires, as Ernest Marwick says, at Yule and at Beltane (May 1), Midsummer and Hallowmas (November 1). So you see we Orcadians have at least four good occasions to get rid of some more burnable bruck, and as fine an excuse as any to arrange more celebrations and dances.

But I digress: I was beginning to tell you that on the night of December 21 – as grand a night as anyone can imagine – fire and fireworks sped into the night sky above the North Links. Refreshments, including a substantial punch, followed in the New Community Centre. Later, at another venue, celebrations continued with music, singing and dancing.

Over the Yule I've made one or two attempts at this letter but, as Robert Burns said, 'The best laid schemes o' Mice an' Men, Gang aft agley.'

I have a reasonable excuse though, and I'm going to blow my own trumpet here by telling you that I have been painting – almost every day that I can and for the past few weeks. Up and down the rocks and beaches, into creeks and crannies, over dykes, stiles and stubble I've travelled with my boards, paints and brushes. And in that time, this year and late last year, I have seen wonderful skies and sunsets, all shades of sea and rock colours and heard the song of the sea, the wind and the birds that frequent the wide-open spaces.

I have to tell you that this has not been achieved without a degree of sometimes considerable discomfort. For despite wearing gloves, a parka and oilskins, the rigours of the winter set upon a motionless body with cruel intent.

Cauld blaws the wind frae east to west,
 The drift is driving sairly;
Sae loud and shrill's I hear the blast,
I'm sure it's winter fairly.

Yes, that's part of a Burns poem. Last year we celebrated the poet's birthday, but sadly not this year. It's funny but as I rough-type this part of my letter, our chiming clock has just struck twelve midnight, which means this is January 25 – Robert Burns' birthday. I was about to say before the clock chimed that there have been arrangements made for a Burns Night, but more of this later when I have something to report. Meantime, at this point in my letter, I shall go back in time to the early hours of the New Year when I actually began a sort of introduction to this letter. I managed this somewhat unusually, after returning from our Hogmanay house next door when I made some notes outside on a cold and frosty moonlit morning. Anyway, here they are for interest, and because they provide some links with the rest of my letter.

Lighthouse

This is New Year's morning and the time is a little after 4am. The wind is blowing fresh and decidedly cold from a westerly direction. In the sky, a little east of south, the moon, although about half spent, still gives enough light for me to see faintly each line as a guide, as I write on the back of our now obsolete calendars of just a few hours ago.

Wreathing the waning moon, scattered high clouds have just a hint of rainbow colours, and on the road, small patches of ice here and there reflect the flash of moonlight.

The westerly wind carries the rumble of restless seas, which are pounding over a rocky coastline, and even with the half light of the moon I can see the dark line which divides the sea from the sky.

As I look around the possible points of the compass along that dark line, not one ship's lights can I see on this New Year's morning. But far more commanding is the sweeping beam of the lighthouse as it swings round and round, lighting up the island every ten seconds and reflecting brightly on Ancum Loch.

As I walk more cloud is beginning to fill in the sky a little, and just now these faint rainbow colours I saw have encircled the moon more prominently, shining against a veil of thin, high, pearly cloud. Where there are clear patches of sky, stars appear for a moment or two before passing cloud hides them from view. And on the road, with its grassy verges, glittering pinpoints of frost sparkle like the silvered decoration one sees on some Christmas cards designed to give that effect. It reminds me of an old festive card I saw earlier on Hogmanay – but the strange thing about the card was that it carried Christmas greetings to a Linklestoon man twenty-eight years ago.

At this point my notes come to an end, but later, once I have given an account of other events, I must tell you the story of the mysterious Christmas card. I suppose it marks the end of an era – or it does in a way. The owner of the card was one of the memorable characters of an older and more traditional Hogmanay, and of a different way of life.

Those other events, which are mainly connected with Yule, began three days before the proper date of December 21. But on that day the now yearly, well-attended and always splendid island Christmas dinner took place.

The affair is organised by the school staff, who manage a great job. On December 24 another enjoyable event occurred. This was the children's Christmas party. Santa this year had no travel problems, and a good turnout gathered in time to see his performance.

Three days later a showing of the film *Treasure Island* provided an introduction to our last official dance for 1996. Tea, sandwiches and homebakes were served after the show, with the dance following. At 3am the evening came to an end with the dancing, by this time in fine form. Hot punch or tea with cakes completed this Christmas occasion.

We seem to be doing things in threes, for three days after the dance Hogmanay was upon us, and what better way to describe this night than by quoting more lines from Robert Burns:

The night drave on wi' sangs and clatter;
And ay the ale was growing better ...
As bees flee hame wi' lades o' treasure,
The minutes wing'd their way wi' pleasure.

The minutes did indeed wing their way, for some, far into the New Year morning – as they did on New Year's e'en. And at that night's venue the dancing extended outside with the stars for celestial company.

These old grey stones, what are they? Pillars reared
By men who lived and died in Orkney land.

Those lines begin Stuart Blackie's poem, which he called 'At the Standing Stones'. The poem comes from *An Anthology of Orkney Verse*, compiled and edited by Ernest Marwick (published in 1949). It has become a very suitable theme poem for our New Year's Day Standing Stone dance, praising as it does those early settlers in Orkney of some five or six thousand years ago.

By the way, before I forget, I recently received two letters from readers of *The Orcadian* enquiring about Duncan J. Robertson's poem 'Songs of the Isles', which I quoted in my last letter from North Ronaldsay.

I will take the opportunity of telling them that this poem, including four others by Robertson, can be found in the anthology. There is also a short biography, and it should be possible to receive a copy, or further information about the poet and author, from a public library.

Anyhow, on New Year's Day, twenty-two dancers made up by a merry mixture of islanders, former islanders, new islanders and visitors, arrived at the Standing Stone. Firstly, we all recited our theme poem, then toasted the New Year, and finished by dancing the first part of the Eightsome Reel round the fourteen-foot-high stone.

At this rate of interest (six new recruits per year), by the year 2000 there could be forty dancers stepping forth – who can tell? Liz Forgan, a supporter of all things North Ronaldsay, very graciously acted as our host when everybody arrived at Neven. There, with Cathy Mahoney helping, tea and cakes were served before Rex Cowan rather grandly proposed another toast. After that songs were sung with piano accompaniment by Liz.

So you see how pleasant an occasion has become this revived custom, thanks to Laurie Taylor, a visitor whose interest in our history, plus his enthusiasm, got us started on this New Year adventure. I have not, though, forgotten my grandmother, who lived until she was ninety-four and was born in 1870. She talked about how islanders used to dance round the Standing Stone – not really so very long ago.

But I should have said all this in a proper reply to Rex's fine toast and added, just to give another mischievous perspective, that the few critics here and there who consider our activities rather silly would be very unlikely to leave any monument or worthwhile mark of their existence, round which the future generations of years hence will dance or pay their respects.

Well, I'm coming very nearly to the Christmas card story, but not before I cover another couple of events. On January 20 Tom Muir from Kirkwall gave an illustrated talk on 'The Folklore of Orkney'. This was one of the Aberdeen University illustrated lectures, held in the New Centre, with tea and biscuits available to complete the evening.

When chapman billies leave the street,
And drouthy neebors, neebors meet.

So began Sidney Ogilvie's reading of Robert Burns' poem 'Tam o' Shanter' at a friendly informal get-together held at Roadside where Sidney and his wife Anne were the hosts. Through the night Burns songs were sung, haggis and clapshot were served, plus a little confined dancing and a few drams. All combined to ensure an enjoyable evening, and also ensured that at least the Bard was remembered.

I'm finishing with an old song – or at least most of it – and the Christmas card story. Both are closely connected, as you will see. Its title is 'Will the Angels Play Their Harps for Me?' and it begins:

I was passing by a churchyard in the city,
And I saw a beggar old and grey.
With his hand outstretched he asked the folks for pity,
And it made me sad to hear him say ...

It's maybe a little strange that I should remember an old song from the Thirties, for that is when the record was made. In fact, it was already being sung in North Ronaldsay in 1931, for, as my father explained, the men who came to the island to build the foghorn that year (bringing the song with them) were surprised to discover that it had arrived before them. The reason for this was that many 78 rpm records had been coming to North Ronaldsay for some years prior to that time – and for years afterwards as well.

It's not a song of my generation. But yet the tune and the chorus mainly remain in my mind.

Three other lines I think I should mention, and they read:

For my feet are growing weary,
And my heart is growing dreary,
Will the angels play their harps for me?

Apart from the rather sad appeal of the words and the attractive melody, one main reason for remembering the song is that it used to be sung so often on Hogmanay. I suppose the last time I heard it must have been on the final Hogmanay that the Linklestoon men made the round together of their toonship houses (there are five other toonships).

That would have been, I think, in the mid-1960s, and at that time I remember fourteen men in the diminishing company. Of that number, eight have passed on, and only five remain living on Linklestoon. And the old traditional round of visits, made by men only, has died out long since – like the Christmas card man I'm going to mention in a minute.

So I'd better begin now and tell you that on this Hogmanay, while on a painting trip, I had laid aside my paints and brushes to retrace my steps of all of these years ago, to a house in the vicinity that I visited on Hogmanay.

The house into which I stepped, with difficulty and some risk, has been empty these past twenty-eight years, and is slowly giving up to the toll of time and inevitable ruin. Its flagstone has partly collapsed and jagged spaces are open to the sky. Across the mantelplace, there's an old brown box still containing spectacles, left there probably on that fateful day twenty-eight years ago.

But most surprising to see was the card, folded outside in and partly protected from the elements in a doorless press. When I opened it, I saw that it was the Christmas card, still bearing its colorful greetings. And still sparkling a little with its frosty glitter effect. Shortly after that card arrived, its owner suffered a serious accident, and from that time until his death some nine years later, he never set foot in his house or saw the Christmas card again.

It was particularly sad to remember those events, and as I left I wondered about times when maybe there is some of that old magic in the air. Nights when the stars are clear and the moon is up in the east with a New Year waiting round the corner. Are the ghosts of those Linklestoon men, I wondered, along with our lost selves, still on the Hogmanay rounds?

And will they be singing 'It's a Long Way to Tipperary' or 'The Dark-Eyed Sailor' or 'Keep Right on to the End of the Road', or maybe they might be singing the song that the Christmas card man used to sing every Hogmanay so many years ago:

Oh a many a mile I've travelled
And a million sights I've seen,
And I'm ready for the glory soon to be,
Oh I wonder, yes I wonder,
Will the angels way up yonder,
Will the angels play their harps for me?

Sailing Away in Realms of Fantasy
June 5, 1997

It seems like a long time since Christmas and the New Year or even since the little celebration that a few of us had on Burns Night when we remembered his birthday.

Over the months that have passed only one community function has occurred, and that was at Easter when Martin Gray gave a most interesting talk on his fairly recent trip to the Falkland Islands. A good turnout of about forty folk enjoyed seeing a quite outstanding selection of slides dealing mainly with bird life of that island group.

This Easter event provided an opportunity to extend a welcome to Sandra and Brian Mawson, and to Sandra's mother Vera Osmonde. The Mawsons are the new owners of Roadside. A great assortment of homebakes with tea and coffee completed this get-together, kindly made possible by Martin Gray.

Martin has now become established as one of a small team of tour guides, who provide guidance and information for nature-loving folks. Such folk travel here and there, usually by boat, to places like Spitsbergen, the Lofoten Islands, the Vesterålen Islands, the Azores (by plane) and the like. The Azores – that very name conjures visions of majestic sailing ships, harnessing the Trade Winds and riding the high seas, or of colorful pirates and treasures from the New World.

The second verse of John Masefield's poem 'Cargoes' further enhances this vision of the Azores.

> *Stately Spanish galleon coming from the Isthmus,*
> *Dipping through the Tropics by the palm-green shores,*
> *With a cargo of diamonds,*
> *Emeralds, amethysts,*
> *Topazes, and cinnamon, and gold moidores.*

But once again I'm away in the realms of fantasy. I was going to say that Martin will, by the time this letter is in print, be sailing on a more extended tour when, during two trips round Scotland, visits will be made to many places. Places such as Oban, St. Kilda and further afield north to Foula and Shetland, finally finishing up in Southern Ireland on the Dingle Peninsula. And after all that, it's way north again to Spitsbergen.

Now I'm going to sail away on another tack altogether – though still on the subject of journeys.

It's a considerable step, both in distance and by comparison, from Princes Street in Edinburgh to the 'oddle' of a North Ronaldsay byre. An 'oddle', by the way, as Hugh Marwick in his *Orkney Norn* states, is 'the channel running along the floor of a byre, or cow house, behind the animals to carry off the liquid manure.'

I was just thinking this recently when dieting out one of our byres, after returning home from my Edinburgh exhibition. It is also almost as much of a contrast between the carpeted floor of an Edinburgh picture gallery and the stony bottom of an island geo – from which I had painted more than one painting on view at my exhibition.

Another interesting comparison, but a more disturbing one, was the sight in Edinburgh of one or two unhappy looking individuals begging for money on out-of-the-way streets, and the sight of a piper dressed splendidly in pipe band uniform and piping away on Princes Street. In his opened pipe box nearby, I saw substantial donations. Most people would hurry past the more dishevelled-looking individuals with their alms box or cap, but the piper would have a good audience.

Sometimes, obviously, tourists would be having their photographs taken alongside the rather magnificently dressed musician. (It was at this time that I had a peep in the piper's box.) I did wonder if this kilted figure was performing for financial reward, or was he simply entertaining the Edinburgh strollers? Anyway, there is nothing so grand as the sound of the Highland bagpipes played in the open air, and they sounded particularly fine on a warm Sunday morning in Edinburgh – such as happened to me when I was there. On a Sunday, I should say, the traffic noise is far less obtrusive than on the more busy week days.

In fact, my trip south was largely one of interesting comparisons in one way or another. In Aberdeen for instance, where I had a spare hour or so, I had arranged to meet the landlady of my digs of my art schooldays. Over a cup of tea and cake we exchanged reminiscences of thirty-five years previous when we had last seen one another.

During our discourse, and since I'm talking about comparisons, it was indeed grand to hear my landlady describe the good days – as she referred to them in the late Fifties and early Sixties when I and others lodged with her. Those were the days when she enjoyed having students, and they in turn enjoyed staying with her. Mostly, in my time, such lodgers came from Orkney and the Western Isles.

As the years passed, both the manners and the attitude of the students apparently deteriorated, until in the early 1980s my landlady was glad to retire, feeling that she no longer wished to work for students who had become, as she said, thankless and even discourteous. I'm not sure what this little story says about some of the new generations of students. Or whether indeed they still come from the Isles. Anyhow, shortly afterwards we exchanged waves as my train left for Edinburgh.

Once in Scotland's capital I had another first-time reunion organised, when I met up with a former contemporary of mine, Ronald Sutherland. For an hour or two during a meal, we talked about 'art schooldays' and our activities over the last thirty years since our stay in Aberdeen. And just to illustrate how time, circumstance and coincidence can sometimes combine strangely, in *The Scotsman*'s obituary column a day or so later I read that one of our college lecturers from those days, Fred Stiven, about whose career and whereabouts my artist friend and I particularly wondered, had just died at age sixty-seven.

Continuing this journey of past faces and old times, I had one other meeting arranged in Edinburgh. This is when I met with Peter Work and his wife Moira (née Lennie), both Orcadians but now living in Kilmarnock. Peter, who had gone on to follow a successful career in engineering had some forty years before shared digs with me and other islanders in Kirkwall.

It was good to remember those far-off days of the Fifties, with memories of those famous lodgings above the old shop of Lipton's, the Boys' Brigade and trips on the steam ships *Sigurd* and *Thorfinn*.

The Works, by the way, were the owners of Holland Farm, Stronsay, which was in those days one of the largest and best-run farms on the island. Peter used to talk, I remember, about their farm with some pride.

A couple of days later I was on my way north again, stopping briefly in Aberdeen where I had an hour or so to spend. In that time, I researched one more comparison which goes back in time some eighty years or more, and which I would eventually complete on my return to North Ronaldsay. That comparison I began (using a notebook) at the railway station, before leaving to catch a plane north to Orkney. In the entrance to the station there is a World War I memorial tablet. Originally it was situated nearby, in the first railway station built at 80 Guild Street. It measures about six feet by three feet, is made of wood and has hand-carved lettering with a gold finish.

On February 15, 1921, the Principal of Aberdeen University, the Very Reverend Sir George Adam Smith (one of a group of brilliant church men of that period) unveiled this memorial which commemorates the men of the Great North of Scotland Railway. They had, as the inscription states, 'laid down their lives in the Great War of 1914–1918.' As I read down the long line of men's names and regiments, I wondered how many people stop to spare a thought for those ninety-three young men who, before the war, worked for such a short time on the railways – less and less, I imagine, as the years pass. But for students of war or for those of us who remember that war time generation, I hope the following will be of some interest.

Of the ninety-three men mentioned above who lost their lives, forty were serving in the Gordon Highlanders, twelve in the Seaforth Highlanders and eleven in the RAMC (Royal Army Medical Corps). The remainder were spread out in very small numbers – ones, twos, threes and five in the following regiments, corps or whatever (apparently some of these units were disbanded after the war): Argyll and Sutherland Highlanders; Cameron Highlanders; Royal Highlanders; HLI (Highland Light Infantry); Royal Scots; London Scottish; RFA (Royal Field Artillery); Royal Engineers; ROD, RE (Railway Operating Division, Royal Engineers) and finally, the RFC (Royal Flying Corps). Three of those men won decorations. One, a sergeant in the Gordon Highlanders, was awarded the Military Cross, and two RAMC soldiers – one a sergeant and one a lance corporal – won the Military Medal.

Shortly after returning to North Ronaldsay one cold, northeasterly day when hail lay here and there and the spring daffodils seemed out of season, I took a walk to our own War Memorial. It is a tall, simple granite cross, and it is with some of its details that I come almost to the end of my letter.

On the supporting plinth below the cross, in lettering cut into the granite, the inscription reads: 'In Memoriam. Died for King and Country in the Great War 1914–1919.' Underneath are the names of those men who died: one in the 2nd Seaforth Highlanders, one in the Royal Scots and another in the Royal Field Artillery. The remaining five were serving in the Royal Navy Reserves (Trawlers).

Although I had hoped to report the date of the Memorial's unveiling and the name or names of whoever performed the dedication ceremony – there were two ministers officiating on the island at that time – I have so far been unable to establish this information. Research is still continuing and eventually I hope to report the final outcome, with sources and names of those who helped. But there was, I discovered from the Orkney Library, a church service held in the UF church, which I will only mention briefly at this time.

During an evening service held in early 1920, two smaller war memorials were unveiled. One was a Roll of Honour and the other was a commemorative brass plaque. The dedication was carried out by the UF Church Minister, the Rev. R. A. Munro. It is interesting too about the three hymns – 328, 306 and 338 – that were sung, and also Psalm 103:13–18. The singing of the National Anthem concluded the service.

So you see how I have travelled in time, seen faces from the past, made – I hope – interesting comparisons and remembered men who died in the Great War. Those men came from widely contrasting backgrounds. On the one hand there were the men who worked for the Great North of Scotland Railway, and on the other hand there were men who had shared communal life in a small island in Orkney.

Let me finish with some lines I've chosen from Psalm 103, which were sung in North Ronaldsay on that evening over seventy-seven years ago. They seem very suitable for the war memorials that I have been describing, although they are situated so far apart in distance and location.

For he remembers we are dust,
And he our frame well knows,
Frail man, his days are like the grass,
As flow'r in field, he grows:
For over it the wind doth pass,
And it away is gone;
And of the place where once it was
It shall no more be known.

Changing Times and Changing Seasons
November 6, 1997

I see almost five months have passed since my last letter from North Ronaldsay appeared in *The Orcadian*. I finished that letter, I remember, with a comparison of the two World War I memorials. One was in Aberdeen and the other in North Ronaldsay.

On looking over that letter, I see that when I was walking along the road sometime in April to inspect our own memorial the wind was in a northeasterly airt and scatterings of hail lay here and there. Today, October 23, the wind is almost due north, and when I was out in the afternoon, a little flurry of hail came flying sharply out of a rolling, purple-grey sky. The air was decidedly cold but the day was fresh, as the northerly always makes it. Occasionally a teewup cried as it rose and banked away on the wind, and the sea to the westward, blue-grey and flecked with white, looked even colder than the north wind felt.

Before proceeding further with this letter and leaving the subject of war memorials, I should say that I have not yet been able to discover when the North Ronaldsay memorial was unveiled, but Alfie Swanney, North Gravity, tells me that he has some papers belonging to his father, a World War I veteran, which refer to the time when he and others were involved with the memorial's erection. Alfie's father Peter was in fact responsible for the building of the very fine back retaining wall. These papers may tell me something about completion of the memorial, so I must pay Alfie a long overdue visit.

I should also mention, just for the record, that I omitted to include the MGC (Machine Gun Corps) on the list of regiments I detailed as being on the Aberdeen war memorial – the Great North of Scotland Railway. It occurs to me as I write that the men on both sides who operated these deadly weapons were responsible for the deaths of many thousands of men.

Well, I began this letter some time ago. At least that is in my mind when first one idea and then another would set me in daydreaming – for that is all that ever came of these good intentions and thoughts. Then in September I actually managed to make a start, and I see when looking over those initial notes that I was writing about various aspects of a poor summer and about this and that. One thing that I mentioned was the lack of sun in May and June, but even so the silage and hay got made as well as ever.

There were many days of sea fog with the accompanying blast of the foghorn sounding away, and sometimes echoing far out to sea. There were also nights of mildew, when low-lying areas of the island seemed to float in grey banks of creeping mist, and houses, here and there, appeared like ships passing by. From some, wreathes of smoke would rise skywards, and the combined effect of chimney stack reek and half-submerged houses reminded me of the old coal-fired trawlers that we used to see long ago, as they passed outward or homeward bound between North Ronaldsay and the Fair Isle.

The thought of those old coal-fired trawlers reminds me of a gift I once got of rather a wonderful model trawler which was driven by a spring-powered propeller. I received this model boat from my uncle on his return from Kirkwall, where he had been on one of those great North Ronaldsay trip-days back in the Fifties. He had, like many North Ronaldsay men and indeed many Orcadians, served on the trawlers of the Northern Patrol during World War I.

At the West Banks there is a little loch which appears mainly in the winter, and whenever I pass by I always remember that little trawler and how realistically it could cross the sometimes wind-rippled water.

> *They're out in the open night and day,*
> *Where the roaring billows sweep;*
> *Lashed by the storm, with mains of spray,*
> *The wild sea-horses leap.*
> *With never a rein to guide their way,*
> *Unbitten, without control,*
> *But ridden by riders as grim as they,*
> *The men of the North Patrol.*

Or:

> *They're sweeping the paths,*
> *When the dawn comes up,*
> *Where the deep sea traders run.*

I think these last three lines are wonderful ones. '*Sweeping the paths, When the dawn comes up, Where the deep sea traders run*' of course meant clearing mines from the shipping lanes.

Yes, I've become carried away again – but quite acceptably so, I hope. However, let me return to my earlier notes, which I shall have to shorten. Apart from the largely sunless summer and persisting sea fogs, about the middle of September we had gales of wind and heavy rain – hairst weather, as they say. Then for a bit the weather improved from the north, drying up battered stooks. But talking about hairst – I mean the real, old-fashioned harvest work – so little of that activity now remains that the number of stacks built on North Ronaldsay are only but a token few.

We were reminded of this change visually when James Thomson (Nether Linnay) was back on holiday from Kirkwall, where he now lives, early in the summer. He very kindly gave a slideshow in the New Centre. The photographs which he had selected were mainly ones of North Ronaldsay folk from the Sixties period and later. Among these photographs was one taken from the balcony of the New Lighthouse over thirty years ago. The island in that view seemed covered in stooks as far as the eye could see. So there is the difference. Another comparison, of course, is the population, which in the 1960s would have been around 160. These islanders were almost exclusively natives of North Ronaldsay, apart from the lighthouse keepers, the doctor and a deaconess. Today the population stands at eighty or just under.

Jimmy's excellent slideshow provided the opportunity for the only community dance (as it happened) of the summer. Tragic events at Westness later meant that other functions planned were cancelled for the remainder of the holiday period.

Looking back at old photographs such as those shown by James Thomson always brings a mixture of feelings and memories – sometimes enjoyable and sometimes sad. I have, for instance, somewhere in my possessions a photograph (in slide form) which I took at sea way back during that Sixties era. In my image of these years gone by, the day is full of sun with not a cloud to be seen in a clear summer sky, and the sea is a brilliant blue. It was taken, I remember clearly, just east of Seal Skerry. In it, Jimmy Deyell's Shetland-built boat, the *Viola*, motors north.

This photo captures for me, and I'm sure other North Ronaldsay fishermen of that period, a time when lobster fishing and indeed any other fishing, was a pleasure, and when time itself seemed to sing a slower and more tuneful song. At the stern of the boat stands John Tulloch, Purtabreck, hand on tiller, and in the middle of the boat Jimmie Deyell, Lochend, facing the camera, is waving his right arm held high, just for a moment in time, against that long-gone summer sky. Early in July James Deyell, farmer and fisherman, passed away. Islanders will remember Jimmie and his elegant dancing at many an island dance.

Well, as I more or less said earlier, hairst is finished – some time ago now in fact – but there was one day when I was building a stack and when other helpers were working away in the field, that I should mention. It happened to be a Sunday and a particularly fine day it was with the sun still pleasantly warm. The sky and the sea were as blue as blue can be and flocks of little swallows were turning, twisting and banking in all directions as they hunted busily away round stooks and stacks. Sometimes they flew below my eye level and sometimes above, as I worked even higher on my stack. It is quite interesting the difference in perspective that only nine or ten feet above ground level can give of the island and round about.

Anyway, to the westward I could see a red-painted cargo ship near the horizon sailing south on legitimate business. But on the east side there was another type of boat altogether, painted black, not a cargo boat, but one of the largest lobster fishing boats in the North Isles. There she worked for some considerable time quite near inshore, hauling hundreds of creels stretching from Dennis Head to the south of the island. Working in and out and among the local lobster boats' creels and only available fishing grounds.

On the north side of the island and elsewhere the same story can be told – for there another large fishing boat from a neighbouring island takes over where the other stops until, in the end, the whole island is surrounded by creels. And just lately we learned that the Orkney Fisheries Association, of which, presumably, those boats crews are members, is actually proposing a closed lobster fishing season around July/August, thereby directly and effectively putting an end to the small inshore boats' limited traditional fishing – not only in North Ronaldsay but all over Orkney. It has been, in fact, those larger types of lobster fishing boats who have been almost entirely responsible for the over-fishing that now forces them to ask for considerable sums of money from the Islands Council for lobster restocking.

But back to the island affairs, where mostly we have a more harmonious lifestyle. Through the summer two picnics were organised by the Community Association. The island's teacher Patricia Thomson, Winnie Scott and others helped with games and so on, and John Thomson, Patricia's husband, cooked almost full time on his barbecue at both picnics. One picnic was held on the springy grass land of the North Links and the other on the school playground.

Then we have Day Club activities for the more senior islanders, with Evelyn Gray and Winnie Scott keeping things on the move. Also, the association and the Community Council employed two wardens – Helga Tulloch, Verracott, and Ingrid Tulloch, Purtabreck – to provide at least some supervised facilities over the summer, for islanders and visitors alike, both at the New Centre and the Memorial Hall.

Communal native sheep punding took place in August and lately, further communal activity is achieving necessary improvements at the Memorial Hall. And even more recently Howie Firth delivered a very fascinating talk entitled 'Standing Stones and Ancient Marriage' (there at least is another excuse for dancing round the Standing Stone on the island). Howie also looked at Celtic and Norse legends in Orkney and how all of these headings interlinked.

On Friday, October 25, the North Ronaldsay Woman's Guild held their annual function to raise money for RNLI funds. A good turnout ensured the usual success, with the president, Isobel Muir, and the secretary, Sheila Deyell, keeping things running smoothly. The treasurer, Evelyn Gray, has just returned to the island with a new baby. As a result of items sold, raffles and donations, at least £600 (exact figures not confirmed) was spent by North Ronaldsay for the Lifeboat Institution. As with Howie's talk, a great selection of homebakes was enjoyed at the end of the event.

Now I must mention a very special occasion which took place on Saturday, August 23. On that evening over fifty folk turned out to see John Tulloch, Upper Linnay, receive a retiral presentation from the island after thirty-seven years of service as postman.

Rosemary Robertson, Holland House, began the evening with another quite outstanding selection of slides. This time the photographs had been taken in Morocco when she had attended the yearly 'Bride's Fair'. Moroccan men acquire a bride at this fair. It was, incidentally, suggested that such a fair in North Ronaldsay would be just the thing for some of the island's old bachelors. Anyhow, be that as it may, after the slideshow a short speech was made tracing the history of the Postal Service on the island dating back to the latter part of the 1800s. For the moment I'll only mention a few details which I hope I have researched accurately. Over that period there have been four sub-postmasters and four sub-postmistresses, with the present sub-postmistress making a total of nine in this office. In the same period there have been six postmen, with the present recently elected office-bearer, making eight in all and making Sheila the first postwoman delivering letters on the island.

Following the speech Bessie Muir, who had returned specially from

Kirkwall where she now lives, and who had been a long-term colleague of John Tulloch at the Post Office, was asked to present John with a very fine gold presentation watch and a pewter tankard. Both gifts were suitably inscribed. Bessie, adding a personal touch to the introduction with her observations, took much pleasure in performing the presentation. Dorothy Henderson, the present sub-postmistress, then presented John's wife Lottie with a basket of flowers. Once those very pleasant proceedings were over, tea and a virtual feast of homebakes completed a memorable occasion.

That short account of John's presentation brings me almost to the end of my letter. I forgot though to mention the Indian summer (in fact two) enjoyed all over Orkney, and just at the end of October and before the Harvest Home, we seem to have a third. A couple of days ago I was surprised to see a fairly large bee flying around quite energetically – such apparent phenomenon certainly shortens the winter. At night sometimes I hear the 'teewups' and the 'whaaps' cry. Golden plover and snipe also call now and then. All of them, night and day, remind me of old North Ronaldsay. They, like the sea and the island, will surely never change.

I began this letter by remembering memorials, and I'm finishing with a poem by George Mackay Brown from a book of poems published in 1989. Its title is 'In Memoriam I.K.' I use it as a poem for the two young folk from without this island, and I use it because it's particularly suitable, and because those of us who live on North Ronaldsay should always remember the two young men who died near Westness this summer.

> *That one should leave The Green Wood suddenly*
> *In the good comrade-time of youth,*
> *And clothed in the first coat of truth*
> *Set out on an uncharted sea:*
> *Who'll ever know what star*
> *Summoned him, what mysterious shell*
> *Locked in his ear that music and that spell*
> *And what grave ship was waiting for him there?*
> *The Greenwood empties soon of leaf and song.*
> *Truth turns to pain. Our coats grow sere.*
> *Barren the comings and goings on this shore.*
> *He anchors off The Island of the Young.*

Looking Back to Past Harvests and Past Wars
December 4, 1997

It's a long way to Tipperary,
It's a long way to go.
It's a long way to Tipperary,
To the sweetest girl I know.
Goodbye Piccadilly
Farewell Leicester Square!
It's a long, long way to Tipperary
But my heart's right there.

So goes the old wartime song and November is a suitable time to quote it. Whenever I hear the song I am reminded of Hogmanay and New Year in North Ronaldsay when it was so often sung during these two great Linklestoon nights of the past.

Three of the men who made up the toonship company were veterans of World War I – two RNR men and the third served in the Seaforth Highlanders. In the 1950s when those memorable end-of-the-year customs were in full swing, the three veterans mentioned were, age-wise, still in their late sixties and early seventies. It's strange to think back to those days in some respects. For instance, folk in my age group who were in their early teens or early twenties thought of those World War I men and their contemporaries as being old or oldish. Yet today we prefer to think that, although we are certainly approaching the same age span as they had reached, maybe fifty or sixty is not so old after all.

However, we have to remember that if those old toonship visits were still practised, then I and my generation would actually be known as the 'Aald Crood' on New Year's night when the young and the old split into two companies.

Away back in 1918 just as the war was more or less at an end, two North Ronaldsay men in the Seaforth Highlanders spoke briefly as they passed one another – one coming back from the front, and the other on his way to the fighting line. The one who had moved up to the front line was shortly afterwards shot by a German sniper. The other – a Linklestoon man – came back to live in North Ronaldsay. Towards the end of his life, I remember him talking once about those days in France and of fellow soldiers whom he had seen blown to bits.

I'm thinking of such things since November is the month of remembrance with Armistice Day not long past. Also I've been reading some World War I poems, and re-reading parts of a book called *The War the Infantry Knew, 1914–1919: A Chronicle of Service in France and Belgium*, assembled and edited by Captain J. C. Dunn. This rather remarkable 600-page book contains a daily diary kept by Captain Dunn from 1914–1919.

On February 12, 1918, Captain Dunn says: 'No-Man's Land was dotted with the dead of their [the French] attempts to regain it. At one place close to the parapet a Frenchman and a German lay as they had bayoneted each other, the throat of one, the chest of the other, pierced through.'

In another image from those desperate battlefields he describes the sight of a long-dead soldier's face, which had detached itself away from the skull. The face, mask-like, was left floating in one of the countless water-filled shell holes that dotted No Man's Land, and into which attacking soldiers had fallen dead, dying or wounded.

Captain Dunn was a medical officer in the Royal Welch Fusiliers. Another medical man serving on the western front was a Canadian doctor and pathologist, John McCrae. It was he who wrote the much-quoted poem 'In Flanders Fields'.

In Flanders fields the poppies blow
Between the crosses, row on row
  That mark our place; and in the sky.
  The larks, still bravely singing, fly
Scarce heard amid the guns below.
We are the Dead. Short days ago
We lived, felt dawn, saw sunset glow,
  Loved and were loved, and now we lie
  In Flanders fields.

This poem, written early in the war, inspired the British Legion to choose the red poppy as a symbol of sacrifice and remembrance, and so it remains almost eighty years after the war ended.

November is also the month when most Harvest Homes were, and still are, celebrated – though far less extensively and with less reason and thankfulness than in the days when oats and bere were the big crops. But the sheaf still remains the symbol for harvest, just as the poppy is the symbol for the dead of the war years.

In North Ronaldsay in the past, not only did the islanders enjoy the

Harvest Home Supper, but they also had a programme of entertainment. In the old minute book of the hall committee for the year 1953 the secretary, Peggy Tulloch, records: 'October 8 – the date of the Harvest Home was fixed for November 6. Question of programme discussed. Tarring of exterior of hall to take place on Thursday 15 if weather.'

Then at another meeting held after the pictures (Rural Cinema film show): 'Friday, October 16 – Harvest Home being the business. Admission to be 3/-, children 1/-. Programme to consist of a sketch, recitations by the schoolchildren, and various musical items. At a further meeting on November 2 held after the cleaning of the hall and before a practice, there was a question of a possible postponement of the Harvest Home owing to the steamer being unable to make a trip with the necessary goods. A large majority voted in favour of going ahead.'

It's interesting after forty-four years to recall that hall committee. They and other committees of these days, when the population of the island was two to three times the eighty or so of today, were involved in organising many more activities than would be possible or successful nowadays. For example, there were concerts or programmes of entertainment for Christmas, Burns Night and the Harvest Home, with evenings of prior practicing, Hallowe'en parties, picnics on the North Links, many more dances, film shows and so on.

The members of the that 1953 committee were as follows: president – Arthur Hughson, principal North Ronaldsay lighthouse (left in 1958); vice presidents – D. McInnes, head teacher, North Ronaldsay School (left in 1956) and Mr. J. Cutt, Gerbo; secretary – Miss Peggy Tulloch, Kirbest; treasurer – Mr William Scott, Cavan; committee – Miss Mary Seatter, Howar, Miss Mina Swanney, Cott, Miss Ruth Tulloch, Senness, Miss Mary Muir, Scotshall, Miss Bessie Scott, Cavan, Mr Robert Thomson, Peckhole, Mr Charles Thomson, Greenspot, Mr Ronald Swanney, Holland, Mr William Muir, Waterhouse. Of these members, Arthur Hughson, David McInnes, William Scott, Charles Thomson and Ronald Swanney are deceased.

All the ladies on the committee are married and are still living on the island except Peggy, who lives in St Ola, and Bessie, who lives in Kirkwall. Robert Thomson also left North Ronaldsay, married, and now lives in Rendell. The remaining two members of the committee, John Cutt and William Muir, also married and live in North Ronaldsay. And of those fourteen committee members, Mina, Ruth and Bessie attended this year's Harvest Home as they had done way back in 1953 – the year of the Coronation.

So there is a piece of history and it has brought me appropriately enough to give an account of the most important event which we hold in North Ronaldsay – the Harvest Home. It took place on Friday, November 7 at the Memorial Hall on as fine a day and night as one expects to have in winter. On that night, with wind light and southerly, the moon in its first quarter, and in a hall seating over ninety, the evening began.

Guest speaker this year was Sandy Firth. Sandy is of course well-known as being very much involved with Orkney's heritage over many years. This involvement has ranged from work with the Sea Cadets to the Orkney Heritage Society, Wireless Museum, Orkney Radio and so on. Sandy was accompanied by his wife Hilda.

Other guests this year were John Copland, manager of the Mart, and his wife Barbara. And representing Loganair, who had flown in a very substantial proportion of the evening's company, was Captain Dave Kirkland and his wife Donella. Guest accordionist this year was Hylton Shearer from Holm. All took part with enthusiasm and enjoyment throughout the evening. And of course Howie Firth was there in good form, playing away on the recorder and spoons and dancing to the music of Lottie, Ann and Hylton.

But back to the start of the evening. After the initial preliminaries with welcomes and acknowledgments, and mention made of the many North Ronaldsay folk who came back to the island for the Harvest Home, with friends and relatives coming from as far afield as London, Swanage and Aberdeen, Howie Firth said the grace. Later, in the second hour, and at the end of the supper, Sandy Firth rose to make his speech. This he did in his own inimitable way, recalling his early days in Shapinsay when an older system of husbandry was practised. Then he talked about the changed face of agriculture on the Orkney Mainland where very little crop is now grown and very few old-fashioned stacks are to be seen – some oats, in fact, only being grown for the straw to make the backs of Orkney chairs.

He went on to describe an occasion of some years ago when he was an itinerant teacher for the North Isles, and instead of landing in Sanday, where John D. Mackay was in his full glory, landed unexpectedly on North Ronaldsay. There at one of the aerodrome dykes a certain dentist was extracting a tooth from a patient who had earlier avoided the official extraction time. Seemingly someone had a very suitable pain deadening agent (whisky) which was also enjoyed by not a few onlookers, who no doubt found the proceedings most entertaining.

These anecdotes and others brought Sandy's speech to a close, and with very splendid drams raised to sparkle briefly in lantern and candlelight, he proposed a toast to the Harvest Home.

Thereafter the evening flew between music, dancing and 'discoorsing', all taking place at one and the same time. Those who wanted to dance danced and those who liked to talk talked. Then there was a swinging Eightsome Reel with Sinclair piping away. Three sets made the Old Hall floor shake. All the time John Swanney very actively played his part as MC, keeping things on the move until more servings of mutton, homebakes and tea gave a welcome break. This interlude allowed Ian Deyell to supervise the raffle when he invited the two most senior ladies present, Mrs Minnie Gorie (eighty-seven) from Kirkwall and Mrs Bethia Scott (eighty-six), to pick the winning tickets.

One of the raffled items came from a beehive in Wiltshire, having been kindly donated by Graham Rendall. Mr Rendall has quite taken North Ronaldsay to his heart and visits the island frequently. Away back in 1873 his great-grandfather, a James Rendall from Westray, was drowned along with two North Ronaldsay men, when the small boat in which they were attempting a landing capsized. And it is this connection that brought Graham, a vet living in Salisbury, to North Ronaldsay.

After more dancing and with time flying and yet seemingly never passing, the Harvest Home came to a close. 'Auld Lang Syne' was sung by almost the entire company who had begun the evening more than seven hours before. The speaker, Sandy Firth, was carried shoulder high round the hall to the singing of 'For He's a Jolly Good Fellow'. Finally, the serving of a Norwegian punch brought the memorable occasion to a close.

I began this letter with a World War I song, and I think I might as well finish with another. Armistice and the Harvest Home seem far away this windy night as I write very nearly at the end of November. The words of the song were suitable back in 1914, and sometimes they are worth singing today when, from time to time, we need maybe to remember that every cloud has a silver lining.

Pack up your troubles in your old kit-bag,
And smile, smile, smile.
While you've a lucifer to light your fag,
Smile, boys, that's the style!
What's the use of worrying?
It never was worthwhile
So, pack up your troubles in your old kit-bag,
And smile, smile, smile!

Standing Stone Dancers Welcome the New Year
February 19, 1998

We've just come in from thrashing 100 sheaves or so which, if anybody is interested, yielded about two and a half sacks of 'aits' (grain). I wonder if I had only mentioned the word thrashing how many folk would have known what I was talking about? Anyhow, when we were working, with the hum of the mill and the thud of the Lister diesel driving engine in the background, I was thinking to myself that I must get down to completing my overdue New Year's letter from North Ronaldsay. As Sarah o' Lochend would have said, 'It's high time and by time' that I did so.

Actually I've made more than one attempt to write a letter, with my first notes having been jotted down very early on New Year's morning. Then on Old Hogmanay (January 13) I made another well-intentioned attempt but, as so often seems to be the case, events catch up with me and delay my efforts.

Today, as I begin again, I see that it is the last day of January – that month of Burns I always think. 'Twas then a blast o' Janwar' Win' / Blew hansel in on Robin.' And through the month I've been browsing through Robert Burns' poetical works. So I might as well begin by saying that on Friday, January 23, we had a very grand little Burns Night, and in a minute or two I'll get round to telling you about the celebration.

This letter will have to be once again one which travels back in time, with its news being somewhat out of date the further I go back. Yet I was just thinking about letters carried on the old sailing ships. Letters for instance, that were destined for Australia. News from the home country would have been some months late in getting there – even at the fastest sailing time of around seventy days. Thinking about the great sailing ships of the late 1800s and early 1900s reminds me of Eric Newby's wonderful account of one of those voyages, *The Last Grain Race*, which took place in 1938. He talks about the Great Southern Ocean, the Roaring Forties and of the daily routine of life aboard ship which he experienced during the race.

Here's a few lines from his narrative, something of the memory of which has been in my mind since first reading the book over thirty years ago. It has taken me some time to find them again.

'A hundred times a day each one of us looked aloft at the towering pyramids of canvas, the beautiful deep curves of the leeches of the sails and the straining sheets of the great courses, listened to the deep hum of the wind up the height of the rigging, the thud and judder of the steering gear as the ship surged along.'

And again: 'From aloft came the great roaring sound that I heard for the first time, and will perhaps never hear again, of strong winds in the rigging of a good ship.'

But, as usual I am sailing off course from our Burns Night account – but then, even Robert Burns was at one time intending to emigrate to the West Indies, so I'm not so far off track, in a way, as one might imagine.

Will ye go to the Indies, my Mary,
And leave auld Scotia's shore;
Will ye go to the Indies, my Mary,
Across t' Atlantic roar?

Those words of Burns bring me back to Friday, January 23 when, with many tartan rugs and tartan spreads, oil lamps and candles, we transformed a little room in the New Community Centre into a very friendly and definitely Scottish-looking venue for a Burns Night. Interspersed between the hanging rugs and spreads were numerous wall pictures depicting scenes from 'Tam o' Shanter' and other poems and songs of Burns. There were a few handy tables with scarlet covers and red candles, and in a little nook, facilities, as Burns might describe them, for 'bousing at the nappy.'

Between forty and fifty folk fitted fairly comfortably into the room and we still had just enough space for a little confined dancing. A portrait of Robert Burns took centre stage, lit on either side by the oil lamps. Once everybody had settled down, Sinclair Scott, playing the pipes, and Winnie Scott, carrying the haggis, entered and made a musical round of the room before depositing the 'Great Chieftain o' the Puddin' Race' in front of our guest speaker, Howie Firth.

Howie delivered a most entertaining address to the haggis, with bits of the haggis's innards flying off his knife at times. Substantial helpings of the traditional supper (cooked by Winnie) were then served along with cider as the accompanying drink. After second helpings and with 'John Barleycorn' being offered in worthy amounts for the toast, Howie gave a most enjoyable and very original 'Immortal Memory'.

Our other guest, Len Wilson, who was accompanied by his wife Lily, followed the 'Immortal Memory' with a selection of Burns songs on his fiddle. Familiar tunes prompted some communal singing and soon the proceedings warmed up with more music providing the inspiration for a little dancing. After tea and a great selection of homebakes, Bessie Muir once again recited 'Tam o' Shanter', followed by Sydney Scott who sang

'Highland Mary' – a song which, as he said, he had last sung on a Burns Night between sixty and seventy years before.

Dancing then continued at a much faster pace. Sidney Ogilvie proposed a toast to the lasses, with Bessie briefly replying, until as in 'Tam o' Shanter', 'The mirth and fun grew fast and furious' with Len's fiddle and Howie's recorder fairly 'kirling and dirling'. Faster and faster they played for a Strip the Willow until the whole scene brought to mind Tam's vision of 'Warlocks and witches in a dance' in the haunted Kirk o' Alloway.

The dancers quick and quicker flew;
They reel'd, they set, they cross'd, they cleek'd.

Flickering candles and lamp light added to the atmosphere of the night, and surely another year, if we are spared, Robert Burns must be celebrated in similar style.

Well, now I'm at my 'Aald Hogmanay' writings. It's a pity, I thought that night, not to put pen to paper before Yule is finished, and so I began the main part of my letter on that day.

Last year it was early on a frosty New Year's morning that I wrote part of my introduction to the first letter for 1997 while walking outside in bright moonlight. On New Year's morning this year I repeated something of the same idea.

Again the silent wheels of time
 Their annual round have driv'n
(Burns, January 1, 1787)

The time was exactly 5.15 and if anybody thinks that is late or early on a New Year's morning, I may say that some first-footers were still very active three or four hours later. Directly overhead the Plough spanned a dark sky which was ablaze with stars. Some sparkled in ever changing colours that seemed to range from reds to green and blue. And as the night had advanced, a slim crescent moon moved slowly to the west from where the wind blew very freshly. It blew, in fact, exactly from the southwest as it happened – I could tell from looking at a very fine little brass bearing compass of mine that I treasure very much.

Resting on a dyke at which I stood, was an old discarded creel, and when looking through its web at the sky (by chance) I could see part of the Milky Way crisscrossed by the diamond shaped loops of the web. Even each individual loop would have, could I have counted them, framed millions of stars as they stretched light-years away and far beyond Earth's vision.

At the same time the interesting comparative thought occurred to me that maybe this very same creel had been set full fourteen fathoms deep at the back of Seal Skerry. And there, on a summer's night in days gone past, maybe, as George Mackay Brown describes him, a 'Mercenary in a dark blue coat of mail' had also looked through the web of the creel – but set instead against the dark green/black water of the North Sea.

The little compass, by the way, I bought in Aberdeen, away back in the 1960s from a veritable Aladdin's cave of a shop down near the harbour. In those days the harbour smelled of fish and the sea, and often numerous trawlers lined the quays on their return from the fishing grounds of the North Sea, the Atlantic or way up in Iceland waters.

It might also be interesting to tell you that the compass is a MK III dated 1940, and it was made in London. The degree card has a beautiful mother-of-pearl finish which, funnily enough as I look at it, reflects the same colour variations I described earlier in the stars. A rotatable and removable glass, marked off in degrees, fits on top of the instrument, and there is a tricky little reflecting prism with a magnifier to enable one to read the compass card with ease. I wonder who owned the compass during the war years? It has a serial number which could identify its owner, I suppose.

But I've been digressing again – too far I think to say anything more about New Year's morning, except to remark that the fresh wind I mentioned became stronger and stronger, until by the time the Standing Stone dancers (yes, we've done it again) got under way at three o'clock or so, it was blowing a fair gale.

Six new dancers joined the company this year, but an equal number of stalwarts found the challenge too much to face – it was a case of the spirit was willing but maybe too much of the Hogmanay spirit had taken its toll. The following Neven party, finishing with an Eightsome Reel, was as grand as ever.

Earlier on New Year's Day I had walked along the West Beach, where the tops of heavy breaking waves streamed backwards in huge showers of white spray, as the gale-force winds faced the incoming sea.

As all this was happening, with the thunder of crashing waves and the howl of the wind, I was still able to listen (on earphones) to a recording made almost sixty years before of the famous black American singer Paul Robeson singing 'An Eriskay Love Lilt'. Those who know the voice of Robeson, and the song from Eriskay in the Outer Hebrides (an island about the same size as North Ronaldsay), will be able to imagine how inspiring and impressive was the combination of such powerful forces of nature and words sung by one of the world's great voices of the past.

New Year celebrations continued at Vincoin later when young and older folk line-danced, country-danced and Scottish-danced the evening away.

Next night Martin Gray gave another one of his very informative and much appreciated slideshows. This time the account covered part of his summer tour guide trip to such places as St Kilda, the Flannan Isle and Foula. He illustrated the talk with wonderful photographs taken at the time. Later, an initially slow dance livened up most enjoyably to launch in the New Year in fine form.

In fact Yule has been quite a busy time, beginning just before the festive season with a whist drive arranged to raise funds for the children's Christmas party. Over £100 was collected and used to run that always successful function.

Also, a little before Christmas, head teacher Patricia Thomson, with the assistance of staff and parents, helped the school children to put on probably the first puppet show ever in North Ronaldsay. With their pre-recorded dialogue being played over a hi-fi system, the pupils operated the puppets behind the scenes. The production took place in the classroom, very cleverly transformed by decorations and a huge room-dividing curtain which isolated the puppet booth quite neatly. A grand spread of homebakes completed the occasion.

On the following day the school's very festive Christmas dinner for the island was enjoyed, and on Saturday our Yule bonfire and fireworks display took place on the North Links. One of the best fireworks shows so far was then followed by hot soup, tea and homebakes, and bar facilities at the Centre, to round off our last get-together for 1997.

So there, I've covered our communal activities since my last letter apart from some native sheep punding managed before Yule. And just to bring everything up to date, we have lately embarked on another session of dancing classes. Wilma Taylor is again very kindly coming out to the island to give a series of evening lessons.

Interestingly, in a book called *Traditional Dancing in Scotland* by J. P. and T. M. Flett, it mentions that in 1891, after a dancing teacher whose name was William Smith had given lessons to folk on Flotta, their rather leisurely dances changed to far more serious affairs. 'There was, indeed, such a craze for dancing on the island following Mr Smith's visit that the lads would even practice the step for "running the reel" when following the plough.'

It would be good if such a craze could sweep Orkney in a similar fashion. Think of the wonderful dances that could result. By the way, Robert Burns says in his autobiography – and I'm waiting for Bobby Leslie from the library to send me a copy – 'To give my manners a brush, I went to a country dancing school'; so there we are.

Well, I think, to use the phrase referred to earlier, 'it's high time and by time' to finish this letter. I do so by remembering another poet, this time an Orcadian one, Robert Rendall (1898–1967). He was born 100 years ago, with his birthday just past on the day before Robert Burns was born. George Mackay Brown describes him as one of the outstanding Orkneymen of the twentieth century.

At a little party held some time ago, when drawing Anne Ogilvie's attention to a favourite poem of mine written by Robert Rendall, she remarked on reading it that she felt somehow it reflected my own feelings about North Ronaldsay. I had never thought of it in that way, but taking a wider view of the poem, I think perhaps, sadly, she was maybe not so far wrong.

Here is Robert Rendall's poem:

Lost Self

To be what I have been but am no more
Or find the shadow of what once was plain
I pace the margin of this haunted shore
Where rocks and stones and echoing cliffs retain
Lost ecstasies, and shouts of natural joy.
Back through a maze of transient gains and griefs
I pick my steps to seek a phantom boy
Who flits from ledge to ledge on these black reefs.
But all the pools have unfamiliar grown
Since those forgotten years, nor can I trace
The distant footprints there that are my own,
Which time can never touch nor tides efface.
  Of this strange world the meaning who can tell,
  Receding thus from those that know it well?

The Man with the Friendly Smile
March 26, 1998

I think it would be an interesting change for once to write a letter from North Ronaldsay which does not include the usual lengthy account of our community activities. It's not, in fact, that we are particularly active on that front, but it's because some months always pass before I get round to tackling another 'saga' and by that time a number of events have accumulated.

On most other islands I should think, and on the Orkney Mainland, much more activity takes place – simply because of the greater number of folk available to take part and help with arrangements. And the community spirit which one writer to *The Orcadian* referred to as being special on North Ronaldsay exists, I'm sure, in no lesser or greater degree than elsewhere in Orkney. The writer who made that observation was no doubt basing his judgment on my letters, which are mainly confined to describing the social events on the island.

I have to tell the writer, however, that North Ronaldsay, just like other places, can have its own little disputes and ups and downs. The necessity being, I suppose, that any such differences in a small community are better resolved amicably, and sooner rather than later. At least so far, we have not resorted to fisticuffs such as I saw once on TV, when MPs in Italy and Japan set about one another with surprising energy.

When I was in the Faroes in 1976 with an exhibition, a friend with whom I happened to be discussing island life told me that when an individual living on the islands got a bit uppity or whatever, the folk would set about taking such a person down a peg or two by making fun of him or her, and often, in addition, thinking up a suitable nickname for good measure. This wonderful local psychology in a way caused some amusement (at my expense) when it became known that I was about to visit a small island not far from Torshavn.

I planned to stay there sketching for a couple of days or so. Only two families lived on the island where they farmed in rather difficult conditions. The lady with whom I was to stay was known as the hangman's daughter. Apparently her father, who was no longer alive, had once applied for the office of hangman in the capital of Denmark. He didn't get the job but was known as the hangman ever after. Anyhow, I was told that I had better be careful or I might never be heard tell of again. I may say that my stay there was most pleasant, and the family with whom I lodged were especially kind.

On the island the only source of light at night was the oil lamp, and in my room by my bedside there was one of those old-fashioned ones with a very tall chimney. With its light I remember first beginning to read a book called *The Stanley Expedition*. I had just, maybe a day before, received a present of the book from the well-known and much respected Faroese sculptor Janus Kamban. The artist, who is now I think well into his eighties, lived in Torshavn where he had a very splendid studio.

This book, published in Torshavn (in English) in 1970, is very fascinating for various reasons. Its full title is *The Journals of the Stanley Expedition to the Faroe Islands and Iceland in 1789 Volume I. Introduction and Diary of James Wright,* one of the expedition's diarists. In the very first part of the diary there is a short account of some members of the expedition's brief visits to Hoy, Graemsay, Kirkwall, Stromness and one or two other areas before being in the Faroes.

Remembering all those bits and pieces and my reference to Hoy brings me back to North Ronaldsay, as you will see. Over Yule I read, and very much enjoyed, John Bremner's book *Hoy the Dark Enchanted Isle*, and often when I think of Hoy I recall the singing of the old song 'Hoy's Dark Lofty Isle'.

At even when glowed the setting sun,
Above the western sea,
A lofty barque her course held on
Full beautiful and brave.

On board the ship was a dying sailor who hoped still to see the land of his birth one more time. 'Land land the wished for land was nigh, Twas Hoy's dark lofty isle.' The song like many of those old sea songs is rather sad, as the sailor died before reaching Hoy.

The singing of this song was mostly associated with Robbie o' Cursiter. I can just remember hearing him singing it on a Hogmanay at Cruesbreck, which must have been in 1946 or '47, since in 1948 we moved from Bustitoon to Linklestoon. From this small croft of Cursiter came six trawler skippers, which surely must be a noteworthy achievement from a family of seven brothers and two sisters.

Cursiter became vacant in 1966 when Robbie Thomson's wife Mary died – she was a lady who probably brewed the strongest tea in Orkney. When cutting roadside weeds I often would stop in by for a 'cuppa'. The croft remained empty until last year when Sidney and Anne Ogilvie took over the house, which they are presently renovating.

But back to the singer, who was generally acknowledged to have been very musical. My father tells a story which illustrates this fact pretty well – but before I go on to repeat the tale I should perhaps relate a bit of relevant history.

Orcadians of round about my age, and older of course, will certainly remember the tinkers who travelled all over Orkney – and Shetland for that matter. They were most colourful characters and interesting folk who probably knew all the farming fraternity in Orkney (and Shetland) and even had a good knowledge of connections and relationships. In addition they were knowledgeable in the medicinal usage of plants, often giving advice on simple problems.

Although the selling of all sorts of clothing was their mainstay, they also, my mother tells me, sold baskets and maybe a few dishes. The making of tin pails, pots and milk utensils formed an important part of their trade before the days of mass production, and they frequently stayed on the island for a bit while they made such varied items to order. They generally lived in tents brought with them, though in later years they might stay wherever they could get some form of accommodation.

The Highland bagpipe seems to have been their favourite instrument, with some of the men having been army pipers during their war service years. But apart from the piping, the tinkers were generally very interested in music, and always I suppose on the lookout for a good tune.

So one day when one of those musical individuals was on his way down the Bride's Ness road, passing by as he did so, with his pack on his back, the croft of Cursiter, he was whistling a new tune only just picked up from across the Pentland Firth (I think that there were connections with possibly relatives living in the Caithness area?).

Outside Cursiter was Robbie, who happened to be listening. When the whistler came back up the road, imagine his surprise when he heard the same tune being played from beginning to end by Robbie on his melodeon, as he sat outside for the occasion.

It's strange how those 'bits and pieces' that I've been writing about very often connect and lead on to something else. Connections can, I suppose, be thought up all the time – sometimes unpleasant, sometimes sad and other times enjoyable. For instance, earlier I mentioned that Linklestoon became our family's toonship in 1948. In front of the home at Antabreck there used to be a little brae where we and others before us often played. Among our old photographs, there is one of Mrs Dawson sitting on that brae. Her husband was the doctor on the island for some years, and they lodged for a time at Antabreck prior to our arrival.

Dr and Mrs Dawson had a daughter who was a contemporary of my generation. We knew her in North Ronaldsay as 'Mary Dawson'. Orcadians and others will know her better as Mary Shearer and for having been in charge at the Eastbank Hospital.

Can I ask folk in Orkney and her medical colleagues, how it came to be that such a person was made prematurely redundant after almost thirty years' service in the nursing profession, and how, as she said, she felt 'worthless and undervalued' by her employers – the Orkney Health Board (as reported in *The Orcadian*, February 5, 1998) and that she felt 'the whole world had fallen to pieces and that everything I had done in my working life was actually worthless'?

Her treatment can only be described as absolutely disgraceful and I hope that the industrial tribunal, who are hearing her case and that of a colleague Enid Street, whose job was also terminated, will surely find that both Health Board employees were at the very least unfairly dismissed. Hopefully the final outcome of the enquiry will in some way recompense the considerable damage done to people who devoted their lives to the business of caring and helping others.

Well, here I am this Sunday morning, nearing the last part of my letter and listening for the moment to a marvelous piece of fiddle music composed by Neil Gow called 'The Lament for James Murray' and it's being played by the well-known Scottish fiddler, Hector MacAndrew. But let's go back to 'Hoy's Dark Lofty Isle' and to Robbie o' Cursiter.

Robbie's mother came from Disher, a croft house long gone with its land being part of Howar since the latter part of last century. It is in fact this connection and this farm which brings me to the final section of my letter, and to remember another personality of bygone years.

Once or twice in past letters I've mentioned the North Ronaldsay trip-days that took place well over thirty years ago and how they were great occasions. Each island in the North Isles had their trip-day, with either the SS *Sigurd* or SS *Thorfinn* sailing to Kirkwall, with North Ronaldsay having their own special day. It meant leaving early on a summer's morning for their destination, returning late in the evening. Those trip-days would probably be the only time that the majority of the trippers would visit the Mainland during the year.

In Kirkwall on such days it was possible, if one didn't know, to tell which island trip-day it was simply by listening to the dialect of the islanders as they walked the streets. On market days on the Mainland of Orkney at that time, the same observation could be made about the identity of folk from the different parishes.

As a wonderful reminder of those days I include a photograph taken in the early Sixties, which shows the *Thorfinn* leaving the Kirkwall pier on its way back to North Ronaldsay. The photograph is in colour and looks as if it had been taken yesterday. Yet more than thirty-five years have passed since that summer's day, and more than half of the folk in the photograph are dead and gone. One face in the company sums up that day I think, and those times somehow. It's the man with the friendly smile – Jimmy Seatter, Howar, was his name. I single him out from his contemporaries on this occasion because his presence in the photograph cannot other than be noticed. That expression was typical of his manner and of his dealings with fellow islanders throughout his life. Very often, for instance, when folk went to visit the Broch of Burrian, which was situated on the farm's ground, the way to this part of the island's heritage would be pointed out if required. Maybe Jimmie, if he was not too busy, would accompany island folk, holidaymakers or visitors alike as they made their way to the monument. Once during one of those sight-seeing excursions when a certain lay preacher along with some other ecclesiastical friends were on their way to the broch, they became aware of the farm's bull who was showing more than a little interest in their activities. Without much delay the men of God vaulted the nearby sheep dyke. Jimmie, who spoke to the party later with a broad smile on his face, told them that he thought they surely did not have much faith.

Around the time of the trip-day photograph, farming on North Ronaldsay and elsewhere in Orkney was still largely in keeping with the full rotation system that had been in use many years, which had made and kept the land in good condition. The man with the friendly smile was one of those farmers, and one to whom farming was a real vocation. That sort of dedication, along with the rest of the family, had won the second prize for the best run farm in Orkney during the early Thirties. Part of the secret of the success was, I suspect, based on the often-made comment by our trip-day personality, that 'even on the smallest farm it would be possible to find something to do every day of the year.' It was certainly a philosophy generally practiced for as long as physically possible by its advocate – ensuring, as it did, that everything was ready for whatever job was on hand as the farming year unfolded.

But at last, time has caught up with me and I think my letter is almost complete. As I write (March 7) I'm looking out through our living room window on the east sea. It's in a turmoil of broken water, and the Reef Dyke – a mile or so offshore – is one long stretch of breaking waves. Across the land, bleak and bare, and along dykes, scatterings of snow lie coldly in the southeast wind. But still for a time my mind goes back to that special photograph. And I'm having another look at the familiar faces there – I know them all. Jimmie Seatter is the man on the right-hand side of the photograph. It was taken almost at the end of the great island trip-days that were so looked forward to. North Ronaldsay at that time was still in reasonably good shape with all those islanders active and certainly in fine fettle, as the photograph shows.

Among the company are men who had served in the Northern Patrols during the First World War. Another saw the German fleet sinking in Scapa Flow in 1919. Here and there, a shopkeeper, crofter, sheepman, fisherman and storyteller – a representative company of men and women on a summer's day long ago who altogether, along with their contemporaries, were part of the history, tradition and way of life on a remote island in the North Atlantic.

This day as I sit and remember those who are gone I know that 'Their like will not be here again.'

Well, Well...
June 25, 1998

Well, well, as my Faroese friend would say. It's time maybe to write another letter from North Ronaldsay. I was in fact making a start a few weeks ago now – on my birthday as it happened. It was, I thought, as good a day as any to focus my mind on the job in hand. For one thing I'm in very good company on that particular day because the day in question, April 23, happens to be St George's Day. It is also the birthday of the painter William Turner and, I believe, the day on which William Shakespeare was born.

Coming back for a moment to my very good friend in the Faroes (Sofus Olsen is his name), I gave him a tinkle on the phone not so long ago and we exchanged island news. He tells me that the fishing in the Faroes has been quite successful these past two years. Cod, of course, is the main fish caught – though he also mentions saithe as being fished. In Iceland, he said, they have had satisfactory catches as well, but for some reason the Icelandic fishermen were on strike at the time of my phone call.

Sofus also let me know that the lady I called 'the hangman's daughter' with whom I lodged so comfortably away back in 1976 – mentioned in my last letter – died some years ago. When I was there this same lady had great plans for tourism on the small island where she and her family and one other family lived. Unfortunately, nothing came of the idea. But all this happened over twenty years ago, and time makes changes – the more noticeable as one gets older.

In today's post Sofus – who is a great supporter of the arts and all things Faroese – has very kindly sent me the other two volumes of the *Stanley Expedition*, which I also referred to in my last saga. It is indeed a real pleasure to receive gifts and letters through the post.

But back to North Ronaldsay where I suppose one might say we've been having all sorts of shenanigans. For instance, we had a wonderful group of young folk who actually called themselves Shenanigans. They entertained us most grandly at Easter with a concert. So I have got a few things to tell you about in a minute.

Before I get involved in describing our community activities, I must mention that Bobby Leslie, chief librarian at the County Library, sent me a copy of rather a remarkable book, *The Complete Letters of Robert Burns*. I had asked for Burns' autobiography, but apart from one very long letter in which he wrote about his life, no such account exists. Instead, there are these 700 or so letters which serve as a personal chronicle of events over his short life.

The letters were written to friends, relatives, doctors, lawyers, philosophers, ministers and so on. Whenever I have a spare minute or more I've been beginning to get into the mind and life of Burns as I read through the book. Anyone who enjoys or dislikes his work, or who admires or denounces his character, should in all fairness read his letters.

There again, and as usual, I have been rambling – I always do. Time though to make a pounce on our varied entertainments or whatever. As I write I'm listening (once again) to some old 78 rpm records of Jimmy Shand, Jim Cameron, Ainsworth and Blue and others. And if you are thinking that I only ever listen to Scottish dance music you're wrong, for I like all sorts: Indian, African, Japanese, jazz or classical.

In that latter category I once heard a retired Aberdonian deep sea trawler skipper choose, on a radio request programme, a favourite piece of mine called 'Morning' by the Norwegian composer Edvard Grieg. It made him think, he said, of being at sea and seeing the dawn break and the sun rise above the long horizon of the North Atlantic.

Anyhow, those Scottish dance band records remind me to tell the person in Stromness that 'her borrowed records' are at least halfway back, since they are at the moment in Kirkwall. They also remind me to tell you about our dancing class, for which Wilma Taylor once again came back to teach.

At Easter we had a grand last night, when we managed to perform the sixteen dances learned – dances such as the Scotch, Axum, Cumberland and Threesome Reels. Some others were the Circassian Circle, Britannia Two Step, One Step and the Keel Row.

To complete that last evening and to acknowledge Wilma's sterling efforts – when for each lesson she had stayed overnight on North Ronaldsay – we all enjoyed a little farewell party. It began with a dram and a toast to 'dancing' after which Vera Osmonde, our most senior pupil, presented Wilma with a beautiful silver bracelet on behalf of the dancing class.

The bracelet had been designed and made by Sandra and Brian Mawson (both had also attended the class). Sandra is, by the way, the daughter of Vera. The Mawsons are now producing a range of their work on the island, and the presentation piece very suitably featured a figure-of-eight design – in keeping with the dance figure of the Scotch Reel.

After the bracelet presentation, which included a basket of flowers, Wilma was invited to present Vera with a flower arrangement as a little reminder from everyone for having baked a cake for each of the dancing classes. It's a pity that the same enthusiasm shown by Vera who, over fifty years before, often danced the evenings away down south during the war years, had not been shared by others, for had they come along they surely would have enjoyed Wilma Taylor's relaxed and enjoyable teaching.

Next came the Lighthouse shenanigans – well, for instance, remember the sensational headlines, 'Isle ire at light slight' or 'Residents on North Ronaldsay are furious', and all sorts of comments that flew around. A classic was 'The Fair Isle had Princess Anne and North Ronaldsay had Ian Scott'. I have no illusions about the possibilities of a compliment there.

The truth is that the majority of islanders were little concerned about the question of which lighthouse should go down in history as the last in Scotland to be automated, or when the flag was lowered, and those of us who had borne the task of preparation for Prince Charles' visit in 1993 were maybe not a little relieved that the razzmatazz finally took place on Fair Isle rather than North Ronaldsay, originally earmarked for the occasion.

On March 30, principal lightkeeper John Payne senior lowered the lighthouse flag for the last time, and then very generously presented the flag to local assistant lightkeeper Billy Muir, who in his capacity as the Community Council chairman accepted the flag on behalf of the people of North Ronaldsay.

The following day, March 31, the date which marked the end of manned lightkeeping in Scotland, and the day when the last three serving lightkeepers and four occasional lightkeepers on North Ronaldsay were made redundant, we marked the occasion in proper style. In a hall decorated with many yards of red curtain drape material, which both reduced and transformed the appearance of the venue, and with bunting, signal flags, oil lamps, candles, memorabilia and a lighthouse flag a grand night unfolded.

As folk arrived, they received a commemorative programme. In it were the names of all North Ronaldsay men who had been involved in lightkeeping since 1854 when the New Lighthouse was lit. In total there had been eleven full-time lightkeepers, two local assistant lightkeepers and eight occasional lightkeepers. Of that number at least four, possibly five, had been principals. Added later to the programme were the names of the last serving lightkeepers and occasional lightkeepers at the station.

After a short history of the lighthouse in North Ronaldsay was detailed, including an account of the Old Lighthouse (lit 1789) – one of the first four to be built officially in Scotland and all working within a period of about three years – Councillor Howie Firth followed with a number of appropriate readings on lighthouses and sea themes. He then presented commemorative books to those lightkeepers and occasionals present who had ended their service in North Ronaldsay.

After the presentations and toast, guest musicians Raymond Scott (recorder and clarinet) and Owen Tierney (guitar) entertained us with some wonderful music, and drinks were very generously provided throughout the night by the Community Council, plus food of all sorts. Eventually folk even danced a little to the music of Raymond, Owen and Howie.

Just before midnight in a symbolic ceremony to mark the end of manned lightkeeping on the island, Sinclair Scott piped in the North Ronaldsay lighthouse flag. It was carried by its recipient, Billy Muir, who placed the folded ensign on a central table. Immediately afterwards, with the pipes again playing, first assistant lightkeeper James Craigie activated one of the station's scheme 'R' emergency lights which had been arranged in a commanding position high in the hall. Almost on the stroke of midnight it began to flash the statutory once-every-ten-seconds of the North Ronaldsay light, symbolising the change from manned service to automation.

This rather moving ceremony, performed by two uniformed men from the station, closed a long chapter of lightkeepers and their families' connections with the island of North Ronaldsay and, as it says in the book *At Scotland's Edge,* 'lighthouse keepers passed into history and into folklore.'

Before I close this account of the lighthouse event, I must refer back to a statement I made about my late uncle, John R. Scott, which I very much regretted afterwards. Perhaps folklore would have it – and I believed it – that John Scott, who was the instigator and driving force in setting up a union for lightkeepers, had to serve many years at rock stations as a result of his efforts.

That sort of statement with all its unfortunate implications was quoted against my express wishes in the *Press and Journal*. If this statement is true, and whatever folklore may imply, then John Scott's widow (a remarkable Shetland lady of eighty-eight years) and the family have made it clear to me that he (John) never once complained, or found fault with the Lighthouse Board throughout his life. And in a letter received from the Board on his retirement in 1964, the commissioners of that era expressed their appreciation of his 'long and faithful service' given over a period of forty-four years.

The Northern Lighthouse Board's letter finished by saying: 'The Commissioners are also mindful of the fact that for over thirty-four years you have acted as a representative of the lightkeepers during which time your wise council has contributed in no small degree to the friendly relations which exist today and to the steady improvement which has taken place in the service.'

Within a few days of the lighthouse event, the group Shenanigans, mentioned earlier, came out to North Ronaldsay to perform at their concert. It was arranged as part of the group's fund-raising activities to help cover the costs of a KGS class trip to Laos.

The group consisted of Kale Askew, Katherine Beaven and Laura Eunson – Laura stood in for Christopher Baxter, who most unfortunately was in hospital. Those three played fiddles, with the fourth member of the group, Lucy Holt, playing cello. The ensuing concert was particularly enjoyable with the musicians giving a polished performance – playing and singing with a confidence gained over many months of public entertainment in which they raised money for their trip abroad.

Once the concert was over, a good little dance got underway with some of Wilma Taylor's dances being introduced successfully. Particular was the enthusiasm of the young people, which included Dr Steven Beaven along with his wife and family – also Adrian Askew and his wife and family. Adrian is, by the way, the leader of the expedition to Laos. Emily Baxter also made the trip out, though very disappointingly because of her brother's illness, parents Liz and Trevor, former teachers on the island, were unable to attend.

Lucy Holt and Laura Eunson at one point most elegantly danced the Highland Fling and through the evening a wonderful assortment of raffle prizes were available – prizes such as Ola Gorie jewellery, Highland Park whisky, wine and fruit hampers. In the early hours of the morning the evening came to a close and remains a most pleasant memory for North Ronaldsay folk and the visitors who attended.

More recently the North Ronaldsay Lifeboat Guild organised a slideshow to raise funds for the Lifeboat Institution. Again Martin Gray projected some very beautiful slides, showing views from North Ronaldsay and his last guided tour to St Kilda, Foula and Spitzbergen – islands featuring mainly.

As with the function mentioned previously, food of all sorts was available and the Lifeboat Guild raised a further £90. (Last season, in the island, over £865 was spent in total between raffles, donations and sales in aid of the RNLI.)

That just about brings the island's activities up to date, apart from two school trips with head teacher Patricia Thomson and assistant teacher Isobel Muir, supervising one trip each during those visits to the Mainland and places such as, for example, the Kirbuster Farm Museum and the Kirkwall Auction Mart. Yet to be enjoyed is the school's end of term Open Day which will happen very shortly.

So you see we have been having a busy time. This letter has been in the progress of being written for weeks. Now we are well into June, and by the time it is in print the longest day will be past and the days on the turn – just think of that.

About a week ago I was walking in our south yard 'knappy' ground as I call it. Knapp (or Napp as we say) – mentioned in Hugh Marwick's *Orkney Norn* – is the name of the farm. Marwick says that the word means a protuberance, hillock or a dry brae, and the house is built on a sort of brae, one might say.

But I must stop this rambling. I was going to mention that when I was at Napp, the call of curlews, oystercatchers and lapwings filled the air, and across a miry piece of ground great patches of shining yellow marsh marigolds made a spectacular display. Such sights and sounds take me back to the days of long ago when we lived within a stone's throw of this area.

Well, you may remember that I was talking about Robert Burns earlier in my letter. He also mentions, in one of his letters, the flowers and birds in rather a fine way. Let me finish with part of what he says:

'I have some favourite flowers in spring, among which are the mountain daisy, the harebell, the foxglove, the wild brier-rose, the budding birk, and the hoary hawthorn, that I view and hang over with particular delight. I never hear the loud solitary cry of the Curlew in the summer noon, or the wild cadence of a troop of grey Plover in an Autumnal morning, without feeling an elevation of soul like enthusiasm of Devotion or Poesy. Tell me, my dear Friend, to what can this be owing?'

Religion, Education, Healthcare
November 19, 1998

When looking at the meaning of the word Hallowe'en one finds that the word is a contraction of All Hallows (hallowed or holy) Eve, or the Eve of All Saints Day. On that particular day, Christians in the western church celebrated the occasion with a feast which commemorated all saints, whether known or unknown.

In pre-Christian Britain, October 31 was the eve of the New Year when the souls of the dead were thought to revisit their homes, and even after it became a Christian festival that belief and other supernatural associations continued to be connected with Hallowe'en.

Ernest Marwick (1915–1977), the distinguished Orcadian writer and folklorist, talks about bonfire customs and mentions a Hallowmas bonfire which used to be an older Orkney ceremony. He goes on to say (when he was writing twenty or thirty years ago) about Hallowe'en: 'It's entirely the children's festival now, but in the old days in Orkney it was the night above all others charged with significance for the young women; for it was the one night of the year when by courage and craft a girl might catch a glimpse of her future husband.' Ernest goes on to detail numerous examples of how such information might be attained.

Fifty or more years ago, my generation and others around our age and even before, will remember Hallowe'en as a time to look forward to, a time when turnip lanterns were made, and when anticipation was in the air. On the night of the celebration we dooked for apples, tried to catch swinging treacle scones by mouth only or played games of one sort and another.

Interestingly enough, for some years it was the Woman's Guild who organised and ran those memorable nights. In fact my father says it was one of the island's ministers who initiated the Hallowe'en celebration in North Ronaldsay. In those early days and later, it was the custom to play various tricks on one's neighbours – shifting farm implements, blocking chimneys and such like.

Today we hear of Hallowe'en as being associated with more disturbing and sinister practices, and even of the 'event' being banned altogether in some areas. I certainly cannot remember anything undesirable or frightening being connected with October 31.

Well, here I am, after four months or so, trying to write another letter from North Ronaldsay. And, not surprisingly, having some difficulty in remembering events. Firstly, I have to think back to the end of the summer term when the school's Open Day took place – an occasion to be enjoyed, as indeed it was, with islanders and additional visitors giving support to the event. Then one sunny day when the wind was in the north, and before the almost monsoon-type weather began from which we have suffered ever since, we tarred the Memorial Hall. Netta Wylie, home on holiday and formerly from Nether Linnay, helped afterwards to serve various suitable refreshments, and many a laugh we all had.

Silage, hay, punding and more recently, harvest work, were carried out with considerable difficulty – even yet there remains some work to tidy away – but of all the crops, possibly the humble sheaf is the easiest to save. Earlier in the summer a successful children's picnic took place with head teacher Patricia Thomson, John Thomson, and Fiona Sinclair supervising. A little later during the holiday period two wardens, Fiona Sinclair and Helga Tulloch, made available facilities for games, both at the New Community Centre and at the Memorial Hall.

Also in the Memorial Hall the one dance of the summer took place. To begin the evening Rosemary Robertson, Holland House, showed a selection of extraordinary and stunningly colourful slides. She had taken the photographs during the Venice Festival when hundreds of people wear the most extravagant of fancy-dress costumes. The dance which followed became quite a lightsome affair.

But the summer proved to be the worst anyone can remember, with almost continuous rain. Hardly a day could be missed no matter the job in hand. If it didn't rain then it was mist, and if it was not one or the other then mostly it was a combination of both.

Returning for a moment to Hallowe'en with its mixture of religion and superstition. Funnily enough, such things remind me of an article in *The Guardian* newspaper of some months ago, and it in a way provides the subject matter for the remainder of my letter. The date was June 20, I see, since I am actually reading the piece. It was written in connection with the National Health Service. The article seeks to compare Britain's busiest and least busy GPs. North Ronaldsay, with the least busy practice, features prominently, with aspects touched on, including old beliefs.

Three themes, it seems to me, emerge from this newspaper article: religion, education and North Ronaldsay's unique contribution to health care.

Taking the first of the themes, it would appear that Christian teaching on North Ronaldsay dates back two or three centuries before the Norsemen arrived in Orkney round about the ninth century. There is, for example, the cross symbol found at Burrian Broch dating back to possibly St Ninian's time. After those early days, records of Christian teaching exist from as far back as 1683. From that date until 1772, for example, six ministers belonging to the united parishes of Cross and Burness and North Ronaldsay visited the island, or had local readers on the island.

Thereafter ministers and their families lived on North Ronaldsay up until the late 1940s. Since then there have been two other ministers, two deaconesses and a lay missionary. After the departure of the last resident preacher various ministers have officiated from Sanday, coming across from time to time to the island, as still happens today.

Hand in hand with religion goes education, as they say. North Ronaldsay's history in this field goes back to at least the mid-1700s. Often, in fact, it was the ministers who recorded much of the way of life in Orkney, and indeed all over Scotland. For example, in the *Statistical Account of Scotland*, published between 1791 and 1799, the Rev W. Clouston, based in Sanday for a time, states: 'There has been no school in the Isle of North Ronaldsay for twenty-five or thirty years past and yet all the young people can read.'

The first schoolteacher was actually teaching in North Ronaldsay forty years before the Scottish Education Act of 1872. During those early days a secondary education outwith the island would have been almost unthinkable, and it was not until the beginning of the 1900s that young folk began to leave the island for further education.

Since then, and up to the present day, at least forty islanders have graduated from universities and colleges, many going on to pursue successful careers. Two of those graduates were Doctors of Philosophy, with one a professor eventually becoming Chancellor of the University of Massachusetts. Fourteen young women that I can recall followed careers in the nursing profession, with three becoming nursing sisters. Another reached the position of matron of Stobhill Hospital, Glasgow, and Senior Examiner for Scotland.

Many islanders pursued careers at sea, with a large percentage becoming trawler and herring boat skippers. Three became masters of sailing ships and one other commanded steam ships. Another two of those who had chosen to go to sea rose to the rank of Commodore – one of the Granton trawler fleet and the other as Commodore Engineer of the NSSC, with others serving as officers on various craft.

Add to those achievements the diverse accomplishments of many other North Ronaldsay men and women who, without a so-called formal education, went on to follow successful occupations and attain positions of importance and distinction throughout the world.

The last of my headings was health care. Already I have gone some way into the island's involvement, referring as I've done to the nursing profession. This medical connection goes back forty-three years before the National Health Service was set up. In those far-off days two nurses from outwith the island served from 1900 to 1905 before an islander, Miss Janet Tulloch, Upper Linnay, took over as a Queen's Nurse.

Nurse Tulloch worked on North Ronaldsay virtually as doctor and nurse from 1905 to 1915 with only a telegraphic communication with the medical officer based on Sanday. Very often in those days the island was cut off from communication for weeks at a time in winter. Though Janet died in 1963 aged eighty-four, she is still remembered as a nurse with affection and respect by those who knew her – not only in her native isle but also in Orphir, where she served with such dedication from 1915 until 1923. When she left Orphir she returned to North Ronaldsay to get married but continued to act as nurse in an unofficial capacity for many years.

Among her personal effects she kept a little case which contains reference letters, certificates, correspondence and newspaper cuttings, all dealing with her work for the Nursing Associations both in North Ronaldsay and Orphir. This material is of such interest and importance that in my next letter I will tell the story of Janet, who was working in North Ronaldsay and the Mainland of Orkney over ninety-three years ago, and who is still remembered as a nurse of considerable ability and dedication.

Well, I'm coming to the end of my letter. November is the month of remembrance and thankfulness, of Armistice and Harvest Homes, and for some of us these last months have indeed been a time of change and sadness.

Not so very long ago I took a fancy once again, as I do from time to time, to visit the kirk where my mother had played the organ for some seventy years or more. In that building, where so many folk over the years attended Sunday school, services of worship, lantern slides or other church functions, only the ghosts of memory remain to haunt the empty pews.

For my mother's funeral held one day in August, my father had chosen the familiar tune for the 23rd Psalm 'Bellarma', but sung to the words of Paraphrase 53. I would like to close with some of those lines. But before I do I must tell you that this very day, November 3, once more folk have made their way to the graveyard, there to attend the funeral of Mary Cutt (née Muir) Gerbo, or – and it doesn't seem so very long ago – the schooldays' Maimie o' Scotsha.

As I walked to the churchyard, which I mostly always do for island funerals, there came out of a cold blue sky, clear for a short time of the grey-purple rain clouds that have been sweeping across Orkney for so long, the far away thunder of a passing plane. Behind the pale silvery jet an ever-lengthening exhaust trail rippled across the sky. Thinking at the time, as one would, about the inevitability of death, the vapour trail seemed to symbolise a lifetime as a long line of memories, clear to those who remembered for a time, but fading soon from the immediate even just as the vapour trail began to dissolve and merge into the changing sky, so that by the time the funeral was past everything appeared as if it had never been.

> *Take comfort, Christians, when your friends in Jesus fall asleep;*
> *Their better being never ends; why then dejected weep?*
> *Why inconsolable, as those to whom no hope is giv'n?*
> *Death is the messenger of peace, and calls the soul to heav'n.*
> *Together to their Father's house with joyful hearts they go;*
> *And dwell for ever with the Lord, beyond the reach of woe.*
> *A few short years of evil past, we reach the happy shore,*
> *where death-divided friends at last shall meet, to part no more.*

Reflections of Past Times
December 24, 1998

Before November, Armistice and Harvest Homes are forgotten until another year, and before Christmas comes upon us, here goes for one more letter.

Last year about this time I remember quoting a verse or two from John McCrae's (1872–1918) 'In Flanders Fields' –

*In Flanders fields the poppies blow
Between the crosses, row on row.*

A more disturbing poem by one of the Great War's distinguished poets, Isaac Rosenberg, who was killed in 1918, is his 'Dead Man's Dump'. This poem conveys the horror of war more clearly than many. It describes a soldier who 'had recently died, his arms still raised, imploring help. A limber (a horse drawn vehicle used to carry ammunition, supplies etc., to the front) rolls over him, its weight forcing the last air from his chest in a weird cry.'

Another poet, more familiar than Rosenberg, was Wilfred Owen, who was also killed in 1918. His well-known poem 'Strange Meeting', where two dead soldiers of opposing sides meet, is a particular favourite of mine.

But let's get back to North Ronaldsay, as I think I'll have to tell you about three fairly recent events. I have also, as promised in my last letter, to add more to the story of Queen's Nurse Janet Tulloch.

Let me begin with the Harvest Home, which was held two days after Armistice. Once again Loganair flew in friends, relations and guests – something which their pilots have been doing these past nine years – but this time under very difficult conditions. The airline was well represented at our celebrations with Captain Seyd and Christine Allan attending, with their respective spouses, Sara and Pat.

Guest speaker this year was Captain Duncan Robertson, who took over as laird of this island exactly fifty years ago. His presence in the Memorial Hall (erected in 1920), which had in fact been bought for the island by his grandfather, William Traill, and which Duncan in his turn had gifted for safekeeping to the North Ronaldsay Heritage Trust, along with the adjacent land, was surely most suitable for such an anniversary occasion.

Another guest we were very happy to have with us was Mary Shearer or, as North Ronaldsay knew her best, Mary Dawson. Many folk in Orkney will recall her disgraceful treatment by the Orkney Health Board and the subsequent success of the enquiry when her unfair dismissal as Nursing Manager of Eastbank and the Ninian Ward was rightly established. Unfortunately neither Duncan's wife nor Mary's husband were able to be with us on this occasion.

Then, as guest accordionist, we had Edwin Flaws (a man with Ronaldsay connections) from Rousay who had very kindly agreed to come and help out with the music. He was accompanied by his wife Itha. Howie Firth's presence completed a most welcome company of Harvest Home guests.

Once the usual preliminaries were over and the supper past, Duncan Robertson rose to make the Harvest Home speech. He began by giving an account of his many connections with the island – even before his wartime service in France where, as he said, he met his wife. The speaker went on to talk about the Crofting Act of 1976 (which allowed crofters to acquire their crofts for a sum equivalent to fifteen times the holding's rent). This Act gave crofters the right to buy their holdings very cheaply in the first instance and then sell very profitably in the second. In North Ronaldsay, for example, almost all of the island had only paid a minimal rent which had remained the same for very many years. This, I may say, was not the case in Shetland or numerous other crofting communities, where rents had increased quite considerably over the years.

The speaker went on to mention incomers – or 'new islanders' as he described them – who had come to the island as a result of those sales. He emphasised the importance of integration and mutual understanding, and how he felt that those new islanders should respect the customs and traditions of the island, which had survived for many hundreds of years. Throughout the speech a number of amusing stories, many island-related, were told. Finishing one, he asked the company to raise their glasses and drink the toast to the harvest.

Councillor Howie Firth then rose to pay tribute to Duncan Robertson, referring firstly to his long association with the island and that of his forebears before him. Mention was made of his wartime service in Burma and later in France.

Incidentally, the first connection with the island (of the Traills) goes back to 1727 when a James Traill, an Edinburgh lawyer, bought the island for £2,222. Howie went on to talk about various aspects of such ownership, one being the importance of continuity, which he believed had very much been the case in North Ronaldsay.

Then completing his tribute, Howie invited the chairman of the Community Council, Billy Muir, to present Duncan Robertson with an inscribed memento of the occasion on behalf of the community. The presentation took the form of a carved wood and red leather-bound edition of the *Orkneyinga Saga*, beautifully made by Sui Generis, Eday.

This ceremony brought to an end the friendly candle and lantern-lit supper which had extended most enjoyably over two hours. Shortly afterwards, with the old floor cleared and Slipperined, a lively Strip the Willow began the dance.

As the evening progressed, tea, served with more helpings of native mutton, sandwiches and homebakes provided more energy for dancing and also time to organise the raffle. A bottle of whisky was very kindly donated by Alan Clouston and his wife, who unfortunately had been unable to attend. A presentation half bottle of Highland Park was donated anonymously. A jar of Wiltshire honey, home-made by Graham Rendall, who visits the island frequently and whose forebears came from Westray, completed the raffle items.

More dancing followed. A second Eightsome Reel swung round the hall in three sets with Sinclair's pipes skirling the traditional reel music. Earlier we had managed, valiantly, a Scotch Reel, and so with more favourite Strip the Willows, Eva Three Steps and so on. The time came at the back of three for 'Auld Lang Syne'. Before leaving the Old Hall to face the November night, a mulled punch was served along with further helpings of native mutton.

Before finishing this section I must mention North Ronaldsay's generous support of two recent events. First was the North Ronaldsay Ladies Lifeboat Guild's annual fundraising evening when catalogue and local goods sales, raffles and donations amounted to a sum well over £600.

Following on from that evening came Children in Need, organised by the school with help from parents. A total of £225.50 was collected and, as with the first event, tea, sandwiches and homebakes were served to complete the enjoyment.

Now, as promised in my last letter, I'm going to tell you more of the story of Queen's Nurse Janet Tulloch. Janet was born at Upper Linnay on December 11, 1879. When she was 19 she became a servant with one of the island's two ministers, the Rev. William MacPherson, MA, BD, who was minister of the United Free Church, as it was known at the time. He writes a fine reference for her dated August 20, 1901.

Leaving North Ronaldsay that year she travelled to Bolton, England, where she successfully completed her three years' nurse's training, receiving high recommendation from Lewis Buck, Medical Officer in charge at the training centre. The next year saw her in Glasgow attending the Maternity Hospital in Rotten Row and gaining her midwifery qualification – a qualification which was to serve her remarkably well, officially and unofficially, for the next forty years. In fact she was to gain an inviolable reputation in this role, firstly in North Ronaldsay, then in Orphir and other parishes where her skill on occasions of difficulty was called upon.

And so at the age of 26, Janet Tulloch returned to her native isle to begin nursing. From 1905 until 1915 she worked in North Ronaldsay, establishing a high reputation in her chosen profession. The population of the island at that time was around 436. With no resident doctor – and with little communication with the outside world, apart from a steamer which sailed from Kirkwall once every three weeks, and often double or more that time during the winter months – she had to bear a considerable responsibility.

Between North Ronaldsay and Sanday a sail boat, based on the island, crossed the often dangerous firth carrying mails and passengers when possible. It was not until 1910 that a PO wireless station was established on the island due to loss of the sailing ship *Isle of Erin* in 1908. On October 10, 1910, a Miss M. J. Sinclair, Sanday, who was one of the first trained woman operators in Britain, made the first wireless communication between North Ronaldsay and Sanday.

Nurse Tulloch's work in North Ronaldsay is best described by quoting from a reference by her Medical Officer in Sanday, Dr Park, MB, ChB, MA. He refers to her as 'a thoroughly capable and highly efficient nurse. During her ten years' service she had sixty-two confinements which she conducted herself with perfect results.' This fact alone, he goes on to say, 'speaks volumes for her professional ability as well as her discretion and common sense.'

Dr Park also refers to the frequent isolation for weeks at a time, apart from telegraphic contact with the outside world. 'She has been doctor and nurse to the island for all these years doing her own prescribing and dispensing in many cases, and invariably treating her patients with intelligence and sympathy. She is particularly good at diagnosis.' He goes on to say that her descriptions of her more serious cases, by letter or telegram, were particularly lucid and informative.

Among her North Ronaldsay papers there are several letters exchanged between the Rev. W. A. Forbes, president of the North Ronaldsay committee of the Nursing Association, and Nurse Tulloch. From the correspondence, for example, we discover that the nurse's salary was £60 per year (1914). One year she received a bonus of £4 and her uniform was paid for by the association. All costs of medicines, surgical dressings etc., were met by the Nursing Association.

By June 1915, Nurse Tulloch's contract in North Ronaldsay came to an end, and on September 11 she took up her new assignment in Orphir (population 734 in 1921), becoming the first nurse to work for the newly formed Orphir District Nursing Association.

The constitution and rules of this association are particularly interesting. An executive committee engaged the nurse, paid her salary, provided a uniform and supplied all appliances and books needed – subject to the approval of the general committee. This general committee consisted of all subscribers of five shillings and upwards to the association's funds. Each month the executive committee met to conduct business and hear reports from the secretary, treasurer and nurse – meetings to be 'strictly private and confidential'.

Members of the association had to pay one shilling and sixpence for the first professional visit of the nurse, one shilling thereafter and 10 shillings to 15 shillings for maternity cases, according to people's circumstances. Non-subscribers were charged four shillings first visit, three shillings thereafter and one pound for maternity cases, a charge also to be made for medicines and surgical dressings.

The nurse was expected to be on duty eight hours per day, to be in her rooms (Orphir schoolhouse) from 3 to 4pm, and was entitled to a month's holiday each year with a half day off duty every second week. The full constitution and rules provide fascinating reading, bearing in mind that they are now over eighty-three years old.

Among the Orphir materials are a couple of letters from J. Wishart, honorary treasurer, one of which details her salary as from November 1 to December 31, 1915, as being £14 15s 8d. Also in his letter he mentions a deduction of four shillings as her proportion of National Health Insurance – I assume this to be for one year or part of a shared insurance payment for one year.

From the newspaper clippings, which are particularly interesting, many facts emerge about the work carried out in Orphir all those years ago. (One must remember that such work was accomplished on foot or bicycle in those days.) In 1917, for instance, John Wishart, honorary treasurer, spoke at a general meeting of the 'great privilege the parish enjoyed in having one of

Nurse Tulloch's experience in their midst'. Her skill was 'equal to that of any in the naval and military hospitals of the South.'

In another report for the year 1918-19, Mr Wishart explained that there had been a great deal of illness in the parish over the past year – principally due to influenza and measles – and it was agreed that members who had frequently employed the nurse should give a donation along with their subscription to help pay a bonus of £12 to be awarded extra to the nurse.

The following year Nurse Tulloch's register recorded 1,700 visits with 256 patients. By the time of her resignation in 1923 – when she left Orphir and returned to North Ronaldsay to marry William Scott, Roadside, postmaster, JP and general merchant – she had, since her duty with the parish began in 1915, had the names of 1,555 patients on her register, to whom she paid 10,357 nursing visits, and cared for 105 maternity cases.

These facts are detailed in *The Orcadian* at the time of her farewell presentation, held on February 8, 1923. At this public meeting the Rev. J. Higgins paid great tribute to the nurse's work in the parish before inviting Mrs Storer Clouston, wife of the distinguished Orcadian novelist and historian J. Storer Clouston, to make the presentation. Before doing so Mrs Clouston described the excellent work which Nurse Tulloch had done in the parish.

One episode in particular she singled out for mention. One night during the winter of 1917-18, when for weeks the snow lay deep and all traffic on the roads ceased, the nurse was called out to attend patients living at either end of the parish. Though the doctors were not able to come out from the town in conditions which, Mrs Clouston said, 'might have tried an Arctic explorer – Nurse Tulloch attended both patients, having accomplished a walk of eighteen miles or thereabouts. It was a splendid performance and one not to be forgotten.'

Nor was it, since when I spoke to two senior Orphir citizens still living in the parish, that was the episode which they both mentioned. Mrs Clouston, completing her tribute as reported in detail in *The Orcadian*, presented Nurse Tulloch with a tea service and tray as tokens of the parish's sincere admiration of the work she had done.

Among the many papers (including, interestingly, a nursing examination paper dated June 23, 1905, with various questions and answers) and letters of Janet Tulloch's remaining, there is still much which could be recorded. But to finish at this time, as briefly mentioned in my last letter, Janet married in 1923 living at Roadside with her husband. At this house she kept a beautiful garden. Janet took part very fully in the communal life of the island, being at one time president of the Woman's Guild – an important organisation in those days. She still continued to act as nurse unofficially whenever called upon, attending most of the island's confinements until in her seventies. In July 1950, her husband died and on January 16, 1963, she died in her eighty-fourth year.

As I come to the end of this long letter, I'm trying to put all of this into some sort of perspective as I think about today's events and newspaper headlines – the difference in any case between then and now is about as great as night is to day. North Ronaldsay in those days and quite a few years later was almost self-sufficient, with bere and oatmeal ground on the island, fish from the sea, vegetables, mutton and pork, milk, ale, cheese and butter. Tea, sugar and tobacco were the main wants, though not necessities.

I have already mentioned the infrequent sea communications. Even in the other islands, in 1923 for example, the connection between them and Kirkwall was only twice a week. The Morse code system was in use for at least thirty years before the public phone service came into being during the early 1950s.

Yet folk were more content – probably happier and arguably healthier. They had to work on the sea, the tangle and brook-laden shore and the land, expending more energy than probably will ever be needed again in the hard and serious business of making a living. They held dances (for a time even at two venues situated at both ends of the island), attended two kirks and took part in many activities planned by the Hall Committee, the Woman's Guild and the Football Association.

Those activities included concerts, sales of work, choir practices and football matches. All those communal events – as well as visiting one's friends and neighbours to play cards, chequers, chess, look over old photographs or 'redd up' relationships and tell stories – served to keep the community close knit and dependent upon one another. It also served to make folk remember their origins, customs, history and folklore – the value and importance of which, as the writer Kevin Crossley-Holland says, 'is the very heart of any island'.

This letter deals mainly with Nurse Janet Tulloch, so I might as well finish with something of hers. When looking through her papers, at the very bottom of a small case of personal effects from which much of this article has been drawn, there was a little crumpled newspaper cutting which I had almost missed. It must have meant something to her. I think I'll finish with its words: they serve as a fine epitaph for Queen's Nurse Janet Tulloch.

Brighter, fairer far than living
With no trace of woe or pain,
Robed in everlasting beauty,
We shall see her once again.
By the light that never fadeth
Underneath eternal skies.
When the Dawn of Resurrection
Breaks o'er deathless Paradise.

Que Sera Sera
February 11, 1999

In 1956, Doris Day sang the hit song 'Que Sera Sera'. I remember a contemporary of mine (we were both born in 1940) singing the song on the last night of that year as the Linklestoon men began their old Hogmanay rounds – but more of this a little later.

Christmas and the festive season seemed long behind me as at last I set my mind to writing another letter. Away back in December, a whist drive raised well over £100 in aid of the children's Christmas party.

Next to take place was the school Christmas dinner for the island. This occasion was as cheerful and magnificent as ever, with the school children giving a short but most enjoyable Christmas presentation. Following on from this function came the traditional children's Christmas Eve party when, after games etc. Santa appeared as mysteriously as ever to entertain both young and old.

Hogmanay was extensively celebrated and on New Year's Day, twenty-six enthusiasts swung round the Standing Stone with the greatest of fun. Then it was on to Neven for a second dram to further toast the New Year. At night, Vincoin carried on the celebrations in suitable style. On the following evening Martin Gray projected some very fine slides of St. Kilda, the Jan Mayan islands, bird life, icebergs and magnificent polar bears. This show began the first dance of the New Year, and very successful it was too. Strip the Willows, Eva Three Steps etc., were danced with three sets of the Eightsome Reels performed twice, adding grandly to the night's entertainment.

Back now then to Doris Day and her song. A few nights before Old Hogmanay (January 12) I happened to be out on foot posting a letter. It brought home to me that one of the advantages of our island life is the unspoiled view one has of the sea and the sky – especially at night. I mean that there are no distracting artificial lights to take away from the grandeur of the sky. And this night was one when, with a touch of frost, everything was at its most magnificent. Stars sparkled brilliantly against the dark spaces of the sky and, although the moon was decidedly on the wane, she still shone brightly in the east. And against the silver of the moon-beamed sea, lower Linklestoon's familiar houses were clearly visible.

As I walked along the road I was thinking, as I often do at this time of year, about the famous Hogmanays and New Years we used to have. Not, I may say, that I was by any means a noteworthy participant. But those days of about forty years and more ago remain fixed in that part of our minds, or at least mine, which believes such times to have been particularly memorable – and memorable in so many ways that can never be experienced again today.

Well, just think of the weeks of brewing and necessary preparations, the long-awaited anticipation of the occasion and Yule generally. How such celebrations and activity lit up and eased for a time a much harder lifestyle and the more severe weather of those old winter nights. Then there was the getting together of neighbours and fellow islanders, who knew each other and had grown up with one another through a less sophisticated way of living, sharing the hardships, trials and joys of a relatively isolated but more strongly community-minded people.

As we age we have, I think, the advantage of making comparisons. On the other hand, later generations will remember their special occasions and events with their own affection. But is it not the case that they are less able to judge and compare the merits of old and new? The question is, which times were actually the best, but who is able to judge? And given a sound opinion, how do we attempt to retain the best and necessary values to enrich future generations?

But here I am as usual, wandering away into all sorts of complications which threaten to bamboozle everybody including myself.

Back to my theme. Never a better night than this, I thought, for the Hogmanay round. And with that in mind, down the Milldam Road I went, intent on walking the old route to pass the doors of each of the eleven or so houses that I recall we visited all those years ago. Milldam was mostly the first house and the collecting point. There I stopped momentarily, remembering again some twenty or more men of the company, the feeling of anticipation, the waiting for everybody to arrive. It was like the beginning of a concert or of some special event, long looked forward to, with the realisation that all the hours of the night were there to be enjoyed.

Then away I went to Barrenha', pausing at that familiar house where now only the ghosts of memory haunt the darkened, uninhabited croft. I peeped briefly through its little south-facing window and for a moment or two transformed the empty room into a lightsome vision of the past. On the open fire a little goblet was steaming away, mulling some ale for one of the older men in the company, a ritual performed at almost every house – yet only a few sips did he ever take. Familiar faces I could see, and voices came back to me for a second or two before the illusion dissolved into darkness.

Scotsha' and Phisligar were the next two houses, where we were welcomed with more ale and refreshments. In Phisligar I always remember being fascinated by a very large ship's telescope fixed up on the wall. Its history we knew, and for me it always conjured up visions of the great days of the sailing ships and of the vast heaving seas of the world's oceans.

Time for the two Greenspots next – joined together as one. Greenspot Number One, with its fallen-in roof opened now to the light of the moon and the stars or to the Northern Lights when they merrily danced across the sky, was particularly sad. For a moment or two everything returned to its former glory – a short visit to One and then on to Greenspot Number Two, now, like Barrenha', dark and empty. It was also the house where, on New Year's Eve the young 'crood' (company) made up of both genders and from other toonships would sometimes meet to begin their visiting spree.

Through its little window, against which overgrown elder trees creaked eerily in the moonlight, I saw in my mind's eye again the two companies–men of the 1956 Hogmanay visit and our own New Year's night crowd. I remember especially the younger first-footers crammed into the little interior, some sitting on the edge of the box bed, some two or three to a chair, others milling around.

The Tilley lamp, with the aid of occasional pumpings, hissed and lit up the proceedings. Pipe and cigarette smoke drifted around the low ceiling and dark bottles of ale continually topped up the glasses. In the midst of all this the sprightly lady of the house moved niftily here and there, serving shortbread or whatever in various Scottish-looking tins. Both companies, on their different nights, flashed backwards and forwards like a moving film in my mind. But in a twinkling all was dark, and I passed then the east window on my way across the fields to North Gravity.

In scattered groups we used to make our way; voices from different directions sounded through the night, dark figures moved along, helped by the moon and the stars or by the old bicycle flashlight. The route to North Gravity was the longest, giving time to experience the reviving night air. Sometimes, I seem to recall, we listened to the chimes of Big Ben ringing out the old year and bringing in the new at Gravity. Ale flowed there too, and the participants by this time were tuning up very finely; but it was mostly Waterhouse where we took in the New Year, and Waterhouse was my next port of call.

Soon I arrived at its door to remember the visit. Once the New Year was in, it seemed to me that the importance of moving on to the next house was a little relaxed – after all, only two houses remained to be visited. In addition, at that stage, the wonderful mixtures and varying strengths of the ales helped to lessen the earlier, somewhat strict routine; but also, the cumulative effect of the evening made it more difficult to get a reluctant company on the move.

But now onto the second last house, Purtabreck. Across the fields we would go, always shortcutting the route. Sometimes at this point I would nip home to report on progress and give some indication of our arrival time at Antabreck.

So at Purtabreck's door I stood for a bit to imagine the company there – by now bravely fortified. The flow of the night then would vary like the tides of the sea, changing direction as the stories and thoughts of North Ronaldsay in the 1950s shifted this way and that as they caught the mind of the jolly crew. Turning my steps northwards, I soon arrived back to where I had started. The walk had taken almost exactly one hour.

Memories of Antabreck remain, of course, more strongly. For we were at the last house on the Hogmanay round and there was no urgency to leave. By this time it would have been well into the early hours of the New Year, after allowing half to three-quarters of an hour at each house. Often the daylight was brightening up the familiar patterns of the island before the last of our closest neighbours finally left to get some rest, carry out essential work and prepare for another round of visits on New Year's night.

Thinking back for a moment to those eleven 'Linklestoon' houses round which I had just made this nostalgic journey, I realised that the total number of folk on the toon at that time, including the Hogmanay company, would have amounted to around fifty or so – well over half the population of North Ronaldsay today. A sobering thought indeed.

By the early to mid-1960s, with the closing down of the mill and consequently no more home brewed ale, those great nights came to an end. Also, by that time the more senior men of the toon were beginning to fail. Such a mixture of entertainment and tradition, as wonderful a combination as ever one can imagine, has slipped away into history.

So it's back to the song: *The future's not ours to see*. Funnily enough, those of us left since 1956 have passed through and seen that future – at least until today. What will it be as we race towards the year 2000, I wonder? Will it be rainbows day after day like the words of the song? Rainbows or not, great work has been achieved in North Ronaldsay recently.

A functional airstrip has been made – amazingly, in winter – through days of rain, wind and difficulty by men from Orkney Direct and with help from the island. That work is partially complete, but the resumption of our vital air service has been secured, and before those council men left they were presented with tokens of appreciation from the community.

Through all of this and the passing months, many other things have been happening. The old Sheep Court has been bravely revitalised and is currently moving ahead with a continuing and ambitious programme of work and development. It is grand to think that in North Ronaldsay, the last remnant of the old Orcadian system of communal agriculture is still alive and firmly under the control of the island.

Like Westray, Papa Westray and other islands, we are looking seriously, I hope – at last, and as we must do, together – towards the future of North Ronaldsay.

Burns Supper is a Memorable Occasion
March 25, 1999

> *Thus seasons dancing, life advancing*
> *Old Time and Nature their changes tell.*
> – Robert Burns

I know that we are now into March, with the month of Burns well behind us. Nevertheless, I am going to quote the poet from time to time and maybe, as the fancy takes me, say some interesting things about the man. You may remember that last year I mentioned the book *The Complete Letters of Robert Burns*. Well, I have been working my way through the book, leaving paper marks here and there so that I can have another look at parts which interest me especially.

Also, later, I must of course tell you about a belated peedie Burns Supper which we eventually managed to arrange for Friday, February 12th. Although almost three weeks late, the weather about that time seemed more in keeping with the wintry seasons that Burns often described so well.

> *Blow, blow ye Winds, with heavier gust!*
> *And freeze, thou bitter-biting Frost!*
> *Descend, ye chilly, smothering Snows!*
> Or:
> *The gloomy night is gath'ring fast,*
> *Loud roars the wild, inconstant blast,*
> *Yon murky cloud is foul with rain,*
> *I see it driving o'er the plain.*

When I was reading through the poet's letters I discovered, for instance, that when he was travelling on horseback as an exciseman, it was not unusual to cover distances of 200 miles in one week. In the little book of Scottish verse edited by Tom Scott, he says of Burns:

'He was plagued by illness, nervous depression, insecurity, anxieties of all sorts, the harassing of exploiting landowners and others. He died worn out with the unequal struggle, an old man at thirty-seven, of rheumatic fever caught on long rides in drenching rain round his territory as an exciseman.'

This writer also says that Burns became the most universally loved of all poets, and his works have been translated into almost every literary language under the sun. He describes Burns as being not only one of the greatest song collectors but also a great writer of songs.

Tom Scott, poet and author, was as a matter of interest encouraged to pursue an academic career by the distinguished Orcadian literary figure Edwin Muir when he was teaching at Newbattle Abbey College near Edinburgh. Two of Muir's fellow Orcadians, Ernest Marwick and George Mackay Brown, also spent some time studying at Newbattle.

Anyhow, as I begin this letter the moon is almost full, and when I looked out a moment ago, she was momentarily encircled by rainbow colours as passing high cloud flew across her face.

It is the moon, I ken her horn,
That's blinkin in the lift sae hie;
She shines sae bright to wyle us hame.

When the cloud cleared, the moon shone with a cold, intense light and it seemed strange to think that man had actually set foot upon her surface. Once back inside, and no sooner had I taken up my pen, then I heard on a tape I happened to be playing 'The Star o' Rabbie Burns'. It was one of the records chosen by Rhoda Bulter from her Radio Shetland programme of *Rhoda's 78s* recorded some years ago. I thought that a coincidence.

Later, Sir Harry Lauder sang 'The Laddies Who Fought and Won', a patriotic and popular song of World War I. It tied in nicely with the Siegfried Sassoon classic book *The Complete Memoirs of George Sherston*, which I am reading at the moment. It is, I suppose, a biographical narrative, dealing in part with that war and Sassoon's involvement as an officer. Most of his life afterwards was spent reliving and writing about those tragic events.

While briefly on the subject of reading, which I mostly do in bed I must admit, before Sassoon's book I read *The Voyage of the Pharos* – Walter Scott's account of a cruise around Scotland in 1814 when, as a guest of the Commissioners of Northern Lights, he accompanied them on an inspection tour of the Scottish lighthouses. Interestingly enough, Scott had met Robert Burns in Edinburgh when he (Scott) was fifteen or so.

You see, I am now away on another aspect – that of connections. Some readers may remember an earlier letter written in that vein when I was telling you about a book. I had been reading the journals of the Stanley expedition – an expedition to the Faroes and Iceland in 1789. At that time, when the expedition's boat left Orkney on her journey north, they passed North Ronaldsay. That same year on the island the Old Lighthouse – one of the first four in Scotland – was being built, and Robert Burns had reached the age of thirteen or so. Twenty-five years later, Walter Scott sailed by North Ronaldsay and its completed lighthouse en route from the Fair Isle. The *Pharos* was unable to make a landing on the island but was able to allow a visit to the Start Lighthouse on Sunday. I merely mention all this because it never ceases to amaze me the number of surprising connections that one can discover on seemingly unrelated topics.

But, like Walter Scott on his lighthouse cruise, I have been sailing, in a manner of speaking, all over the place and it's high time, as Sarah o' Lochend would have said, to tell you about our little Burns Night. And as I begin to think about writing up this event, another day has come, and very cold and bleak it is. A night of strong easterly wind, now fast backing to the north, has transformed the east sea into a heaving mass, breaking all along the shoreline, north and east, and lining the submerged Reef Dyke with great tumbling waves.

> *I saw thee seek the sounding shore,*
> *Delighted with the dashing roar;*
> *Or when the North his fleecy store*
> *Drove thro' the sky.*

I always think that atmosphere plays a great part in the success or failure of an event, and for Burns Night lamp and candlelight especially suit the period. Scottish-looking drapery and illustrations from the poems of Burns lightsomed our homely venue, and after the usual North Ronaldsay delay in starting, in marched the piper, Sinclair Scott, playing away briskly. He was closely followed by the chief cook, Winnie Scott, carrying the haggis. (It just occurs to me this letter seems riddled with Scotts, but that is another coincidence.) The piper's dram was almost forgotten but managed in a twinkling as Alastair Henderson, recently retired lightkeeper, tackled the address to the haggis.

When the traditional supper was finished, our invited speaker, Brian Murray from Stromness, a retired schoolteacher and formerly a headmaster in Ayrshire, gave us the 'Immortal Memory'. His tribute to Burns covering as it did the poet's life was much enjoyed. He elaborated on the Bard's achievements: the preservation of some 250 Scottish songs in one way or another, the important contribution he made to keeping alive the Scots dialect, and his recording of old words. Brian also referred to the legacy which Burns had left – his exposure of hypocrisy in controversial places and his resolution in matters social and political. At this point I will write out a statement made by Burns which pleases me finely and supports Brian Murray's summing up of the poet.

It is contained in a letter to John Francis Erskine 27th Earl of Mar, dated April 13, 1793. His letter refers to an instruction from his superiors in the excise service which stated that Burns' business was to act, not think, and to be silent and obedient:

'Does any man tell me that my individual efforts can be of no service, and that it does not belong to my humble station to meddle with the concerns of a nation? I can tell him that it is on such individuals as I that a nation has to rest, both for the hand of support, and the eye of intelligence. The uninformed MOB may swell a nation's bulk, and the tilted, tinsel, courtly throng may be its feathered ornament, but the number of those who are elevated in life to reason and reflect, yet low enough to keep clear of the venal contagion of a court – these are a nation's strength.'

At the conclusion of his tribute to Burns, Brian asked everyone to be upstanding and to toast the Immortal Memory. Next came the Toast to the Lasses and the Reply. Both were amusingly accomplished by two islanders and one-time school classmates now living in Kirkwall – Jimmy o' Nether Linnay (Thomson) who proposed the toast and Jenny o' Cavan (Mainland née Scott) who made the reply.

At this point in the programme Howie Firth, who had come out specially for the occasion, rose to pay tribute to Sydney Scott on his retiral after thirty-two years' service as agent for the North Isles Shipping Company. Sydney, he said, had been working on the North Ronaldsay pier in 1929 when he was just fourteen years old. (At that time the Orkney Steam Navigation Company ran the North Isles shipping service. They were replaced by the Orkney Islands Shipping Company, who were in their turn superseded by Orkney Ferries.)

Howie mentioned the many years that Sydney had worked on the North Ronaldsay pier, 1999 taking him into his seventieth year of service. He had to get up early on many a morning in winter or summer to attend to his duties, and for the thirty-two years as agent, he faced the responsibility of bringing the ship to the island or otherwise. He went on to mention Sydney's fifteen years as miller, the many games of cards and other games of one sort and another that used to be played in the mill at slack times, and the playing of the pipes on his way home after a day's work.

Howie referred to Sydney's fiddle-playing at island dances, the organisation of concerts, his stone-building skills and the keeping alive of North Ronaldsay's heritage through stories and song. Completing his tribute, Howie and Brian Murray each presented Sidney with personal gifts of books. Then Howie, mentioning the privilege it was for him to make the island's presentation, handed over the various gifts – an automatic camera, an inscribed pewter quaich, Captain Sutherland's book '*Romiosini*' and book tokens. Sydney thanked everybody for the many gifts he had received, bringing those pleasant proceedings to an end.

A selection of Burns songs followed before Howie, in splendid form, gave an energetic and most enjoyable performance of Burns' masterpiece 'Tam O' Shanter'. A couple more songs were sung before Alastair Henderson, shortly to leave North Ronaldsay along with his wife Dorothy to live in Stromness, ended the first part of the night with a recitation of 'To a Mouse'.

The rest of the evening saw an assortment of lively dances – the confined area making them particularly lightsome. Wilma Taylor, our dancing teacher of last year and before, would have, I think, been very pleased indeed to see a reasonable performance of North Ronaldsay's Axum Reel, revived and taught by her. Tea and homebakes made a welcome break. Later Sydney sang 'O Wert Thou in the Cauld Blast' and a little later still Sidney Ogilvie recited his own special poem as an additional tribute to the lasses. More dances followed until, between one and two in the morning, 'Auld Lang Syne', a song collected and preserved by Burns with the addition of two verses of his own, brought a memorable occasion to a close.

Well, I've worked away at this letter for most of a particularly unpleasant and very cold day. Even as I write, near on one in the morning, the wind is sounding loudly in the chimney and swapping over Antabreck's slate roof. Every now and then fierce showers of rain laced with sleet come rattling down from the north.

> *When biting Boreas, fell and doure,*
> *Sharp shivers thro' the leafless bow'r;*
> *When Phoebus gies a short-liv'd glow'r,*
> *Far south the lift,*
> *Dim-dark'ning thro' the flaky show'r*
> *Or whirling drift.*

I was listening to some Scottish dance music and thinking of a dance practice we have often talked about, when among the tunes being played was a medley of World War II songs. They brought to mind one other sad event for North Ronaldsay, as on Tuesday, March 2, a veteran of that war, lifetime shopkeeper Hughie Swanney, past agent for Alginate Industries and a well-known island personality, unexpectedly passed away. Today, Friday, March 5, on one of our finest days of the winter, Hughie was laid to rest. From the West Banks, much frequented by Hughie in earlier times, came the sound of the restless sea, and from the north the wind blew coldly.

Should auld acquaintance be forgot
 And never brought to mind?
Should auld acquaintance be forgot,
 And auld lang syne!
For auld lang syne, my jo,
 For auld lang syne,
We'll tak a cup o' kindness yet
 For auld lang syne.

Remembrance
June 10, 1999

Last year I began writing one of my letters from North Ronaldsay on my birthday, which falls on St George's Day, April 23. This year on that day my father was laid to rest, and only eight months before, my mother had passed away. Nineteen years ago, I remember happier times. My parents were still working away. The creel boats were being got ready for the lobster fishing season and two of us (fishermen) were attempting to renew our youth by returning to the 'high seas'.

With such a thought in mind I was working next door where my sister and her husband live, helping to prepare the boat from which we would set sail to seek out those 'blue denizens of the deep'. A dumpling had been prepared for my birthday, the weather was fine, with the spring work about finished and it seemed as if there was still time to return to days of former pleasures – I think that from now on St George's Day will never be quite the same again.

Since last I wrote, North Ronaldsay has been involved with the remaining springtime activities. The school pupils have been away on various educational trips to the Orkney Mainland. There have been sheep meetings, development meetings, Community Council, Community Association and millennium meetings – with more to come, involving all of those organisations. *Well, well*, as my Faroese friend would say.

At Easter, a special evening was arranged for Howie Firth in order to acknowledge his work as councillor for the island. The event proved a great success. Two musicians, Raymond Scott (clarinet and recorder) and Owen Tierney (guitar), once again very kindly came out to provide a focus for the occasion. They began the evening with a short programme of music made up of Irish, Scottish and contemporary material, playing in a relaxed but very professional way.

After this musical introduction, the main business of the evening got under way when an account was given of his most notable achievements as councillor for North Ronaldsay. As time passes it becomes difficult to remember all the things which have happened during one Community Council's term of office, let alone two, but over that period a number of important decisions were made by Orkney Islands Council which directly benefited North Ronaldsay. Howie was responsible in no small way for bringing the issues to the council and in persuading councillors to vote for North Ronaldsay's interests.

One of the first real benefits for the island's residents was the greatly reduced air fares and, very importantly, securing the subsidy from the council to keep the airline in operation. Another notable achievement was the island's development plan, where up to twenty-five percent assistance on projects became available from the oil reserve fund and the Department of Economic Development. Other more advantaged islands, that is those with roll-on/roll-off ferries, received much less by comparison.

In 1993 there was the sheep dyke disaster brought about by severe weather early in the year. Great stretches of dyke were devastated allowing hundreds of native sheep access to the inside land. Orkney Enterprise and the council's Economic Development Department gave £2500 each to assist with the purchase of fencing posts and wire, ensuring protection where the dyke could not be easily rebuilt.

And again, both sources provided a very substantial sum of money to set up the company A Yarn from North Ronaldsay. Jane Donnelly was appointed manager of this venture which involves the marketing of the native sheep's and other related products. As well as arguing for those and setting in place those overall island projects, Howie helped with many individual developments on the island.

His efforts were instrumental in assigning 'seedcorn' money for all community councils, with North Ronaldsay benefiting considerably. For example, help was given for various Community Council projects costing £5000 and covering such undertakings as marketing the North Ronaldsay native mutton, sheepskin curing and the employment of an accountant to research the lighthouse project – a real potential in attracting young families to the island.

This latter project involves the setting up of a trust, which it is hoped will take over the responsibility of this complex undertaking. Again, Howie was the driving force behind the idea. The concept relates in many ways to the formation of a policy document for Orkney's islands called 'A Vision for Orkney', adopted on April 7, with which Howie was very much involved. Once that idea gets underway, less favoured areas such as North Ronaldsay will again qualify for help.

Then there was the vitally important hardcore runway on the aerodrome ensuring our air connexion, without which North Ronaldsay would arguably be unable to survive. And during the time when the island was without

Loganair's service, as a result of the waterlogged runway, a helicopter link was established. This expensive service was strongly backed by Howie with the support of Jeremy Baster, Director of Development and Planning.

At the pier a new store, waiting room and toilets were completed recently and apart from important run-of-the-mill work which also involves guidance and help, those are probably the main achievements with which our councillor was involved. Mention was also made of many other schemes beneficial to Orkney generally which Howie enthusiastically helped to progress through council, and also the many occasions when he had supported community functions on the island, taking part with great energy and enjoyment – all of which had helped to give him the insight and understanding of the needs of an island, and had also won him the respect of its inhabitants.

At the conclusion of this tribute Peter Donnelly, representing his wife Jane and on behalf of the business 'A Yarn from North Ronaldsay', presented Howie with a beautiful rug woven from the wool of our native sheep. The next presentation was made by the chairman of the Community Council, Billy Muir, who on behalf of the island unveiled an oil painting (by Ian Scott) of North Ronaldsay's particularly scenic West Beach.

Howie then thanked everybody for their kindness and generous gifts. He went on to tell various amusing stories connected with his long involvement and knowledge of council work and promised to come back to North Ronaldsay whenever the chance presented itself – Harvest Homes being high on his list.

To complete those very pleasant proceedings, substantial drams were served and a toast proposed, when the good wishes of North Ronaldsay to his future endeavours was extended. The evening progressed with much talk and enjoyment. Raymond Scott and Owen Tierney continued to entertain everybody with some great music. There was a little singing and a little dancing from time to time. Howie joined in with his recorder and later, by special request and in splendid form, repeated his Harvest Home performance of some years past when he danced the samba while at the same time playing two recorders.

Finally, in the early hours of the morning, with candles, lamps, coloured bulbs and curtained walls of red, blue and green creating a cosy atmosphere, 'Auld Lang Syne' brought this memorable occasion to a close. Down in Elgin, where Howie has his new home, a presentation bouquet of flowers was arranged to be delivered to his wife Sidsel from the community.

I began this letter by remembering events which at some time affect all our lives. In an island such as North Ronaldsay, I always think that when someone dies North Ronaldsay also dies a little – I'm thinking about each lifetime's experience, each generation's stories, each individual's personality and contribution to the life of an island. A few days ago, I was listening to my father's voice on tape. He was singing one of his old Hogmanay songs – intended, you'll understand, to liven up the proceedings. If you know the song, then there was never one better. It took me back to those great nights I've often tried to describe in previous letters. Also on the tape is my mother's voice helping with the verses of another song he sings: 'The Leaving of Stromness'.

After her passing, I was looking through one of her favourite poetry books. She had left a coloured marker at rather a sad poem by the Victorian poet Christina Georgina Rossetti. Its first lines begin:

Remember me when I am gone away
Gone far away into the silent land

and it concludes

Better by far you should forget and smile
Than that you should remember and be sad.

But I'm going back once more to those nights brought vividly to life as I listened to the singing of 'A Capital Ship':

A capital ship for an ocean trip
Was the Walloping Window Blind!
No wind that blew dismayed the crew
Or troubled the captain's mind
The man at the wheel was made to feel
Contempt for the wildest blow-ow-ow
Though it often appeared
When the gale had cleared
That he'd been in his bunk below.

Most of our toonships men were in their prime, in their grandest form during those Hogmanays of the Fifties. The song was being delivered with the energy and gusto it demanded amidst the swirl of tobacco reek and the flicker of our old 'Modern Mistress' stove. A Tilley lamp lit up the scene, and near the fire sat one or two of the more senior men.

Among the company went my mother serving North Ronaldsay mutton from a large ashet and making sure ale mugs were full. Round the table, strewn with the hospitality of Hogmanay, were 'the crood' (the company), talking, drinking, laughing or joining in the chorus of 'A Capital Ship', and two noteworthy characters, Arnold and Philip, who each tried to get the better of one another verbally, going at it in style.

Even as the years slip away, those nights will surely always remain in my mind, but such a 'mixter-maxter' of sound, atmosphere and fellowship, made up by a company whose presence represented the very heart and history of an island, I do not think we will ever see again.

Then blow, ye winds hey ho!
A roving I will go!
I'll stay no more on England's shore
So let the music play ay-ay!
I'm off for the morning train
I'll cross the raging main!
I'm off to my love with a boxing glove
Ten thousand miles away!

It's those last words of the song, somehow they capture the mind – 10,000 miles away. Is it an idea of time and distance I wonder? Maybe just simply the imagined vision of a capital ship, all adazzle in white sails voyaging far away. Or maybe it's simply a memory of a time lost.

I'm off to my love with a boxing glove 10,000 miles away.

School Open Day
July 15, 1999

On Friday, June 25, the North Ronaldsay primary school held their end of term open day. A good turnout, which included Day Club members, attended the event. The Community Centre was brightly decorated in keeping with the summer project, the study of plant life. Large sunflower motifs – a particular flower which the pupils had studied, dominated the stage area, along with an assortment of plants which had been looked after by the school during the term. Along the walls were displayed various flower paintings, drawings, text, diagrams etc., carried out for the school project. One of the most interesting areas studied was at Holland House – which at one time had extensive gardens with all sorts of plants, trees and flowers.

Head teacher Patricia Thompson welcomed everybody to begin the proceedings and went on to introduce the afternoon's main attraction: a mini concert performed by the school children. The pupils began the concert by each giving a short description of plants familiar to island folk which included the wild iris. Segy boats used to be made from the long leaf, and one or two were on display, with leaves available for further examples to be made.

The hymn 'All Things Bright and Beautiful' was sung followed by other songs and poems, including recitations related to the term's project. A short history of the national flower emblems of Scotland, Wales, England and Ireland was related by the children, who also displayed illustrations of the four emblems. Another interesting part of the concert involved audience participation, when folk were asked to provide answers to various riddles.

Throughout the programme, which included short mime sketches performed in plant costumes, all the pupils – Louis Craigie, Joni Craigie, Richenda and Thomas Brookman and pre-school nursery pupil Heather Woodbridge, performed well and made very confident use of a microphone system.

Finally to finish the mini concert, all the school children danced a seven-step polka. Patricia Thompson and her assistant teacher, Isobel Muir, helped with the dance – as indeed they had done throughout with the various items presented.

To complete the open day tea, a very large assortment of homebakes was served. Parents and staff had all helped with the baking, much of which had been decorated by the pupils with, appropriately enough, flower motifs.

On sale were various cards with pressed flowers which had been made at the school, and their sale along with a number of raffled items plus donations realised a sum of £125 for the school's funds. This concluding event brought to an end a very successful and enjoyable occasion.

Slideshow
August 5, 1999

Recently, Captain Andy Alsop (a pioneer pilot with Loganair's Inter-Island Service), accompanied by his wife Glenys, gave a slideshow in North Ronaldsay. The venue was the Memorial Hall and the subject was 'A Pilot's View of Antarctica'.

Andy's work, as one of a team of pilots who take various scientific expeditions to that area, supplying and moving them around, provides him with a unique opportunity of viewing mostly the British section of this vast continent.

His slideshow of photographs taken from the ground and the air gave a very comprehensive impression of Antarctica. The slides projected were excellent and the commentary was particularly informative, covering the flying aspect of the work, geology, climate, wildlife and finishing with some spectacular views of icebergs, animals, sunsets and of Antarctica generally.

A dance followed the slideshow with eighty or so folk – young and old, visitors and islanders, all enjoying the evening. Sinclair (bagpipes) and Lottie and Ann (accordions) provided the music, with John O' Westness acting as MC. A raffle brought in £64. 90 for the NRCA. Tea, sandwiches and a very grand selection of homebakes provided extra energy for the dance, which went on until the early light of the dawn touched the sky.

The next day a North Ronaldsay trip steamer took back many of the night's participants and may do so again when another proposed slideshow and dance will take place in the New Community Centre in a few weeks' time. Helga Tulloch, Community Association Village Hall Scheme's Warden (Orkney Tourist Board-assisted project) was much involved with the organisation of the event, as she will join our next community get together.

Yemen Slideshow
September 16, 1999

The second community function of the summer took place on Saturday, August 7 in the New Community Centre, when Rosemary Robertson of Holland House gave a talk and slideshow on Yemen.

The range and quality of her work was excellent. She has an eye for composition, colour and especially portraits of the indigenous people, as we have seen with her other slideshows. A lively dance followed, which improved as the night wore on. A raffle of many choice items, including a donation from the Frozen Food Centre in Kirkwall, raised over £50 for the Community Association. A number of visitors attended the function enjoying, in particular, Strip the Willow in very fast time and Eightsome Reels. As with the last event a number of the evening's revellers returned to Kirkwall on a Sunday trip steamer.

The following day, Sunday, Helga Tulloch the community warden and organiser of the dance and slideshow, ran a successful barbecue at the West Beach. John Thompson, Schoolhouse, was kept busy all afternoon cooking on his barbeque. A bottle stall raised £26 for NRCA's funds.

Next on Helga's list of events was a Car Treasure Hunt which attracted eleven cars, with well over fifty folk participating in teams of five or so – cars and minds were set to work for a few hours. First prize was a bottle of Highland Park whisky donated by the Highland Park Distillery. It was won by Michael, Graham (Scott) and Brian Mawson (Burrian Inn). Little medals for first, second and third were presented and, along with the last year's medals, they will be displayed in the Burrian Inn. Presentations took place in the Memorial Hall where tea, cake and biscuits were available, rounding off what is becoming a popular event. A further raffle raised over £20.

Over a period of six weeks or so Helga Tulloch has been quite busy as, apart from activity mornings for children, open nights etc., she organised a picnic on the North Links with a sandcastle competition and games. A snooker competition also took place in the New Centre when Bertie Thompson emerged as victorious over the fourteen or so competitors who took part. The Burrian Inn donated a bottle of whisky as first prize.

More recently a netball evening was greatly enjoyed, with Patricia Thompson, head teacher, acting as referee over a very lively match indeed. To complete the warden's period of supervision and organisation, Helga ran a children's final activity morning, finishing with a little party. Otherwise, as with all of Orkney, North Ronaldsay has enjoyed marvellous weather for silage, hay, wrapped bales and such like. Of all these activities only the making of the old fashioned cole with a fork (a peedie stack-like gathering of loose hay used to head stacks of square baled hay) remains of the haymaking that used to be long ago. Today across the Orkney landscape, rows of shiny black plastic-wrapped bales of grass lie detached and unsympathetic, in sad contrast to the haystacks of old.

Community Functions
October 14, 1999

Two community functions took place fairly recently in the New Centre as part of the Orkney Science Festival. Howie Firth arranged the occasions which were well attended and greatly enjoyed. Firstly, Dr June Morris, who was accompanied by her husband Gerald, gave a fascinating talk called 'North Ronaldsay's Native Sheep'. Both June and Gerald are biologists working at the Manchester Metropolitan University and have been visiting North Ronaldsay for many years. The native sheep are the source of an in-depth study both on the island and at the Morris's home, where June has a few island sheep as well as some other primitive breeds.

June gave a particularly enlightening talk linking the North Ronaldsay native sheep with other likely relatives, for example in St Kilda, Norway and France. She dealt at length with their interesting biology (their body adaptation to eating seaweed and so forth), their high intelligence compared with other domestic breeds, their waterproof wool, the significance of wool colour and many other general observations concerning the islands sheep and other primitive breeds.

Following the talk, illustrated by overhead colour projections, a lively discussion took place with many of the island's sheep owners taking part, whose working knowledge of the sheep covers generations. Missing from the talk was Bill Carstairs, veterinary advisor to the North Ronaldsay Sheep Court (he subsequently, as billed, teamed up with June for the complete presentation in Kirkwall). Another year, it is planned to have Bill, June, Gerald and others visit the island to discuss further this most interesting of subjects.

A few days later the second of the two festival events took place when the audience was entertained musically by Hamish Bayne, a former member of the well-known McCalman's folk group and Frank Gray, a music teacher working in Orkney. Hamish Bain began the evening with a video and talk on concertinas, describing in detail how he actually makes one of these musical instruments – a dedicated and highly skilled occupation which takes some 800 and more hours to complete. Not many people actually make the concertina, and Hamish is one of the very few. As well as demonstrating the versatility of the concertina, Hamish also performed as competently on the tin whistle and sang a few songs. Fran Gray accompanied on guitar and played accordion. Both in fact provided excellent and professional entertainment for an appreciative audience.

During the evening Hamish's wife Freda, who is a weaver, demonstrated her craft by using an ancient Egyptian method of weaving dash. Taking a loom to North Ronaldsay is too difficult by plane, so Freda had brought out a few examples of her weaving, which gave an idea of just some of what can be achieved in this line of work.

Before these two festival events, RSPB officer Eric Meek, along with his colleague Andy Knight, gave a talk illustrated by slides and diagrams on wetland management. At all of these functions there were the usual refreshments, giving time for further discussion and general enjoyment.

Finally, the North Ronaldsay primary school, along with headteacher Patricia Thompson, have been visiting the Orkney Mainland. They attended two Science Festival events and also, during a second trip from the island, visited Skara Brae and the Tomb of the Eagles. Swimming, music, PE and art were additional features of the children's educational visits to the Mainland.

Such excursions in the days of open boat trips to Sanday and once every two weeks sailing by steamer to Kirkwall would have been unthinkable in pre-Loganair days (1967).

Thoughts During the 'Heuld' of the Night
November 4, 1999

Here I am writing another letter from North Ronaldsay. It seems a long time since my last. But at least I have from time to time, given short reports on our island activities just to let readers know that we are still to the fore in Orkney's Ultima Thule.

Over the passing months, having decided for a time to cover local events separately, various ideas of what I might write about have come to mind – often when I might wake up on the 'heuld' of the night, or even round about the crack of dawn. Such thoughts seemed likely material at the time, but I've quite forgotten the swing o' them. I should have, as John Firth did, noted down the gist of my ramblings when they came to mind.

John Firth, since I've mentioned his name, wrote *Reminiscences of an Orkney Parish* (together with old Orkney words, riddles, proverbs). He was born in 1838 and died in 1920, aged eighty-two. His book is described as a fine piece of ethnological writing, dealing with life in rural Orkney as it was down to the middle of the 19th century.

Of considerable interest is his list of old words. Whenever such a word was heard or came to mind, he noted it down – even if, as he says, 'the temperature should be zero', he would 'extricate himself from the warmth and comfort of the blankets ... [and] put it down in black and white.'

The word 'heuld' which I use above – 'the heuld o' the night' – is described as midnight by Hugh Marwick (the distinguished Orcadian scholar). I always myself thought the word to mean much later at night, and mistakenly used it in that context.

Querying the usage locally, I had some support for my understanding of its meaning. Maybe it's one of those words, the exact meaning for which has changed somewhat. But on the other hand, I was reminded that the old folk were not in the habit of being up late (like I tend to be, and is maybe the case generally).

They rose early in the morning to take advantage of the short winter daylight, and were in bed early to conserve fuel, both for light and heat. I think too that 'heuld' somehow has a winter ring to it – whatever, it is a grand word in the North Ronaldsay dialect.

Further to those ideas, Walter Traill Dennison (1825–1894) whose important contribution to our knowledge of the old Orcadian way of life (traditional and historical) is a wonderful legacy, mentions the midnight horn as the 'heuld horn'. He says that in Saga times, when the guests had been in bed some time, the lady of the house (making a round of the bedrooms) offered the guests a warm spirituous liquor. This was called the heuld drink.

Dennison also refers to this custom in his account of Orkney weddings and wedding customs – although I find it difficult to believe that weddings were over by midnight. Maybe sometimes they all had a bit of a rest and then went at it again 'pell-mell'. Hugh Marwick, in his book *The Orkney Norn*, mentions other references (including Dennison's) to this very descriptive word.

Well, now you see I'm away on the track of old words – not, I hasten to add, that I am at all very knowledgeable, quite apart from having a memory, as Burns said, 'no worth a preen'. But this word *heuld* has taken possession of my mind for the moment and got me back to re-reading John Firth's book and getting to grips with Marwick's *Orkney Norn*.

Jakobsen's studies led him to conclude that the Shetland Norn was still a living language in the middle of the 18th century. In Orkney, by comparison, Marwick estimates that the Norn was spoken by only a few Orcadians during the early part of the same century – fading out it seems, not surprisingly, somewhat earlier than in the more remote Shetland Islands.

In Marwick's introduction to *The Orkney Norn*, where he quotes from various sources on the use of the Norn language during the 15th and 16th centuries and later, he says that songs are normally retained longer than any part of a language. In light of that statement and his estimation that the Norn language was no longer in common use early in the 18th century – in fact, he says that anyone who had the ability to speak the old language was described as an 'auld Norny body' – he goes on to mention that in North Ronaldsay our famous old Saga poem was still remembered in the native Norn as late as 1770. The poem was known on the island as 'The Magicians' or 'The Enchantresses'.

Marwick cites this as a remarkable instance of how much the old legends were respected and remembered, even seven and a half centuries after the event. The poem, which was sung in North Ronaldsay, is closely connected with the decisive and bloody battle of Clontarf (1014). It marked the end of Scandinavian supremacy in Ireland.

In fact, Walter Scott was responsible for recording this information. When he was briefly in Orkney during his 1814 voyage round Scotland's lighthouses at the invitation of the Lighthouse Commissioners, he heard that in North Ronaldsay a clergyman, when reading a version of the poem (based on a translation) by Thomas Gray, was told by some islanders that they had often sung the song in the Norn language to him personally.

Intending to find out more about this great battle, I thought there might be an account in the *Orkneyinga Saga* because in the fight Earl Sigurd was killed. In fact, there is only a minor reference to the event, but in the books and notes it mentions 'Njal's Saga' (Magnus Magnusson is a co-translator of this famous Icelandic saga), where there is a graphic account of the battle. The Icelandic translation of the poem, which is different from Thomas Gray's version, would of course be nearer the original as remembered in North Ronaldsay. Its English translation is contained in the saga. Marwick and Jakobsen both researched and recorded words which they knew to be of Norse origin. John Firth, on the other hand, noted down words which were both Norn and Scottish.

Another writer who has collected old words for some time is Gregor Lamb. As a basis for his *Orkney Wordbook* (revised 1995) he uses the Orkney Norn but adds all other words and phrases which cannot be found in a standard English Dictionary.

In North Ronaldsay, Peter A. Tulloch (1899–1985) in his book *A Window on North Ronaldsay* included a list of over 550 words or so, which he says were in regular use beyond the end of the last century. Many of them, like Gregor Lamb's collection, are of Scottish origin, but when I have more time it would certainly be worthwhile to try to isolate those of Norse origin.

Considering in this letter only the words listed by John Firth, Peter Tulloch and Hugh Marwick, but particularly Marwick's since they are of Norse origin, it's interesting to get some idea of how much has been lost over the 100 years or so that have passed since their collection. I will, in this limited experiment, have to use myself as an example of the third, going on fourth, generation's knowledge. When I have another chance, I would like to find out the range of other islanders' memories of Norn words – particularly the next generation and those older – or indeed those younger.

Taking John Firth's list of old words (I feel that there must have been more in his original notes), I find that I know about one-quarter of the 500 or so recorded, but many are, as I said, Scottish or of Scottish origin. Of Peter Tulloch's list, as one would expect, being a fellow islander, I am familiar with the majority. Nevertheless, there are about 150 or so that I do not know.

On the other hand, the *Orkney Norn* contains over 3000 words of Norse origin (Marwick notes the words he thinks are of Norse origin) and those are the ones I am particularly interested in. Going carefully through the dictionary word for word, I find that I know somewhere between 450 and 500, which indicates a considerable loss in over 100 years for someone of my generation.

My knowledge, by comparison, of Jakobsen's *Shetland Norn* is much less, though I have yet to read through the two volumes containing on average from ten to eleven thousand words. Interestingly there are, even with limited study, some which are similar to North Ronaldsay words. As just one example, the word *oot-rugg* which we use and which has no mention, or even a part explanation, in Marwick's *Norn*, does have a connection with Shetland.

The word *rugg*, as recorded by Jakobsen, has various meanings, one of which is a strong tide. In North Ronaldsay an *oot-rugg* means an undercurrent, or tide even, which is caused by the rebound of beach waves. A sheep, or a person for that matter, could be caught in the *oot-rugg* and dragged out to sea.

Jakobsen's statement regarding the Shetland Norn in which he refers to the loss of language, and with which Marwick agrees, is interesting. He says that 'many old words which have survived relate to the state of the weather, the wind, and the sea ... nouns betokening something visible – living objects or things without life – survived somewhat longer.' He mentions 'a special and very rich class – i.e. jocular or derisive terms or words expressing anger, ill humour, behaviour ... words for cattle and sheep colours, sheep marks.'

Words for example like the North Ronaldsay sheep marks, *hemlin*, and *stooed*, or the word *gimmero* – a two-year-old female (from the Norse word *gymbr*, ewe lamb*)*, or *moorit* (a reddish-brown colour) or again, *murled* (spotted face).

There are very many words describing the weather and the sea, a few of which are still in use locally, e.g. *flum* (passing shower), *hoolin* (very strong wind), *kruttle* (a ruffling on the surface of the water) or *a kruttle in the throat* (a slightly rattling sound), *rugg* (close drizzle) or the word *teebro* (flickering seen in the air especially over rising ground), *kukwacks* (stormy weather in May), *leaper* (sweltering heat) and *skethur* (passing shower).

Four other sea terms to mention, though there are a number used locally – *miracles* (phosphorescence seen best in the dark on raw fish, newly hauled creels or even sometimes on the surface of the water); *swaar* (frothy broken water inshore) – the derivation seems complicated (see *The Orkney Norn* and Jakobsen's explanation); *rost* (tide race – a contrary wind giving rise to dangerous steep overfalls); *bod* (a long run of sea) – a *westerly bod* and so on.

While on the subject of the sea there are only a few boat terms I can mention, *bilge-kod*, *buls-kod* (a strap or straps of wood fastened on the outside of the bilge of a boat for protection when hauling and possibly for some stability); *back* (seat in boat – *fore or aft back*); *tulfers* (floor boards); and *wiring* (strap of wood round inside of boat six inches or so below gunwhale).

Examples of descriptive words connected with people are numerous. Here are a few that I am familiar with: *munyo* (pith, strength); *ruize* (praise); *domaless* (stupid); *ravsy* (ill-dressed, careless, slovenly); *nuither* (to speak under one's breath); *ramist* (various: ill-at-ease, cross and peevish rash, hurried – I think, as in the Shetland usage – cross and peevish through want of sleep); *ill vedgid* (intending to do evil); *glafter* (loud silly laughter); *trowie* (weakly).

Then there are a mixture of words still in use which would come under a general heading: *fang* (a catch) – something of worth, North Ronaldsay; *fain* (like) *I would fain see something* or *I dunno fain the leuk o' the sky*; *talvers* (tatters*); wanfine* (destruction*); guppen* (amount one can hold in one's hands when forming a bowl shape); *feesked* (gone bad, mouldy); *ackaspire* (spotted with mouldiness); *feutries* (superstitious beliefs); *kruggle* (to crouch down); *urter* (pasture that is very bare); *veekalty* (out of order); *sanlo* (ringed plover); *chalder* (oystercatcher – we say *shellder*); *snysin* (coot); and *horse-gok* (snipe).

Many of those words will shortly be forgotten, simply because they relate to work or whatever no longer extensively practised or used nowadays. Farm work is a good illustration with the changes in animal management: *bar* (grain end of a sheaf); *shos* (awns or beard on head of a bere); *corn* (North Ronaldsay) *stiggle* (poor, thin crop of grain); *diss* (small stack); *koom* (dust of meal); *buil* (lying place for cattle); *bizzy* (place where a cow stands in a byre); and *whum* (temporary covering of sheaves on a stack – we might say to 'home' in the stack – maybe it was too late at night or rain was threatening).

The old words of Norse derivation are in the main no longer used except occasionally by older Orcadians; a few, I suppose by my generation (born 1940) and folk now in their seventies and eighties or older. They would naturally know many more but again, their use of old words would only be infrequent. *Smeeo*, from the old Norse for instance, is a word probably no longer often used, meaning a small hole in a dyke for shifting sheep. In North Ronaldsay moving native sheep from the sea side of the dyke inland – and the word *tuzzi-fae* (middling) – is not recorded in the Orkney Norse or Shetland Norse or, it seems, the Scottish dictionary.

The above selection of words is taken from Marwick's *The Orkney Norn* with his spelling and meanings. The particular local vowel sounds used – particularly, 'a' and 'u', I won't try to explain. I have chosen them not because they are particularly special, but to illustrate the aforementioned theory concerning the durability of certain words.

Well, now you see where this word *heuld* has led me. I hope its direction has been interesting. I've certainly found the research so. Firstly, re-reading John Firth's book, then *The Orkney Norn*, browsing through Gregor

Lamb's dictionary and Peter Tulloch's book, beginning to work my way into Jakobsen's two-volume study, and when I got to bed – on the *heuld* to be sure – reading some of W. T. Dennison's stories.

You would think that's enough to be going on with on a winter night, but let's not forget Walter Scott's *The Pirate*, with the author's interesting notes at the back of the book on Orkney and Shetland, and last but by no means least, the *Orkneyinga Saga* and *Njal's Saga*.

I was going to tell you about other things – especially the *hairst* work – little as it now is. It occurred to me often when we were working, of how lightsome those activities can be when the weather's fine and the shearing easy. And how in the early Sixties, I suppose, at least thirty crofts would have been involved with the work of the hairst. On moonlit nights, hundreds of friendly stacks would cast their mysterious shadows across stubbled fields. But all of this will have to wait until a later time – maybe when I write about the Harvest Home.

Thinking back to the theme of my letter – the dying out of our old words, and coupling that with disappearing traditional work on land and sea – I'm reminded of some words written by George Mackay Brown. They were quoted again recently in *Northern Lights – A Poet's Sources*, published by John Murray.

He writes: '... time is running out. The culture of the cities is everywhere taking root in Orkney ... instead of listening to the stories on winter nights, people read *The Sun*. The horses of Edwin Muir's poetry have all but vanished ... The ethos and outlook of the islanders have changed greatly since I was a child. People are more prosperous, but the community spirit has everywhere slackened, and the language becomes increasingly impoverished. But sea and islands and hills are still there, and I am thankful that I saw those everlasting things with a child's eye, and the vivid people who lived among them, and their ancient benign rituals ...'

I remember an expression not used much nowadays but often spoken by the old folk. It seems an appropriate way to finish this particular letter with its emphasis on Norn words. My grandmother's generation frequently made use of it when one was leaving after a visit. They would say *Guid be wi' thee* – meaning of course 'God be with you.'

Millennium Needs a Touch of Magic
December 30, 1999

I'm beginning this letter with a poem written by the eminent Orcadian poet Edwin Muir, 1887–1959. Its title is 'Merlin'. Merlin was a wizard who practised magic, as most folk know, and I'm thinking some magic is needed for the millennium.

> *O Merlin in your crystal cave*
> *Deep in the diamond of the day,*
> *Will there ever be a singer*
> *Whose music will smooth away*
> *The furrow drawn by Adam's finger*
> *Across the meadow and the wave?*
> *Or a runner who'll outrun*
> *Man's long shadow driving on*
> *Break through the gate of memory*
> *And hang the apple on the tree?*
> *Will your magic ever show*
> *The sleeping bride shut in her bower,*
> *The day wreathed in its mound of snow*
> *And Time locked in his tower?*

During a spell of fierce, cold and windy weather, 'the gods smiled favourably' and gave us a fine day for the North Ronaldsay Harvest Home. This always very grand occasion was held on Friday, November 19, with the Memorial Hall once again vibrating to the music of accordions, bagpipes, dancing feet, and eight very lightsome hours indeed.

I've often thought, especially nowadays, that the word 'Harvest Home' has a certain ring of magic to it. For myself and mainly my generation and those older of course, this celebration reminds one of a time when corn and oats were the king and queen of the harvest. A time when, during the last months of the year, the main work of the season was finally completed. Its returns provided for the farm animals during their long winter sojourn indoors. The thrashing of the sheaves gave seed for next year's harvest, and indeed, not so long ago, enough also to mill, ensuring that islanders had sufficient meal for baking until the following season. The corn grain, in addition, provided for the making of home-brewed ale, necessary for many occasions of neighbourly help and times of festivity.

During the hairst, binders travelled up and down the many fields of oats and corn; before that, reapers; and before the reapers were the scythes, when sometimes teams of men would work in lines cutting down acres of crop. Sheaves, stooks and stacks followed, with help being given whenever required. Then on one great night of the year islanders got together to celebrate the safe gathering in of the harvest's bounty. Today, the straw decorations with which we decorate the Old Hall are symbolic of that older, more communal and neighbourly system of fanning – now almost disappeared. But those decorations also represent, even in the late traditional Harvest Home month of November, the year's much earlier and almost exclusive returns of silage and hay.

Jim Wallace, Orkney's MP, MSP and Deputy First Minister of the Scottish Parliament, was the guest speaker at the North Ronaldsay Harvest Home, accompanied by his wife Rosina. Two other guests, reminding us of our sea connections and representing the shipping company were Orkney Ferries senior captain Kenny McKay and second captain, Kenny Nicolson. Both were accompanied by their wives, Julie and Molly respectively.

Our guest speaker, as one would expect, gave a very fine and immensely entertaining speech. He began by saying how happy both he and his wife were to be able to attend a North Ronaldsay Harvest Home, and after a few more opening remarks went on to tell a number of particularly amusing stories.

One which was especially entertaining concerned an election campaign of some years ago, when a certain Tory candidate visited the island to canvass for votes. On his way back to the Mainland via Sanday, when crossing the North Ronaldsay Firth, (those were the days when connections often had to be made by an open post-boat) he was explaining, with considerable satisfaction, to the island's two boatmen how, because of a very full attendance at his meeting, he felt quite confident that at least North Ronaldsay would be voting for him. He was told in a typical Orcadian way that the island had already voted by postal ballot the week before and that Jo Grimond was their man.

The speaker went on to talk about his position in the Scottish Parliament, and of how he had to be very alert to increased public scrutiny and criticism. He spoke about the importance of small communities and how it is often argued that such places cost so much to maintain. Yet many of the services mentioned and their costs, taken for granted by the public at large, are often non-existent in isolated areas.

Jim Wallace continued his speech, mentioning the harvest and other aspects of island life. He singled out in particular the success in the overall marketing of North Ronaldsay's native sheep with their wool and meat. Concluding his tribute to the harvest, with almost eighty folk rising to their feet and holding quite grand drams at the ready, Mr Wallace proposed the toast to the harvest.

Thereafter the night sped on, developing into one of our most successful Harvest Home dances. Substantial raffle items were on offer: Loganair's Captain Seyd (one of last year's guests) had very kindly donated whisky and gin, with Orkney Ferries' two captains each gifting whisky. Howie Firth, who had been unable to attend, sent his good wishes along with a further bottle of whisky. On swept the dance with everybody, including visitors and all our special guests, participating with lively enthusiasm, as did two very new islanders, Norman and Carole Bayley from Breckan. Between times a Scotch Reel was performed.

Tea and refreshments, with more native sheep mutton on offer, was arranged between Strip-the-Willows, Eva Three Steps, Palais Glides and what not. Two Eightsome Reels were danced with four sets to the second reel. A set of young dancers performed, if not elegantly, with the greatest gusto, verve and enjoyment. All the while the bagpipes blew very finely, to be followed swiftly by accordions, tip-tapping sticks and even more dancing.

By three in the morning it was time for 'Auld Lang Syne'. For me this song is one of parting, remembrance and of old times, and whenever it is sung I remember North Ronaldsay folk from all the toonships – Linklestoon, Abby, Easting, Nesstoon, Bustie, and Holland's Toon. Many now, like that last Harvest Home of this millennium, have passed into time and memory. To complete a very fine occasion, more mutton from the beaches of North Ronaldsay was served along with hot soup before finally folk left, stepping outside into the changing light of a peeping silvery moon.

In my last letter I referred briefly to the past harvest, thinking at the time that I might add something extra when next I wrote – and so I will!

As it transpired, this last 'hairst' turned out to be one of the easiest and best for some years, though, as I mentioned before, such work has almost become a thing of the past. But I will always believe the harvest time to be the lightsomest of all the year's farming seasons, leaving many unforgettable memories of those days of years ago – memories of windy, sunny days when fields of oats and corn would go rippling in moving waves up and down the length of the land. To the east and west, according to the time of day, dark blue seas would flash like silver as the autumn sun crossed the sky. And when the work of shearing began one would, unusually, see the land, sky and sea through turning binder wings; even sometimes spectacular sunsets and blue islands to the west would flicker through the binderman's changing machine-vision.

I'm thinking too about the rattle of binder blades as they flashed through stalks of grain and the click-clacking of the packers and needle as the sheaves came into being, to be thrown out and fall in long lines ready for stooking; of sheaves, stooks and stacks in good and bad weather; cups of tea, scones and cookies gladly taken out in the fields whenever there was a welcome break – or something stronger when helping hands might come along; of working sometimes in sharp pelts of cold rain and having to shelter in half-built stacks behind a hastily held protective sheaf; or of building stacks sometimes by the light of the moon.

Special too were the times when a helping hand was given. Those occasions were probably the most enjoyed, for nothing, I believe, can ever compare with communal work, good company and the will to work together.

Once long ago I remember, as an example of such times, helping to build stacks at another croft house. The wind was so strong that the first line of defence in such a situation was to lay some sheaves, bar (the grain end of the sheaf) outwards on the side of the stack facing the wind, thus presenting a streamlined face to the elements. On this occasion such evasive action was not enough, as sheaves flew like kites up and over the stack. Iron pinches or anything heavy or handy had to be placed on the windward side, as one worked ever upwards to the crown.

All of this had to be accomplished in the mirking of a hairst night. Other stacks were also being finished, with the last loads of sheaves coming in from the stubbled fields. Spare helpers in the yard got nets ready as stacks were completed. Imagine the relief of climbing down from the top after such a battle, and knowing that we had finished leading.

Finally, everyone would come together in the comfort of the kitchen (I'm thinking on this occasion of a particular house), where a coal fire crackled and burned redly. Amber coloured drams would be poured and served as the sun goes its round, with a toast to a good crop being made before eating began. Then later, under the light of the Tilley lamp and with suitable additional refreshments being served, the evening would unfold so very grandly. The swirling reek of pipe and cigarette would add to the atmosphere, with conversations taking place in complications of two or three going on at the same time. And as the night wore on, many were the memories to treasure of those old hairst days and nights, wherever one worked.

There, I've told you a little about our harvests of not so very long ago. Without the sort of help I have just described our reduced but presentable crop at Antabreck could never have been managed.

But now, briefly, back to today's affairs for a moment. Recently the island remembered the RNLI when the North Ronaldsay Lifeboat Guild once again arranged an evening of sales and raffles. The total spent by the island, which included the raffles, sale of local goods, donations and catalogue items (sold in aid of the Lifeboat Institution) amounted to a very splendid sum of £776.38. Tea, with a grand spread of homebakes and savouries, gave an enjoyable ending to a well-attended function.

In my last letter a few errors crept in, as they can often do. My father used to say that when building in stone it was always prudent after a spell of work, to take a few steps backwards and view one's handiwork from a distance. That way, he said, mistakes could be more easily seen, and therefore remedied, before it was too late. The same, I think, applies to anything worthwhile, whether it be writing or building a dyke.

By the way, also in my last letter, the word *smeeo* (wrongly spelled, as it happened) was not a word, it seems, much used in North Ronaldsay. Apparently it was a Rousay one brought here by a family from that island who worked the farm of Holland for a time. I knew the word from my father, who, I'm just remembering, left a list of old words in his desk that I must look at one of these days. However, a number of such small closeable holes (*smeeos*) exist round the island for the movement of animals in and out of the surrounding sheep dyke, and there must therefore have been a North Ronaldsay word for such an important convenience.

In fact I received little praise for my last letter on the subject. The idea was simply intended to draw attention to the two great scholars of the Norn language in Orkney and Shetland, and to show roughly what has happened to the use and memory of old Norn words over a period of about 100 years.

A fisherman from Westray, with an interest and knowledge of old words, phoned me up one night mentioning a few, and I have yet to think about their possible origins. (Ask the Library for a copy of Hugh Marwick's

Orkney Norn and Jakobson's Shetland dictionary of Norn words, I say to my Westray communicant.)

One of the Westray words I knew well, though funnily enough, when trying to recall the word for my few examples of boat terminology given in my last letter, I stupidly could not think what it was. It is the word used to describe the wooden oar-stops which fit into the gunwale of a boat, thus allowing oars to be worked. *Touals/Toualls*, if that is anything like the spelling, is the name of those hard wood oar stops. Interestingly, it does not, I think, appear in either of the books mentioned above.

But I had better stop all of this right now or I'll be writing another letter on the subject. Well, here we are as I write (Saturday, December 4), speeding over the last days of this millennium at an alarming rate and wondering where time goes – there is no doubt that time seems to travel faster as we grow older. The year 2000 seems an *unkan* way to describe a year. It has a ring of the future, science fiction and the unknown about it. It is a word that stops the mind for a moment and then gets the imagination going.

And in that respect, we are planning great things for the millennium celebrations: dance practices, carol singing (as of old), looking at hundreds of slides depicting North Ronaldsay at times past and times present, and compilations of video footage shot over the years (images of North Ronaldsay folk working, and at leisure – some are still here, and others have gone). On Hogmanay a bonfire and fireworks display to frighten away all the bad spirits and undesirable thoughts of 1999 – traditional, mind you, for at Yule the old bonfires used to be lit. All of this before dancing away the last hours of the year in the New Community Centre, and to crown it all – yes, on New Year's Day – round the Standing Stone many will go. Then on to the Memorial Hall for whatever transpires – mulled punch and hot soup to begin with, and then maybe a few swirls round the old silvered dancing floor. Who knows, many folk are specially here for this once in a millennium occasion and anything might happen. I mentioned imagination a little back – that's what all of this is about.

Edwin Muir, a very great Orcadian, about whom I've been reading lately, believed in 'the absolute necessity of imagination in all forms of human communications', as I'm sure also did George Mackay Brown. Both men towards the end of their lives wrote about the memory of their parents. George writes a very beautiful and moving essay about his mother in particular. Edwin Muir also mentions his mother at length. He says, 'perhaps I shall meet her again ... I do not know how to conceive immortality, though I still believe in it. If I meet her in another world, I know – and that is the infinite comfort – that I shall see her as she is, at last, the Imperfections of mortality past ...' I myself cannot imagine immortality. It seems that it surely should be, for I do not think that the power and complexity of the human mind can only exist for however long a lifetime might be, and then disappear forever.

George Mackay Brown ends his essay about his mother quite beautifully. He says: 'I have a deep-rooted belief that what has once existed can never die, not even the frailest things, spindrift or clover scent or glitter of star on a wet stone. All is gathered into the web of creation, that is apparently established and yet perhaps only a dream in the eternal mind; and yet, too, we work at the making of it with every word and thought and action of our lives.'

Well, those wonderful words of GMB bring me almost to the end of another letter, and the last I shall be writing in this millennium.

During the past few days King Winter has begun to frown menacingly from the north and cold has been the wind with morning ice and scatterings of hail. Across windy skies great purple and grey clouds fly, with sometimes brilliantly white snowy clouds lighting up the island from unexpected airts, and huge misty sheets of sleet or hail go sweeping past, far out to sea. Even the lapwings (or teewups) call sadly, wap-wapping up and away in the mirking, or unseen in the night – mostly when they are suddenly disturbed. They always look particularly smart in their iridescent green and black and white plumage, wearing a little tuft of head feathers – like a fine hat – just to set off their appearance. But their plover cry is a lonely one I always think. In the spring though, when the daylight lengthens and summer seems just around the corner, I'm much happier with their call. But let me finish as I began with some more words taken from a poem by Edwin Muir:

> *We have such hours, but are drawn back again*
> *By faces of goodness, faithful masks of sorrow,*
> *Honesty, kindness, courage, fidelity,*
> *The love that lasts a life's time. And the fields,*
> *Homestead and stall and barn, springtime and autumn.*
> *(For we can love even the wandering seasons*
> *In their inhuman circuit.) And the dead*
> *Who lodge in us so strangely, unremembered,*

Yet in their place. For how can we reject
The long last look on the ever-dying face
Turned backward from the other side of time?
And how offend the dead and shame the living
By these despairs? And how refrain from love?
This is a difficult country, and our home.

Appendix: Days at Sea

Days at Sea: Memories of Traditional Lobster Fishing

August 24, 2000

Away back in the Sixties I remember one day in particular. It would have probably been after the 'ku-whacks' – stormy weather that usually comes sometime in May, after which the lobster fishermen thought it relatively safe to begin working their creels on the north side of North Ronaldsay. Anyway, it was one of those warm, sunny days early in June. The wind was from an easterly direction, and it carried a particularly distinctive smell across the island.

At the time, I happened to be at the south yard crossroads known as the Harriet slap (gate). I wonder who Harriet was? I seem to have a shadow in my mind of having been told once. On that morning the word had gone around that the creel boats were out. I think that in the Sixties there would have been seven boats in total working – three on the north side and four on the south side, which included the 'Wast Banks' to the west.

When I stopped at the crossroads to 'discoorse' to Willie o' Scotsha – he happened to be coming up the Nesstoon road at the time – we touched on various topics and the fact that the fishing boats were out. I remember mentioning the unusual smell that was in the air which somehow, on that day, I associated with the creel boats. Unthinkingly, I imagined that the smell was connected with the creel bait, and that it was being carried on the wind from the direction that the boats were setting part of their drifts. Willie, smiling a little, explained that the smell was that of wasting 'brook' – decaying seaweed. Well, of course I knew about brook and the various 'tangs' it can have – but on that particular day! In any case, the time is so clearly fixed in my mind with that combination of the senses one sometimes gets. The smell of the sea and the banks; the memory of a fresh, bright day, with the wind blowing from the east; the 'crack' with Willie, sitting on his tractor with his pipe; and especially the thought of this wonderful world, I imagined, the creel-men entered once they put out to sea.

You may remember the fairy story that mentions the little folk who were sometimes heard tap, tapping away underground, mending fairy shoes or whatever. Well, the connection I'm about to make I suppose you might think to be somewhat fanciful. Never mind, I enjoy those thoughts, and in any case I always felt that there was something magical in the life of the lobster fishermen. In the old days many boats were working, and the island was alive with folk. The north-yard boats oaring their way out from the Hole o' Brue, Peul, possibly Garso Banks, Hell Banks and Sae Geo, the pier at Bewan, Geo o' Rue and the Noust at Sandbank; with the south-yard boats setting out from the Galt and Hooking, Bridesness, the Noust at Howar, Scarfie Geo, and sometimes boats would also work out of Dew Geo – a wide geo situated at the risky west banks and used only in very settled weather. In fact, one older retired fisherman told me creels set there in the old days were usually brought back to safer ground before night.

But there you see I'm away again – never mind. I was going to say that during the long winter nights, if one happened to pass by the crofts of the creel-men, you would hear tapping and hammering as creels were being made or mended – just like in the fairy story, I like to think. Lights from Tilley lamps, gas or oil lamps, or later (in the Sixties) from Startomatics, would shine in the night from the little windows of sheds or smithies where the creel-men were working. Sometimes a passing visitor or two might step in by for a visit, to talk about the day's events, or whatever, and very possibly also enjoy a bottle of beer.

One of those 'wark-hooses', if you will, that I remember in the Sixties (it belonged to Willie Muir, with whom I was to spend a few years as his fishing partner), was like a veritable little Aladdin's cave. It was divided in two by a wooden partition, with one part of the building being darkish, but all the more intriguing, the other part in daylight, when lit by a window just above a lengthy workbench. Along the walls in both areas were ranked rows of creels stacked one top of the other. Some were big, some were small, with most being two-holed creels – that is, a creel having two entrances for the lobster to explore, one on each side of the creel, advisable when a rock face might block an entrance hole.

A few others only had the one entrance and were usually smaller. Among those creels would be special ones, creels that were famous in their way, great fishing creels, maybe a few years old but nevertheless still taking a trick. Then neatly stacked beneath the work bench, or where convenient, would be the creel ropes, some about seven fathoms long (a fathom is six feet), some twelve and others twenty or more for use in deeper waters. Hanging up on the walls or from the couples would be thin coir, heavily corked – seven-fathom light ropes (coir ropes were made from coconut fibre) designed to give additional flotation in deeper water and strong tides, and they could be added when required to the twenty-fathom ropes. The much shorter creel ropes in the early days, when the deeper and more tidal water of later years was not fished, were made from coir but of a heavier gauge.

This rope, although it had a floating nature, was not very resilient when the sea got up. When such adverse weather did come unexpectedly creels were driven ashore, or worse, against the rock faces (particularly on the more rugged north side) where the ropes and thin coir-twine creel covers were easily cut over or badly damaged.

Later, stronger ropes called sisal and manila replaced the coir. These were made from two plants: the agave plant and the abaca plant, whose fibre was used for rope making. Both types of rope were initially factory treated with a tar mixture, then locally each year used to be soaked in creosote in the Voar-time (springtime) for preservation purposes, and sometimes a little heated tar might be mixed in with the creosote, adding probably to their strength and lasting properties. For a couple of weeks or so, those tarry/creosoted ropes used to line the dyke-tops round the crofts of the creel-men, so as to dry out in the wind and sun. For a few days at sea those ropes were not very clean to work with, and rubber gloves were used for a time. The sisal/manila was in turn superseded by synthetic ropes – a particularly durable material standing up to surprising wear and tuction, the most commonly used being an orange-coloured rope. Though there were other colours, orange was considered the best. I think of various names – polypropylene, nylon, spunstron. There were different makes and different colours, but I think it was generally agreed that the orange polypropylene proved to be the superior rope mostly used.

All the ropes were corked every two feet or so, measured from the hand to the oxter, initially using the old net corks which had to be cut and shaped from lengths of cork available from the local shop. The special shaping gave a more streamlined end to better face the tides, with less drag. This natural material made from the bark of the cork tree would become progressively waterlogged at sea. Eventually, the ropes and creels would be brought ashore through the fishing season for drying out and to kill off the various types of seaweed that grew on the rope itself.

Another reason for taking the creels ashore for a time – especially the old coir-covered creels and coir ropes which were very prone to marine growth – was to have the creels fresh and ready for the next round of fishing. This spell ashore, generally common practice in the early days and up to the mid-Fifties or so, allowed folk to manage their hay and any other necessary land jobs and to bypass the period later in the summer when numbers of lobsters were casting their shells. But by this time – late Fifties and early Sixties – deeper water was being explored with the longer, more durable ropes. In addition, the creels were larger and covered with a stronger twine (treated with a green solution whose trade name escapes me), to be followed by the very durable courlene twine (another synthetic material), and this practice of taking creels ashore was more or less abandoned.

However, the ropes were still changed when necessary, being replaced at sea with fresh ones. Incidentally, a single creel rope was divided into three thicknesses: heavy below where the most wear occurred (three to four fathom), less heavy for the main part (maybe ten to twelve fathom) and then lighter for the top six or seven fathoms. Around the Sixties, thousands of synthetic corks started to come ashore in North Ronaldsay and elsewhere. They were known as Russian corks and were quickly utilised, replacing the older cork type. Those new replacements hardly ever absorbed water and were particularly good at helping the already more buoyant couralene ropes to float and to rise much faster out of the tide. Then there were the all-important buoy heads made up of seven or more corks which, with their different colouring for each boat – red and white, yellow and red, blue and white, black and yellow, and so on – distinguished ownership and also gave additional buoyancy to the creel ropes.

But I see I'm away again into all sorts of detail. Let's get back to the 'wark-hoose' with all its treasures that I was meaning to tell you about. There were oilskins, a ship's bell, sou'westers, stack nets, pitchforks, seaboots, relics from beachcombing – old ship block tackles, samples of dyewood from the wreck of an East Indiaman (the *Svecia*, 1740) – and a hundred and one other bits and pieces to capture one's curiosity.

And hidden away in dark corners were creels which had been the brief watery prisons for many bold and colourful lobsters, and which had been set in all sorts of promising inshore 'slunks', 'trinks' and 'leys' (narrow clefts or crevices) and at many a deep rock face; creel wood of various shapes and sizes – durable pieces for bottoms; particularly strong wood for the three cross-pins which formed a sort of cage over which the web was stretched; extra protection pins for the web which stretched over the cross-pins; then wire rings for the entrance 'hole-traps' of about five and a half inch diameter on which swung 'snitters' – two fixed wire legs designed to pivot on the entrance ring which only opened inwards, so that when the lobster entered the creel there was, in theory, no way out. Collections of heavy beach stones used as weights – necessary for holding position in the strong tides – to be fitted and fixed by heavy galvanised grid on to the bottom of the creel; heavy gauge galvanised rod for the three half-circle bows, on which were tied the three pins mentioned above; webs knitted by hand from couralene in black, white or orange colours ready to cover old or new creels (diamond size loops of about two inches by one and a half); needles (old wooden ones or made of plastic) for weaving the web; awls, drills, pliers, hammers, saws, nails, staples and nippers – all used for the making of a creel. Such items and more were required to make a good, durable, strong creel, which had to withstand the rigours of stormy seas.

Our creels varied in size, with the largest wooden ones measuring about eighteen inches wide by two feet long, and with their 'sinking-stone' they (the creels) weighed some forty or more pounds – around twenty-five kilos. They were slung from the centre. To haul creels slung from the middle top bow was hard work when sometimes lifting the creel from deep water – from around twelve to maybe fifteen fathom. It was thought that the centre-slung creel stood up to adverse weather by better holding its ground, but also creels were slung from the creel-end which made the hauling by hand much easier, as the creel tended to glide up through the water. The three galvanised rod half-circle hoops (one quarter inch or heavier diameter) – one at either end and one in the middle – were about fourteen inches high. Another advantage of the end-slung creels was that it made it easier and safer to pull a creel to safety when its long rope could be caught. Often with a heavy land sea an inside creel had to be brought to safety. I might say that the ropes mentioned above with the three different sizes were around five-eighths diameter for the heavy lower rope (more exposed to rock faces), with the main rope about three-eighths diameter. The light top rope would have been two-eighths of an inch diameter. All three ropes, I think, would have been just that bit greater in diameter.

But back to the 'Aladdin's cave'. In another corner were two slim-looking Seagull outboard engines with small, fitted petrol fuel tanks, which had replaced the earlier power of oars and sail. They looked to me impressive at the time in their silvery finish with their business-like propellers. Finally, through a peedie window above the work bench marked with a thousand and more cuts and scratches – the result of at least two generations of creel-men's work, sawing wood, cutting ropes and twine, shaping corks and so on – one could see the sea through the day and at night. Maybe a faraway ship's lights would flicker and twinkle as she carried sea-going men of a different calling to unknown and distant destinations.

A year or two later I was fortunate enough to enter the world of the 'lobster fishermen'. In those days there seemed to be time for 'every purpose under heaven' – or at least folk of my age (twenty-four) and younger thought so, and probably they will always do. I remember very clearly the day the bargain was struck for my involvement. It was in the Voar-time and my father and I were sowing a piece of ground at the 'back o' the yard' – quite early in

March it was that year. We stopped for a bit so as to discuss the proposal in hand. Here was a chance to enter, as I thought, this wonderful world of the sea – not only in the activity of creel work, but to actually be working on the very element I had, as an artist, painted so often. Only now I would be in the fascinating position of being able to watch, study and enjoy the many moods and changing colours and understand something of its power. The bargain was struck with the caveat that I would, as well as being the 'bait man', be able to handle the boat. In an emergency, we both agreed, it was essential that each boatman could take over and control and work the boat in all conditions. My fishing partner and I, during our five-year or so partnership, worked day about – one day as 'bait man' and one day as steersman.

Of all the work connected with making a creel, I suppose the weaving of the hole (entrance channel or funnel) is probably the most important. This hole has to be the right size, give the proper angle for the backward sloping ring – facing slightly away from the centrally placed 'maet-band' (a narrow double twine band in which the bait was fixed with a slipping toggle) – and be the correct distance into the creel itself. It also requires a comfortable flattish and attractive entrance path for its very cautious customer – the lobster.

And so, to another memory connection. Often, whenever I happen to be in our front shed when the wind is in the east, I'm reminded of my first all-important lesson given in hole weaving, when a reasonable number of my new creels were ready for this process. This piece of work for a novice as I was required careful instruction and some practice. A badly knitted hole meant a poor fishing creel. In fact, the evening was a sort of special occasion, and I can still feel something of the interest and anticipation of that night. But to get back to the memory connection, the reason for this recollection is firstly not a particularly romantic one, since it depends on the smell of the 'iper' (sewage drain from a byre), which was noticeable in these days when the east wind, as it was that night, coincided with the shed and our old front byre outside drain-away channel. Another reason for remembering that occasion was a sad one, as the four of us in the shed that night (Willie o' Waterhouse, John o' Purtabreck, my late father and myself) learned that an islander, Stewart Swanney, only forty-nine years old, had died. At one time he had been the local baker, and indeed a very good one, before becoming more involved with lobster fishing and farming. In fact, four of the island's inhabitants were to die in that year of 1964: Stewart Swanney, Kirbist; Mary Tulloch, Breckan; William Scott, Cavan; and William Muir, Waterhouse.

When my token drift of creels and ropes were ready, the next stage was to carry out any necessary repair work on the fishing boat before tarring and painting. This was usually done in April or May, once all the spring work had been completed, and was always a lightsome occupation with the thought of a new season about to begin. But for me on this occasion the first season, and a step, as they say, into 'uncharted waters'.

Let's think though for a moment about the boats that were used mainly between the wars and after. The type of creel boat that came to be used fairly extensively, though not exclusively, was the North Ronaldsay praam. Early praams were small (round about twelve feet or so long) with little spring (bow uplift), and not suited, or indeed used, for open-sea work, though they were used for inshore and fine-weather fishing.

More seaworthy of course, and widely used in the early days, were the old skiffs and yoles. Most of them, with their sharp stem and deep keels, were more difficult to handle on the land and had the disadvantage of not being so well-suited for outboard motors; nor could they, with their deeper keels, manoeuvre as easily among creel ropes. They could however sail and pull by oar much better than the larger and flatter-bottomed praams that came to be built, even with their pre-engine-days deeper keels, necessary for sailing, which was managed when a suitable opportunity arose. But those more able praams (built after World War I) were ideal for lobster fishing. They were much larger with a relatively high stem and less depth of keel than the skiffs and yoles, with less again once outboard engines came into use after World War II.

All those changes in design made them very suitable for easy beach landing, hauling and launching. They could turn easily, virtually on their axis, and were therefore particularly manoeuvrable when setting and hauling creels in congested areas – either when working by oar or engine. All those attributes combined also made the boat quickly answerable in the event of having to meet tide-lumps and suchlike. The design of boat was first conceived by Hughie Muir, Sholtisquoy, early in the 1920s. He had seen the larger and more graceful Norwegian praams on board a passing ship from that country. After apparently taking a few measurements on the ship, Hughie then embarked on the building of a boat suitable for North Ronaldsay's special needs.

A number were built beginning in the 1920s, initially with Hughie's collaboration with the local joiner, Willie Cutt, Milldam. One or two were built by others with varying success. Then a little later, I imagine, seeing how the praams behaved, Hughie set about building his own boat – with help no doubt from Willie – in which he finally brought together all the important features he'd studied, resulting in the most successful of all the praams. This boat, known as the Sholtisquoy praam, *Ruth* (length 15 ft 9.5 in, beam 5 ft 10 in, transom 2 ft 11 in wide), is still looked after by her owner, but no longer lobster fishing. Today, three relatively new boats based on the Sholtisquoy design have been built but two of them are much bigger, with an overall length of 20 ft, beam 6ft 7in, transom 3 ft 6.5 in wide. They have the advantage of more carrying capacity, more working room and are more able or seaworthy with their greater freeboard, beam, height of stem and powerful 25 hp engines. On the other hand, they depend almost entirely on their engine power, are heavier to manhandle on land (though in time, methods of hauling and moving on land were resolved with tractor power) and cannot be as well propelled by oar – whereas the standard models were fairly reasonably managed on the land and by oar. The third one mentioned above is near enough the size of the first boats (14/15 ft). All three were built in the early 1980s by the Shapinsay boatbuilder Ivan Hourston, with the first praam, the *Mary Jane*, built in 1980.

Incidentally, after World War II there was a boat (*Viola*) built in Shetland in the Fifties for a North Ronaldsay fisherman – Jimmie Deyell, whose father was a Shetlander – and brought over for lobster fishing. The boat measured 18 ft overall, beam 7 ft with a transom stem of just over 4 ft wide. She was fitted out with a second, more powerful inboard engine in the mid-Sixties, which superseded the outboard (the Seagull engine) used initially. Her first inboard engine was a Britt, with the second a Lister. Despite being an able boat with her fine Shetland/Norwegian stem and being able to hold more creels when wanted with more working space, there was always the problem of handling such a boat on land, with no safe harbour or anchorage.

But back to 1964. Before the creel fishing began in earnest, a night at the cuithes was considered advisable for me so that I might begin to get my sea-legs. I seem to think that in addition a few creels were worked on the more settled and safer east side for practice. In any case, the great day arrived early in June when our drift of creels was to be set on the north side. Well, it was down to reality that day for sure. This formidable piece of water was beginning to show just a feeling of the 'colours' (as Willie Muir, boat-owner and my sea involvement teacher, described the north side sea) it can unfurl when the wind is in the north. When we came up to the 'mooth o' the soond', a passage between Seal Skerry and the land, the heave and distinctive motion of this exposed area took its effect – in short, I was sick! No time then to think about the magic of the creels, nor time to waste being unwell – no, it was nose down to work among the less than romantic smell of oily bait and continue with the job in hand. Unwind rope, lift creel, set, unwind rope, lift creel, set, on and on, creel by creel, and then back to land for another load or two. I'm glad to say that this first real initiation cured me once and for all from any ordinary sea-sickness – an affliction with which I was well acquainted on the many sometimes rough, uncomfortable boat trips we made to and from Sanday in the undecked 'post boat', which carried the Royal Mail, and to Kirkwall or North Ronaldsay by 'steamer' (cargo/passenger boat fuelled by coal) – well before the days of Loganair.

Fishing boat *Jessie Jim*, in Dog Geo.
L to R: William Cutt, Gerbo, and William Tulloch, Cruesbreck, early 1930s.

L to R: Willie Muir, Waterhouse, Ian Scott, Antabreck, packing lobsters for shipping, early 1960s.

Three NR praams hauled up at Sae Geo, 1960s. Photo Ian Scott.

NR praam, Ruth, at Sae Geo, 1960s. Photo by Ian Scott.

NR praam, Ruth, hauled up on Sae Geo Ayre, 1960s. Photo by Ian Scott.

Viola fishing north side in the 1960s. L to R Jimmie Deyell, Lochend, and John Tulloch, Purtabreck. Photo Ian Scott.

Viola fishing north side. L to R Jimmie Deyell, Lochend, and John Tulloch, Purtabreck, early 1960s. Photo Ian Scott.

L to R: Ian Scott, Antabreck, and John Tulloch, Purtabreck, 1980s.
Photo by Thomas Tulloch, North Ness

The creel boat *Mary Jane* built 1980 by Ivan Hourston, Shapinsay.

L to R: Graeme Scott, Cruesbreck, and Ian Deyell, Vincoin, c 2000. Photo Helga Scott

Days at Sea: Memories of Traditional Lobster Fishing
August 31, 2000

And so at last those memorable days began, working firstly from Hell Banks on the north side, from what in effect was a long, wide, flat and gradually sloping rock, which forms the side of a narrow geo – not at all a very safe landing place when there was any land sea running.

For a time in the Sixties, three boats on the north side worked from Hell Banks – a somewhat restricted area – before all eventually moved to Sae Geo near the Old Beacon. Those boats' – all prams – names and crews were: the *Pearl*, Jimmie Deyell, Lochend, and John Tulloch, Purtabreck; the *Iris*, Willie Thomson, Neven, and Peter Thomson, Neven; the *Ruth*, Willie Muir, Waterhouse, and me, Antabreck.

The new base to which we moved had a number of advantages, not least being the fact that it was safer, and the boats could access the main fishing ground on the north side faster, without having to pass through the 'soond' – a somewhat shallow, narrow passage (affected when there is sea on) between the shore and Seal Skerry. This passage connects the north side proper with the fishing grounds to the west of Seal Skerry, Garso Wick and Lens Wick.

During the days when the Seagull outboard engine was in use – particularly the models with which I was familiar in the early Sixties – more oar-work was generally required, particularly when hauling creels inshore with ebb tide. The reason for this was the design of the propeller which tended to catch the exposed or semi-submerged blades of seaweed. Interestingly, I believe this was not a problem with the first Seagulls that became available just after the Second World War (in fact I think that they were wartime surplus), as they had more rounded-edge propellers. Then the new, slightly more powerful Seagull engines (Silver Century I think was the name) that became available were not so successful when working among seaweed. In fact, they were also problematic engine-wise and only were in use for a short time. They in turn were superseded by new makes of engines – six to twelve hp Johnsons and Yamahas (and finally twenty-five hp Yamahas for the twenty ft new praams). Those engines were fitted with 'weed-less' propellers (more rounded blades) which mostly got over the difficulty of seaweed entanglement.

When the boats were engaged working inshore among exposed and semi-submerged seaweeds in the earlier days, often the engine was not in use. Then there would only be the sound of the sea, the hungry cries of herring gulls and blackbacks waiting for discarded creel-bait, with the clunk, clunk, clunk and splash of the oars. Also, on still days without the noise of the outboard engines, one could hear the voices of the creel-men carrying lightsomely across the water – even at considerable distances. And in the days of the less efficient rising ropes and less powerful engines, many were the delays waiting for ropes to rise out of the tide. This was a particular problem in the fierce tidal areas round Seal Skerry, where the ropes were totally submerged by flood and ebb. At such times, with the prospect of long waits for the tide to slacken, we frequently landed on the skerry to take a 'piece' (a cookie or whatever) with milk, or tea from a thermos flask.

I used to enjoy the little visits to the skerry where, during this adventure, one could have a look at the numerous scarfs' nests that were a feature of the area, keep an eye open for a bit of unusual drift and watch the many seals that give the skerry its name. As one approached the landing through a deep known as the Boat Geo – so called, since at a certain stage of tide a boat could pass through to the other side of the skerry and into Garso Wick – it was often possible to see the seals close at hand and also, spectacularly, under water as they shot like green, luminous torpedoes out to sea.

Then all through the early fishing days, when working in the famous Sholtisquoy praam, and later in one of the new and very able twenty ft boats, there were always the great sights of the sea and sky that all boatmen witness. The power and danger of the sea was evident on many a day, and at times those dangers were frighteningly near. Indeed, so close were they that when they passed by one was very aware of the few inches of freeboard between ourselves and the ocean, and it was a number of seconds before one's senses and body regained full composure. I'm thinking about the many occasions when we would have to negotiate the rearing lumps of water experienced in the subsidiary tides, such as easter tide, waster tide, north or south tide. When the wind was strong in the face of those tides – and with stream tides in particular – they could become extremely formidable and dangerous, breaking all over the place.

Yet there was a certain degree of enjoyment in managing the hills and dales of those angry tides, and balancing in a boat that danced and jumped across the tideways. On the other hand, negotiating a passage through the main, and extremely powerful, tides of ebb and flood with the wind in our faces as we swept past the main points with increasing speed, was an awe-inspiring experience only to be understood by having been there. And there are a number of times that remain very clear in my mind connected with such confrontation or when sudden 'hoolans' (a very strong gale) came out of the blue or when confronted by threatening waves.

Three especially unforgettable instances are fixed in my memory when we came face to face with imminent danger. One was on the east side of the island during the back-end fishing – September, October time – when sudden, extremely strong 'whinners' (blasts) of wind can come out of the blue, and usually it would be an offshore wind. On that occasion it was the older boat (the Sholtisquoy praam, *Ruth*) with my turn on the engine, powered by the 4.5 hp Seagull, coming in from the North Riff (Reef Dyke), a submerged reef over a mile long, extending southwards and well over half a mile to fully a mile's distance offshore – depending on how far away one might be from the nearest point of land in relation to where the boat might be fishing along the length of the reef. Not very far, you might think, but in an open boat facing gale force winds with the daylight beginning to fail, the distance has a very different aspect altogether.

Those less sophisticated engines were prone to taking water into the carburettor in adverse conditions and stopping, and this is what happened. So powerful was the wind that it was almost impossible to bring the oars back for a stroke in order to keep the boat's head up to the wind – let alone even thinking about flying to lee. On that occasion Willie was struggling to maintain the boat head on to the gale force wind. Fortunately, after a few frantic pulls on the starting cord the engine started, and we continued to edge our way very carefully inshore.

The other two times involved the same boat with the sight of huge, powerful-looking waves approaching, rising menacingly, black and turning green, as they powered towards us. There was no time or seaway for any escape; we could only watch with a sinking feeling the frightening sight, and hold the boat's head to the oncoming sea. Again, fortunately on both occasions with Willie, as I remember, at the engine, the first time inside Seal Skerry, and the other near the Reef Dyke, the great waves went hissing past, exploding thunderously beyond the boat.

Decisions to be taken in such situations (if one had the time) came under the heading of a calculated risk, and were mostly always agreed in advance by the two-man crew, as indeed was the more considered decision to 'snatch' creels from dangerous inshore positions when the sea was up.

But let's proceed some further with this account. How, for instance, does one know where a hundred or more hand-hauled creels exactly are, once they are out at sea? They would be set in twos and threes, sixes and eights or more, in line or singly, and in all sorts of areas – inshore, middle and outer ground. Well, the answer is that their positions have to be committed, as well as possible, to memory with every passing day's change of sets. This is achieved by memorising marks taken on the land which pinpointed at least the first creel, and if possible, the last in the line. For example, the middle lum (chimney) of a croft in the distance directly in line with some other distinguishing feature at a close point on the land, or the lums of two crofts in line; lighthouses together (the Old and New Lighthouses); the foghorn on the Quoy of Bewan; or two crofts a 'cartslap' apart, and so on.

There was also, of course, the cross mark to remember – recording the distance out from the land. In the more confined and restricted north side (because of the excessive depth of water for single creels relatively near the land, and the strength of tide), those combinations of marks in every detail were not absolutely necessary. But on the shallower, more extensive east side, with its greater distances in all directions, it was imperative that as many as possible of the outside marks were remembered. To forget them, especially if it was only three or four creels set on their own away out in the bay, was very frustrating indeed and caused considerable delay.

And then, what about mist? Again, a similar system of memory ability was required, but this time one would draw on the recollection of exactly how the creel looked – what were the distinguishing features, which one belonged to whom and in what sequence? All this knowledge was of course very useful when the creels became scattered as in a 'turl' (a spell of rough weather), or when they drove ashore. I'm sorry to say that my ability in this respect was extremely poor, for apart from my memory being, as Burns says in one of his poems, 'no worth a preen' – especially for this sort of detail – it would often fly away on other things, like the birds that followed us from day to day.

As time went on with our new twenty-foot praam, more creels were worked with more pinpointing marks to remember. And so, with my very inadequate memory getting progressively worse, I concentrated on dealing with the creel-working aspect of the fishing, but I missed the satisfying handling of the boat and the joy of sailing along and picking a way through the ever-changing seaways with the salt spray flying. My consolation was that I knew I could still take over if required or in an emergency. But the system of each to his job gave the steersman a much better ability to watch and memorise the marks of creels set – maybe lines of six, eight, ten, more or less, here, there and everywhere – thus arguably making for a more efficient fishing. This was, after all, the main purpose of our enterprise – far more important at the end of the day than my more romantic ideas and maybe my preoccupation with the wonderful sights of sea and sky that related to a different calling.

However, apart from creel-marks, there were vitally important marks that had to be committed to memory. Those were the safety marks required to avoid underwater reefs or rocks, making a safe passage round dangerous points or negotiating short cuts and main seaways. One also had to remember the alterations to many of those marks to compensate for land sea which extended the danger areas, not only for the above passages but also, for example, when hauling inshore creels when there was a land sea running (heavy inshore breakers).

I should mention one other frightening episode when working, this time, in the *Mary Jane*. We were coming round Kirk Taing and Dennis Taing, having completed our creel work on the north side, and were on our homeward journey. The wind was in the north and strengthening more and faster than we anticipated. It was blowing in the face of the ebb tide which was 'making up' running north and getting more powerful by the minute. Even with our 25 hp engine our progress seemed slow, and as the ebb increased in strength so the sea began to become quite dangerous with over-falls breaking in great, high upheavals of water here and there. Any particularly dangerous-looking wavetops we had to momentarily turn and face, as one break would have been a barrel or more of water which would have half-filled the boat. With each safety manoeuvre we made, the boat of course lost headway going backwards with the tide. This frightening passage took quite a long time as the ebb tide increased in velocity, with the lumps of water breaking ever more frequently and becoming higher and higher. After what seemed a very long, somewhat frightening battle – prolonged by evasive action, first losing ground with the tide, then back again against the tide in our effort to get clear of the ebb – we finally got out of a situation that, for me at least, took some time to overcome, with a certain weakness at the knees and time to regain my composure. I think we both felt mightily relieved at our escape.

But let me continue by recalling some of the special memories, wonderful scenes and less pleasant times too, all of which make the fishing days part of that magic I mentioned at the beginning of my account. There were the days in the 'croon o summer' when it could be very warm on the sea – even when the salty breezes blew.

On such days, my early days with the old Seagull outboard, and after hours of work, it was hard to keep one's eyes open during the long, slowish trips from one area to another. I'm thinking especially of the few times when we would be hauling creels at the Riff (Reef Dyke), and then having to motor over five miles round the north of the island, then west to the 'holes of the Grey-stane' (special inshore creel sets). I can still almost feel the heat of the sun, visualise the blue of the sea, with the blinding flash of the sun's reflections, flick, flick, flickering every second on the broken sea surface. That, combined with the constant hum of the outboard motor, had an almost hypnotising effect.

But there was also the comfort and enjoyment of those sunny days, and many others extending over the years: time between hauling creels to watch the great panorama of sea and sky; time for discourse, with talk about this and that; stories told; the sound of the crying birds and the sight of hundreds of calling kittiwakes ('kittiwhakoes') and terns ('pickie-ternos'), rising in white clouds and wheeling away from Selkie Skerry, the Green Skerry, or Summer Ayre; the sight of the 'solans' sailing past in the sky, out at the 'Riff Dyke' or at the back o' the skerry or at the North Breed; of seeing them sometimes diving suddenly, like a falling stone, for fish and plunging underwater in spectacular form.

Add to that the occasional appearance of puffins, skuas, stormy petrels and guillemots – and who can ever forget the flight of the common fulmar, with its streamlined body, forever gliding and skimming over the waves. Away they would go up in the sky with wings hardly ever moving, and then in a long, lazy, controlled sweep, back they would come without a single word out of their heads, banking this way, that way, forever riding the air waves and following their destiny.

I'm remembering too other days in September, October and November time when, on awkward chilling days, cold spray, rain or hail lashed the face and body, when hands and feet were painfully cold and it seemed almost a relief to dip one's hands in the sea after handling creels and bait. Days when it 'tuimed' (poured) with rain, with arms, neck and more being uncomfortably cold and wet – despite a full set of oilskins with their hoods, and warm clothing underneath.

And the times, when coming ashore, so powerless had one's fingers become that it was a major job to untie and re-tie the cord which held the lobster box secure. But to compensate for those experiences there were the many other occasions such as, when setting out to fish, returning from a day's work or simply making a passage between lines of creels, when the sheer joy of thudding along through choppy blue seas – or any colour of sea, with the salt spray flying, and a face-tingling fresh wind spinning away the wave tops – constituted the very greatest of pleasure.

I recall especially the great sights of the sea and sky in all its moods. Days when the sea might be a pale powder blue and as smooth as silk, with hardly a surface movement save that of the boat's wake stretching in long rippling angles backwards. Times when it would be as blue as blue can be, or battleship grey, dark and black, emerald green or burnished coppery-orange from the rays of the setting sun – a thousand colours for a thousand days, and a thousand skies. Sunsets of red and gold, purple clouds with fiery reflections, dark, misty-grey days with the mournful sound of the foghorn – but nevertheless serving as a necessary guide in treacherous waters. Crimson and orange sunrises seen, not long after the crack of dawn, with cold seas heaving in the east, or at other times above a calm and summery ocean.

As I think and write, I can remember those days so very clearly. Who, for instance, has seen a thunder-plumb or pelts of hail at sea? The grey surface of the sea jumps in every square inch or less, and the cascading sound rattles the very air. Spectacular too are the great arcs of rainbows that often appear – sometimes two or three – in passing showers, and even the little boat-rainbows seen when the sun reflects through the bow or stern spray as the praam goes clipping and slapping along; seals playful and curious but guilty too of making a 'peswisp' (a bad tangle) of inshore ropes when they have nothing else to do; 'paalos' (porpoises) flashing through the water and maybe a huge basking shark slowly passing by with quiet deliberation.

And then there were the times when the moon rose, amber-coloured or ghostly white in the eastern sky, and times when her ever-brightening light would transform the boat's homeward journey into that of a magical experience. On such nights, and others too as it got darker, little sparkles of greenish phosphorescence might be seen on cuithes, creels, ropes or whatever.

And what about the days when the sea is up, working within a stone's throw of land breaks. Watching great waves rearing ever higher, cannoning landward and exploding in huge expanses of white foam, and sometimes, when viewed from the side, seeing the long tunnel which appears, for a second or two, before the wave finally turns over and breaks. At the 'back' (the seaward side of Seal Skerry) when hauling creels from some of our deepest worked waters – ten or fifteen fathom or more – in heavy weather, rare sights are to be seen. Often in the huge swells, the praams seem to be from time to time in great, deep, watery valleys, with nothing to see but the sky and the sea. The land and the tall New Lighthouse easily disappear in the deep swells as the powerful waves go heaving ever higher, thundering towards the skerry. And when, in such conditions, stream flood or ebb comes in with a strengthening wind in either's face – well, then indeed, one sees the full power and majesty of the sea and knows that to be there in an open boat, by unintentioned chance or engine failure, both men and boat would disappear in an absolute maelstrom of fearful destruction.

There are many other recollections that I could tell you about. Two in particular often come to mind. Firstly, thinking back to 1966 and the 'hairst time', I remember the day as clearly as if it were yesterday. Folk had begun to sit up with a North Ronaldsay resident, Mary o' Cursiter, living on her own, who was failing in health that hairst, and by early November she had died. In former days many were the times when she had hoisted the 'waft' (a signal) on a tall pole nearby to let the island's postman and residents know that the 'post boat', which carried the Royal Mail, was in view coming back from Sanday. Cursiter and nearby Howatoft (whose residents had originally attended to the signal) commanded a good view of the North Ronaldsay Firth, across which the post boat made many a rough passage.

Anyhow, at Antabreck we were just finishing off work for the night. My father and I had been cutting a shift (field) of oats with the binder, and there still remained a short spell of daylight before the night fell. That year the hairst fishing on the east side was good, and with both myself and my fishing partner, John Tulloch, Purtabreck (for that particular hairst fishing), being young and intent on catching an extra lobster or two, or just for the 'deevelment' of it, (as John would say), we decided to set sail.

It was away to the Noust o' Sandbank, where we worked from that year, without another thought and quickly afloat as it began to mirk. Not far distant was a piece of good inshore fishing ground called the 'Galt'. I suppose we may have hauled a dozen or so creels before it became too dark, and whether we caught anything worthwhile or not I can't remember. But what will always remain in my mind is a sight I'd not seen before, and that I never did see again. As the boat left the noust not a lipper of sea disturbed the surface of the water, and streaming out on either side in the wake of the boat we saw the luminous fire of the 'miracle' (phosphorescence), dancing and shimmering almost all the way to the Galt.

The other occasion was on one of the marvellous moonlit nights of a few years ago now, when returning from fishing at the Riff. A combination of factors made that event special. In the western sky the last crimson streaks of a sunset still lingered briefly before turning purple and darkening; the night was calm but yet there was the slap, slap, slap of the boat's fast-moving hull through the water. All the while the climbing moon cast a long, following path of sparkling silver, and then suddenly, as I happened to look round, our sister praam, the *Diana*, K471 and her two-man crew, Jimmie Deyell and his son Ian, crossed over the moonlit path, silhouetted just for an instant in time, black against the intense brightness of the sea.

I'm just about at the end of this account, the writing of which has given me considerable enjoyment but also some sadness too, as I relive old times, and particularly when I consider what has happened to our traditional fishing grounds over recent years, and is still happening today. They are relentlessly exploited by large boats from elsewhere, dwindling down the number of those wonderful 'blue denizens of the deep', as George Mackay Brown describes them.

The account of traditional lobster fishing which I've written is by no means complete, and others, I know, with their memories, wider experience and greater knowledge could tell as much and more. But I hope that what I have written will give you some idea of the work, involvement and mystic feelings, if you like, of what it meant as our small open boats set out to fish, hauling creels by hand, in the dangerous waters round North Ronaldsay. For that experience I want to acknowledge the two men who each gave me this opportunity at different times.

Firstly, for five or so years (1964–1968), Willie o' Waterhouse (Muir), who inherited the *Ruth*, K52, from his grand-uncle, Hughie o' Sholtisquoy – the architect and builder of the boat from which the next generation of praams would be based. Secondly, for sixteen years or so (1980–1996) with John o' Purtabreck (Tulloch) in our own boat, the *Mary Jane*, K496. Both seamen often had to put up with a fishing partner whose mind and attention, more often than not, would be like the flight of the fulmar, gliding here and there.

But there are times in my imagination, especially at the time of year when the boats used to be getting ready for the fishing, when I think that maybe, on some fine early summer's morning – a morning when none of us are yet up or even awake – the ghosts of the old lobster fishermen will be on the move once again, loading up their boats with bait and sail and pulling out to sea. There will be no sound to disturb the peace of the morning, nor their discoorse, save that of the birds and the clunk and splash of the oars. If there is a morning breeze, then it will carry the smell of the men's pipe reek and their voices inland, or far away out on the deep. Possibly the sea, that always sings, will be 'hushing' just a little louder from the skerry and matching the colour of the dawn. Will they still catch a ghostly lobster or two and feel the thrill of it all again I wonder? And will they be back again to their favourite sets – up to Seal Skerry and the Swallow Rock ley, the Sholtisquoy ley, or the Blue Pow ley, or away to Back Ness to look for the Kirn o' Rue? Maybe, but more likely, I think, when they cast a discerning eye backwards to the land of their birth, they might feel very sad and disappear, like the mysterious sea-fogs that often come and go.

www.ingramcontent.com/pod-product-compliance
Lightning Source LLC
Chambersburg PA
CBHW041304110526
44590CB00028B/4244